ARNHEM UMBRELLA

ARNHEM UMBRELLA

Major Digby Tatham Warter DSO

NEIL THORNTON

FONTHILL

For Digby and Jane

Fonthill Media Language Policy

Fonthill Media publishes in the international English language market. One language edition is published worldwide. As there are minor differences in spelling and presentation, especially with regard to American English and British English, a policy is necessary to define which form of English to use. The Fonthill Policy is to use the form of English native to the author. Neil Thornton was born and educated in _____; therefore British English has been adopted in this publication.

Fonthill Media Limited
Fonthill Media LLC
www.fonthillmedia.com
office@fonthillmedia.com

First published in the United Kingdom and the United States of America 2022

British Library Cataloguing in Publication Data:
A catalogue record for this book is available from the British Library

ISBN 978-1-78155-882-9

Typeset in 10pt on 13pt Sabon
Printed and bound in England

Foreword

This book follows Digby's life. It describes his early military career and frustrations at his lack of involvement of early action in the Second World War, especially as his sister, Kit, and brother, John, were heavily committed from the outset. It then focusses in on Operation Market Garden that was to establish Digby as an intelligent, proactive warrior who took risks, always confident that events would work out in his favour. After the war, he went out to Kenya, married Jane, and bought and developed two farms over the next thirty years. During the Mau Mau insurgency, he raised a mounted infantry section that patrolled the Aberdares and had great success in restricting the movement and activities of the terrorists. One of his original men in the mounted infantry section was Tony Nuttall, my stepfather, who was responsible for introducing me to Digby.

Digby was an outstanding horseman, breaking his own ponies, playing polo at an international standard, designing both show jumping and cross-country courses, indeed the Tatham Warters became leaders in all matters equitation in Kenya. His foresight, in partnership with Hilary Hook, to start luxurious photographic safaris, demonstrates a vision of conservation that was unusual in the sixties and seventies, but is so relevant now.

This book is a very well-researched story of a man of many qualities and talents who, in the opinion of some of those interviewed, was 'slow to develop and considered dumb', 'never very diplomatic', 'mad as a hatter', 'a man of calm and ingenuity', and 'a complex character'. Whatever one's opinion of Digby Tatham Warter, there would be others who might disagree! I described him to the author as 'exceedingly arrogant and upset a lot of people', but he was an important mentor to me.

On leaving school, I spent eight months with the family. Digby and Jane went out of their way to make my stay instructive and developmental. Our friendship was to span twenty-five years, his influence on me has left a lifetime impression.

Initially Digby came across as a very organised, but very private family man who did not let many into his inner circle. He was a delegator as well as a doer. He liked to ask questions and through discussion put across his knowledge. He would explain what he wanted, whether to his safari staff or other employees, and then allow them to get on with it. This was on the understanding that whatever the task, the result had to be as he foresaw. His style of leadership, which he demonstrated in Holland in September 1944, was unique. When reading Neil's book, I could think of many examples in Digby's later life when that style resonated. Essentially, he allowed people to develop within his vision, if they made mistakes they would learn and grow.

The Tatham Warter family is a very solid institution. Jane was Digby's utterly necessary safety catch, to be applied when he had been on the sauce or was being intolerant of others! Jane always put on the catch with good firm spirit, which brooked no argument. Jane and Digby have three daughters who are in the mould of their parents. They are all immensely popular. They are undoubted achievers in their own worlds and have produced grandchildren who will forever carry the unique Tatham Warter spirit.

The book is a tale of its time. It is about a man who rose to the occasion when it was required and then continued to extract the most out of life, whilst making his mark in the world and influencing the lives of many.

Colonel Michael Kingscote LVO

Colonel Michael Kingscote LVO was commissioned into the 17th/21st Lancers and served with the Sultan of Oman's Armed Forces, UK Special Forces, and finally with The Queen's Bodyguard of the Yeomen of the Guard, some fifty-one years as a soldier.

Preface

In times of war, both the best and worst of mankind emerge. The sheer cruelty and brutality inflicted on one's fellow man is hard to comprehend, but alongside the horror and butchery sits duty, devotion, comradeship, and self-sacrifice. A man, or indeed woman, will think nothing of risking and in many cases sacrificing one's own life in order to save or try to save another.

A mutual respect between enemies born of shared hardship can also grudgingly surface, as was the case at Arnhem.

Heroes and villains invariably come to light, as do those few special men who stand out above their peers for, among other things, their strength of character and bravery. In Digby's case, these attributes together with a large dose of eccentricity mark him out as a unique individual whose name will forever be linked to the Battle of Arnhem and who will continue to be remembered by the Parachute Regiment with pride and honour.

Other men share traits that were not too dissimilar to those shown by Digby. The renowned Second World War Commando 'Mad Jack' Churchill who fought the war with a longbow and sword is among that number. Churchill, who bore no relation to war-time Prime Minister Winston Churchill, believed that any officer going into action without his sword was improperly dressed. In addition to his longbow, Churchill went into battle with a set of bagpipes with which he was seen bursting out of a landing craft at Vågsøy in Norway while simultaneously throwing grenades at the enemy as he advanced.

A huge admirer of war, 'Mad Jack', who was awarded the Distinguished Service Order (DSO) and bar and the Military Cross (MC) and bar, was sorry to see it end and later claimed, 'If it wasn't for them damn Yanks we could have kept the war going another ten years!'[1]

When describing Adrian Carton de Wiart, *The Oxford Dictionary of National Biography* stated: 'With his black eye-patch and empty sleeve, Carton de Wiart looked like an elegant pirate, and became a figure of legend'.[2]

With only one eye and one hand, de Wiart did resemble something of the stereotypical pirate. A long-serving British Army officer born to Belgian parents, he obtained the rank of lieutenant-general before his retirement in 1947. In the First World War, he was awarded the Victoria Cross where, in the midst of a fierce battle, he was seen pulling the pins out of grenades with his teeth. Modesty prevented him from mentioning anything about his VC or the act for which it was awarded when he wrote his memoir.

Adrian Carton de Wiart served in many conflicts including the Boer War, First World War, and Second World War and was wounded multiple times. He was shot in the face and head, lost part of an ear and an eye, was shot in the stomach (twice), and received other wounds to his hip, legs, and arms. His fingers were all but destroyed and when a surgeon refused to amputate the mangled bits that remained, he simply bit them off instead. He survived two plane crashes, broke his back, and escaped from an Italian POW camp, spending many days on the run before being recaptured.

In his autobiography, *Happy Odyssey*, Adrian Carton de Wiart wrote of 'the unconquerable spirit of the Britisher who is at his best when he is losing', while acknowledging that 'war manages to be a universal provider of funny situations and that unfailing sense of humour which can rise above everything'.[3] His observations are undoubtedly true.

In times of great pressure, when the odds are stacked against him, the British soldier will invariably crack a joke and smile. Never were these traits more evident than on the streets of Arnhem in September 1944 when, faced with a hopeless situation, the British paratroopers joked and absorbed their predicament with good humour.

The humour of the British Tommy can be dark and often comes at their own expense. At other times, it is directed towards the enemy.

The Arnhem operation was a costly failure and the number of casualties horrific. Many men lost their lives and many more were captured, a large number of them wounded. Yet throughout the battle, their morale and humour remained firmly intact. Interrogation by their captors presented the British paratrooper with a golden opportunity to play the fool. One wag, when asked by a German officer to provide his occupation, replied that in peacetime he had been a professional ballet dancer. Following his lead, a comrade explained that he had been an opera singer, while another told the interrogating officer he had been a lion tamer at a circus before the war. A further batch of prisoners, when asked to provide their names, reeled off a series of Disney characters instead. If these men are to be believed, Mickey Mouse and Donald Duck had fought at Arnhem as paratroopers.

Battlefield humour comes in many forms and takes place for a variety of reasons. On many occasions, it was simply boys being boys who, without fail, will always find something, or someone, to laugh at, no matter their surroundings. But deeper more meaningful reasons also exist.

Humour is a great personal coping mechanism and the saying 'If I don't laugh, I'll cry' is only too true. When one particular paratrooper holed up in a battered building at Arnhem began shouting mockingly at the Germans to inform them they had missed him and should shoot closer next time, his comrades began to get understandably vexed. Upon being persuaded to stop shouting, the culprit then took to singing at the top of his voice, somewhat badly at that. It was soon realised that this man's erratic behaviour was his outlet and his way of dealing with the stresses of battle. Realising this, his comrades left him to it.

Some of the stronger characters will adopt humour as a means of uplifting the morale of comrades to improve their resolve and fighting spirit when most desperately needed. Thus inspired, the British soldier will laugh harder and inadvertently fight harder. The positive impact these jokers can have is immeasurable.

British humour does not go unnoticed to those belonging to other nations who serve alongside our countrymen. At Arnhem, American ground observer Lt Bruce Davis, who had been tasked with scouting locations for a US Air Force signals operation, was caught up in the fighting and witnessed first-hand the British soldier with his back against the wall. 'I saw men who were hungry, exhausted, hopelessly outnumbered, men who by all rules of war could have easily surrendered and had it all over with,' noted Davis, 'men who were shelled until they should have been hopeless psychopaths, and through it all they laughed, and died, and kept fighting.'[4]

Davis continued:

> They absorbed everything—mortars, tanks, S-P guns, machine guns—everything in the book, and kept coming up for more. The German infantry was scared of the Red Berets and would not attack without the help of armour or big guns.... And the amazing thing about the British was that they carried on with the light-hearted abandon of a Sunday-school class on their first spring picnic.[5]

Digby Tatham Warter was not your stereotypical joker. He was a serious man whose mannerisms and attitude were absolutely proper, but beneath the surface lurked a ripple of uniquely dry humour. Those who knew Digby often wondered if he was actually attempting to amuse or if his actions came effortlessly as part of his character.

The personal accounts of those who fought at the bridge show the remarkable influence Digby had on the men he commanded, including those from other units who were not familiar with who he was.

His calm and stoic behaviour was vitally important and his umbrella a symbol of defiance and resilience against the odds. At one stage of the battle, Digby wore a bowler hat. This peculiar sight caused at least one man to erupt into laughter, despite being in the midst of battle.

Upon his death in 1993, an obituary stated:

> Tatham-Warter's striking appearance was particularly valuable when the British were fighting against impossible odds at Arnhem. For within the perimeter were soldiers from other detachments, signals, sappers and gunners, who would not know him by sight as his own men would, but who could not fail to be inspired by his towering figure and unflagging spirit of resistance.[6]

No German account of 'the man with the umbrella' exists, but it is likely that any enemy soldiers who saw him felt a certain degree of bemusement as to why a British paratrooper was scurrying around the battlefield wearing a bowler hat and carrying an umbrella.

One of Digby's most memorable traits was his complete confidence in his own ability, as was noticed by his fellow officers as soon as he joined the unit. Digby proved to be an excellent soldier and a solid if somewhat unconventional leader of men. At Arnhem, he gave hope and confidence to the already battle-hardened veteran paratroopers in what was his own first action, instilling in them a sense of utter defiance against their enemy. His calmness under fire and stiff upper-lip attitude in the face of adversity stood out as a highlight of the battle and was a huge source of morale.

But there was far more to Digby than dry humour and a large dose of eccentricity. As the officer commanding 'A' Company, 2nd Parachute Battalion, 1st Airborne Division, he would spearhead the division's advance for the Arnhem road bridge. During the course of the battle, he would be wounded and knocked unconscious by a blast from a Tiger tank, have the rear of his trousers 'blown out', and was generally battered and bruised, yet at the bitter end he would still be on his feet, commanding the small band of men who remained in the fight before issuing his final order of 'Every man for himself'.

Pulled from an aqueduct at the point of several SS bayonets at 10 a.m. on 21 September, Digby became a prisoner of war. Feigning wounds that far outweighed those he had actually received, he was taken to hospital with other casualties but promptly escaped by jumping from a window.

Following his escape, Digby made contact with the Dutch Underground, and over the course of the next four weeks, he would put into motion an audacious and ultimately successful plan known as Operation Pegasus, designed to evacuate 140 'evaders'—men who had took to hiding since the collapse of Operation Market Garden—back across the Rhine into friendly territory. During his time behind the lines, Digby, with his usual air of confidence, travelled around the Dutch countryside in civilian clothes armed only with a fake identification.

For his actions in the battle and subsequent evacuation, Digby was awarded the DSO. His performance at the bridge, notwithstanding his later actions in planning the evacuation, had been more than enough to warrant this high-level award, second only to the VC.

Digby's commanding officer, Lt-Col. John Frost, described him as a 'Prince Rupert of a man' and thought he would have made 'a great cavalry commander on the King's side in the war with the Roundheads'.[7] In his book *A Drop Too Many*, Frost also highlighted Digby's humorous tendencies, writing that with men like Digby around, 'there was no lack of ribaldry and tomfoolery'.[8]

Maj. Dover considered Digby 'a cool, calm and collected man', and described him as 'tall, a little aloof and full of confidence'.[9] It came as no surprise to Dover 'that it was he who astonished the Germans by carrying an open umbrella during the battle'.[10]

The maverick Canadian officer Leo Heaps, who would be closely associated with Digby during Operation Pegasus, wrote: 'Tatham Warter walked calmly round the battered positions quite unconcerned about his personal safety, cheering the wounded and organising his men in the shelled houses'.[11]

The commander of the 1st Airborne Division, Maj.-Gen. Urquhart, who took part in the operation but was not at the bridge itself, heard all about Digby's exploits from those who were there. In his own aptly named book *Arnhem*, Urquhart wrote that 'Major Digby Tatham Warter waved an umbrella as if it were a symbol of invincibility. On another occasion when the mortaring was heavy, he was seen sheltering under it'.[12]

Urquhart considered Digby a 'lively' individual, whose 'influence on morale at the Bridge had proved incalculable'.[13]

Urquhart was quite correct in his assessment.

Author Notes

Official documents, books, and countless other sources spell Digby's surname as Tatham-Warter, with hyphen. Yet it will be noted here that the name lacks the hyphen and features as Tatham Warter. It was explained to me by Digby's immediate family that, despite common misconception, Digby himself did not use a hyphen. Upon exploring the matter and seeking out a number of Digby's signatures, it became clear that this was indeed the case. Clarification if it were needed can be found on the cover of Digby's self-published short booklet *Dutch Courage & 'Pegasus'*, published in 1993, and on various documents signed by Digby himself, some of which can be found in this book. Therefore, I have omitted the use of a hyphen in my main narrative. Primary sources and quotations, however, have not be edited or tampered with, and as a result do incorrectly feature the hyphen.

As for pronunciation: Tatham is pronounced as 'Tay-thumb' and Warter as 'Water'.

This is a biography of one man who fought at Arnhem and should not be taken as a detailed history book that aims to cover the whole operation. I have endeavoured to concentrate on the actions and individuals relevant to Digby's story. As a consequence and so not to spoil the direction of this focus, some notable characters involved in Operation Market Garden may not feature if not directly linked to the flow of this narrative. The same applies to the various units and sub-units involved, the detail for which I did not want to get bogged down with. Should any reader wish to undertake further reading into this fascinating subject in minute detail, there are plenty of books fitting the bill.

All efforts have been made to locate the title of the book by Thady Ryan; the excerpt used was obtained as a scanned image via email correspondence with Tom Lawrence, and was under the header 'The Years of Strife–Mau Mau and the Emergency'. Unfortunately, I have since been unable to make contact and thus have been unable to find the title of the book from which the scan is from.

Acknowledgements

First and foremost, I must thank Digby's family for their inspiring enthusiasm and immense contribution to this book and for their 'warts and all' approach, which, in my opinion, is the only way for a biography to be written. Their hospitality and kindness in inviting me out to Kenya to stay with them was an experience I shall never forget. Not only did they materially assist, they also opened many further avenues of research by putting me in touch with others who had known Digby.

The input from Jane Tatham Warter, Digby's wife (who never remarried after Digby's death in 1993), was priceless, and her recollections and family photographs, many of which feature within these pages, proved invaluable. Sadly Jane passed away before this book could be published. She was a remarkable lady whom I am honoured to have met.

The same applies to Digby's daughters—Caroline Holdcroft, Joanna (Jo) McCallum, and Belinda (Binny) Oldenburg—whose hospitality and stories of their father (many of them humorous) were fantastic to hear, as were those provided by Digby's son-in-laws—Tim Holdcroft and Danny McCallum—both of whom added much to my knowledge regarding their father-in-law. For their splendid hospitality, I also thank Simon and Tana Herd (Digby's granddaughter).

The reader may be interested to hear that upon meeting Digby's family, it quickly became apparent that they had no idea of Digby's reputation and popularity outside of the Parachute Regiment.

I must also thank Alice Oldenburg, Digby's granddaughter and daughter of Binny, who was the first family member I was able to contact.

Jane Randle, Digby's niece, also played a very important part in this project with her stories, photographs, and in producing vital information regarding the family history as well as details on Digby and his siblings, particularly John and Kit.

The input of Digby's nephew, Anthony Barkas, added greatly to this book and his recollections provide the reader with an extraordinary insight into Digby's character and personality.

Early in my research, I contacted Arnhem enthusiast Debbie Betts, the niece of Steve Morgan, who, as a member of Frost's 2nd Battalion, had fought at the bridge. Steve saw Digby at various stages of the battle, yet felt he could not add anything useful. Thankfully, Steve's recollections were excellent and very useful indeed, and I am indebted to both Steve and Debbie for their assistance.

For permission to quote from a recorded interview featuring Steve Morgan, I am indebted to Rick and Will Everist. For providing recollections of their fathers regarding Digby, Graham Toze and Phil Spring receive my thanks.

David Charters, who served under Digby in Kenya in the 1950s during the Mau Mau Rebellion (calling him 'a born leader of men'), also receives my warmest appreciation for his input.

In Kenya, in addition to those already mentioned, I had the pleasure to meet the following people, all of whom shared their recollections and memories: Ulf Aschan, Sue and Dave Brown, Paul Benson, Rose Caldwell, Eddie Fernandes, Tim Lawrence, Michael and Gilly Littlewood, and Irralie Murray. Sue and Dave Brown receive my additional gratitude for their hospitality and for a magnificent day spent at Lewa Conservancy visiting Digby's grave—a day I will never forget.

I must also thank the following people whose fathers served at Arnhem and who provided invaluable information: Virginia (Ginny) Arbuthnot (*née* Lathbury) and Annabel Johnston (*née* Lathbury), the daughters of Brig. Gerald Lathbury; Lt-Col. John Frost's daughter, Caroline; Charles Dobie, son of Lt-Col. David Dobie; and Adrian Heaps, son of Lt Leo Heaps, not only for allowing me to quote from his father's book, but for his sterling efforts in providing access to a series of audio recordings of Digby describing events, as recorded by his father.*

This book hugely benefited from the input of Dicky Wildeboer, daughter of Bill Wildeboer, who, as the leader of the Ede Resistance, sheltered Digby after his escape from captivity and who, alongside Digby, played a leading role in planning Operation Pegasus. Likewise, Hiltje Van Eck provided valuable assistance from the Netherlands, as did Ruud Slangen who truly went above and beyond in providing live video footage of specific routes relating to Operation Pegasus made necessary after my own plans to travel were scuppered.

For providing contemporary documents and primary sources and for some major assistance with editing and labelling images and photographs, Paul Pariso receives my gratitude, as does Don Rooken-Smith for his excellent contribution in providing information and recollections regarding Kenyan polo.

Additionally I would like to thank Geoff Baulk, Mr Matthew Broadbridge, Bryan Burnikell, Rob Clark, Robert Collingwood, John Connor, Beverley Cooper, Alex de Groot, Mark Hickman, Dair Farrar-Hockley, Bart Houx, David Frampton, Lt-Col. Jonny Hipkins, Darren Kaye, Rene Kemna, Sebastian Mills, Dave McCall, Revd Graham D. Phillips, Secander Raisani, Paul Raison, Lt-Col. David Reeve, Michael Tremlett, and Adam Whitefoord (Digby's nephew).

The following organisations and associated individuals provided great assistance: Airborne Assault Museum, British Medal Forum, Gelders Archive, Imperial War Museum, Kenyan Police Association Archive, Parachute Regiment Association, and the Pegasus Archive.

I would like to thank the artists Steve Noon and Eric Thornton (my father) for producing artwork specifically for this publication, Jean Winch and the family of artist David Shepherd, Brian Sanders for permission to reproduce his painting, and last but not least, Damien Lewis, for reading my manuscript before submission and for his kind words, and Col. (ret'd) Michael Kingscote whose close bond with the Tatham Warter's together with his military connection put him in the perfect position to write the foreword to this book.

Regarding copyright: every effort has been made to seek permission from copyright holders. Any omissions are accidental and will be rectified in future print-runs and editions.

* Ranks correct at the time of Arnhem.

Addendum

Sadly, Jane Tatham Warter, Steve Morgan, and David Charters all passed away during the writing stage of this book. All three are remembered with great fondness.

Contents

1
Family

The surname of Tatham can be traced as far back as 1208 and is believed to have originated from the Yorkshire area. Many generations later, the Tathams would marry into the Warter family whose origins stretch back to before the Norman Conquest. Rooted in Shropshire, the original bearer of the name would have resided by a river, lake, or other prominent body of water. Variances of the name include Water and Waters.

The two families were connected through the marriage of Digby's maternal great grandparents, Henry de Grey (de Grey is an old variance of Diggory) and Harriett Warter (*née* Benbow)—the daughter of Conservative politician John Benbow.

Together, Henry and Harriett had two children: Henry de Grey junior (1834–1903) and Mary Eliza (1835–97), who, throughout her life—and from this point forward in this book—was known by her middle name of Eliza.[1] Young Henry tried his hand at being a comedian before forging a career in theatre, first as an actor and then as a stage manager and stage director, managing many of Gilbert and Sullivan's comic operas and other productions of the D'Oyly Carte Opera Company. Estranged from his father and wanting nothing to do with him or his inheritance, Henry had adopted the stage name of Richard Barker. He outlived his father by seventeen years, and after a long stage career, an American wife, and bankruptcy, he died virtually penniless in 1903.

The breakdown of relations between Henry and his son left Eliza to inherit her father's estate. In 1860, she married Meaburn Smith Tatham (1832–70), a solicitor who was in business with his father. Meaburn passed away in 1870 at the age of thirty-eight, having fathered seven children with Eliza: five girls and two boys. Of the two boys, Charles, born in 1865, died suddenly when only four months old. Their surviving son, Henry de Grey Warter Tatham (1862–1927), was Digby's father.

Interestingly, both Henry and Charles had been baptised with Warter as a middle name. Then, in May 1884, seven months before her father's demise, Eliza changed her name by deed poll from 'Tatham' to 'Warter Tatham'. It is believed this change took

Left: Richard Barker, comedian, stage manager, and director who was written out of his father's will, *c.* 1901.

Below: Baptism records for Digby's father, Henry, show his full Christian name as Henry de Grey Warter. Later, when Warter was added to the surname, his full and correct name was in fact Henry de Grey Warter Tatham Warter.

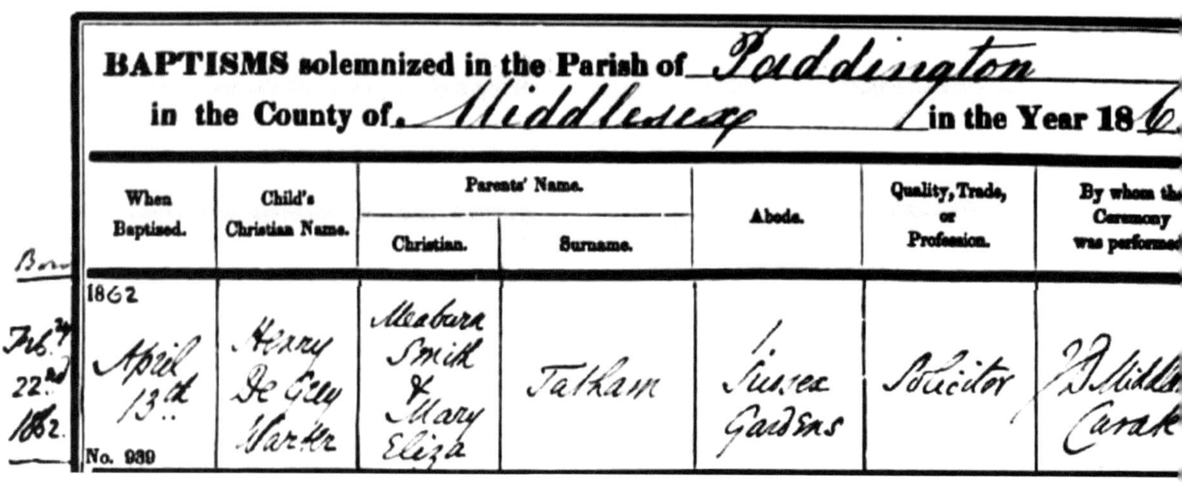

BAPTISMS solemnized in the Parish of Paddington
in the County of Middlesex **in the Year 18**62

When Baptised.	Child's Christian Name.	Parents' Name. Christian.	Parents' Name. Surname.	Abode.	Quality, Trade, or Profession.	By whom the Ceremony was performed
1862 April 13th No. 939	Henry De Grey Warter	Meabarn Smith & Mary Eliza	Tatham	1 Sussex Gardens	Solicitor	[illegible]

place for reasons of inheritance and was a stipulation made by her father who, since his son had abandoned the family name, did not wish to see the name die with him. When Eliza's father died in December 1884, she succeeded him at the grand twenty-five-bedroom family home, Longden Manor, in Pontsebury. At this stage, Digby's father, Henry, was now a young man.

Educated at Eton and Trinity College in Cambridge, Henry was known to be extremely kind and pleasant. He was also a talented athlete and a particularly good sprinter. His friends and at least some members of the family called him 'Harry'. He later became a very successful businessman, owning vast swathes of land and various estates in the South West of England. When in his thirties, he married the much younger Kathleen Maude Dearlove, a very bright and very pretty young lady who was the daughter of an associate, Thomas Dearlove Griggs, and his wife, Mary Meredith (*née* Nicholson).

Kathleen, Henry's future wife, was just thirteen years old when Henry first set eyes on her. As a successful farmer in Cambridgeshire, Kathleen's father had taken Henry under his wing to teach him about land management after Henry had inherited some land of his own. This had also prompted Henry to apply for a place at the Royal Agricultural College at Cirencester in Gloucestershire. Henry had become immediately smitten with Kathleen and had decided that he had to marry her. Thomas was horrified but her mother, Mary, saw it as a good thing, for Henry was extremely wealthy. After his initial scepticism, Kathleen's father began to come around to the idea.

Henry waited five years for Kathleen to come of age. In 1900, at the age of thirty-nine, he married Kathleen who had just turned eighteen.

Digby's mother, Kathleen Dearlove, was just eighteen years old when she married Digby's father who was considerably older. Henry had fallen in love with Kathleen the moment he had laid eyes on her when she was just thirteen and had vowed to marry her when she came of age.

Above left: Kathleen's father (Digby's grandfather), Thomas Dearlove, who, as a pedigree farmer, helped Digby's father to learn the ropes after he had inherited farmland.

Above right: Henry Tatham Warter, Digby's father, was much older than his wife. He passed away in 1927 when Digby was just eleven years old.

Longden Manor in Shropshire, built by Digby's grandfather, Henry de Grey Warter, between 1863 and 1866, was the couple's first marital home. The impressive property and surrounding grounds spanned many acres (over 260 acres by the end of the nineteenth century). Here they started their family. Between the years of 1901 and 1918, they had seven children: Mary Yolande, born June 1901; Joan Kathleen, born November 1903; Kitty Meredith, born October 1909; Diane, born July 1913; John de Grey, born July 1915; Allison Digby, born May 1917; and Angela Mary Beatrice, born July 1918.

Longden Manor was a spectacularly huge mansion and Henry and Kathleen deemed to be too large for their family. By April 1911, with three of their seven children born, they had moved to smaller Hinton Hall in Pontesbury that was more suitable for their needs. The property boasted sixteen rooms, and five servants were on hand to tend to the household. The family would remain here for approximately fifteen years until around the time of Henry's death.

Allison Digby Tatham Warter, the sixth of seven children, was born in Atcham, Shropshire, on 21 May 1917. He was known by his middle name of Digby but whether or not this was the case from the birth or was something that Digby initiated from a young age is not completely clear.

Digby was one of three siblings to be born during the First World War which had begun in August 1914. Digby's father was fifty-three years of age at the outbreak of war and deemed too old for frontline duty. The common belief that he served in the trenches and suffered a premature death from the effects of being gassed is incorrect. The family believe that over the years, the service of other family members has been confused with Henry's. Since there are numerous men named Henry in the family—some of whom did serve in the trenches—there is a strong possibility that this is the case.[2]

The impressive Longden Manor, Shropshire; home of the Tatham Warter family. The vast twenty-five-bedroom manor house was considered too large for the family's needs. By 1911, they had moved to a smaller property.

Buckland House, residence of the Tatham Warters. Digby's father, Henry, passed away here in 1927. He is buried by its gateway.

A room from one of the Tatham Warter residences, quite possibly Buckland House, adorned with evidence of Henry's hunting expeditions.

Pencil drawing of Longden Manor by Henry Warter.

Right: Henry Tatham Warter (Digby's father) seen here during the First World War as a member of the King's Shropshire Light Infantry. Contrary to popular belief, he was not gassed in the trenches.

Below: A wartime postcard of Henry's showing the Hornchurch camp of the Royal Fusiliers Sportsman's Battalion where he was stationed.

Henry initially served as an officer in the Royal Fusiliers' Sportsman's Battalion based in Hornchurch, London. Since postcards sent home show him wearing the cap badge of the King's Shropshire Light Infantry, he must have changed units at some point.

Henry's business dealings continued after the war and he travelled frequently, particularly to India. Often, Kathleen would set out with him and disembark *en route* at Mombasa to visit family including her sister in Kenya. On occasion, particularly during the school holidays, the children would accompany her to Kenya to see their cousins who, at other times, would travel to England to visit the Tatham Warters.

Comfortable lifestyle aside, Digby's childhood did not come without difficulty. He was slow to develop and considered dumb. Moreover, his older brother, John, was the apple of his mother's eye and could do no wrong. Their mother made it clear that of her two boys, John was the favourite son who she saw as the 'golden boy'. Digby very much lived in his brother's shadow and suffered to some considerable degree because of this.

John was two years older than Digby and a school prefect by the age of fifteen. This was partly due to ability but was also an attempt to curb his mischievous ways and leg-pulling for which he was well known. John had a wicked sense of humour and loved to play tricks on people, but his popularity allowed him to get away with things that others could not.

At the age of sixty-five, after suffering a series of strokes, Digby's father passed away at the family-owned Buckland House in 1927. He was buried by the gate to the property. Digby at the time was just eleven years old.

A subsequent announcement regarding Henry's death and distribution of his will was soon published. One particular newspaper gave sympathy to his wife and children, including his 'daughter', Allison. It is doubtful that this was the only time that Digby was wrongly identified as a female.

Not long after Henry's death, a young girl by the name of Ann arrived to stay with the family. The Tatham Warter children were already familiar with Ann since she had been to their home on many occasions to visit the family. Henry, before his death, had spent a lot of time with Ann and had been very fond of her. She was, the children were told, the daughter of one of their nannies' sisters. Digby adored Ann and was very good to her, but the other siblings did not make things easy and regularly teased her and made fun of her accent.

Horses had always played a large part in the family's life, particularly with Digby's mother, Kathleen, who was an extremely talented rider and very passionate about horses. Digby and his siblings were taught to ride from a young age. They became members of the young riders group at the Cattistock Pony Club where their mother was the district commissioner. They raced competitively and regularly contended for silverware. In their races, Digby was often pipped to the post by his brother, John, who invariably saw to it that his younger brother had to settle for a silver medal instead of gold.

One particular saddle-race in 1931 for ages fourteen to sixteen ended with John as the winner, with Digby, who was one of the youngest riders in the race, coming a close second. During the same event, Digby rode in a four-person under-fifteens relay with

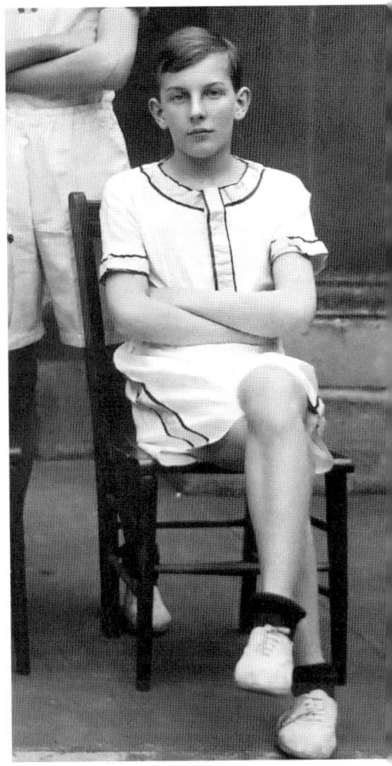

Digby throughout his school years.

Above: Digby, looking younger and considerably smaller than his teammates, stands far right with other 'Winners of P.T. comp. Summer 32'. His brother, John, stands second from left.

Left: A young John de Grey Tatham Warter. John was a very popular boy and two years older than Digby.

Above: John Tatham Warter stands far right. 'School Prefect, Xmas 1933' is written on the reverse of the original photograph.

Right: A day at the beach. *From left to right*: Digby's father, Henry, shortly before his death, with some of his children, Joan, Diana, and Angela, with Digby sitting in front of his sisters.

Above: A young Digby aka 'Digs'.

Left: Digby Tatham Warter, approximate age seventeen.

his sister, Angela, and two other teammates, winning the race and taking the gold. Digby and John then faced off in the thirteen to sixteen-year category, but yet again, John just beat his brother over the line to win the gold. Between them, John, Digby, and Angela had further successes that day, and, as usual, almost all the races had at least one Tatham Warter sibling in the top three.

But when it came to horses, it was Digby's sister, Kit, who was the most naturally gifted of them all. Kit—an utterly fearless rider—would go on to enjoy a long and distinguished equestrian career as a leading figure in the sport, representing Great Britain in the European Championships in the three-day Eventing, and riding competitively for several decades. In 1949, she would be described as 'the leading rider in the country'.[3] She is also credited as being one of the first people in the country to breed Rhodesian Ridgebacks after they were introduced to Britain in the 1930s.

Digby too would ride competitively for many years, including post-war in Kenya where he would set up his own young riders club and teach children how to ride. Digby's interest in horses would also result in a passion for polo, which he would later refer to as 'snob's hockey'.[4]

As a youngster, Digby had always been very small for his age, but a growth spurt around the age of sixteen saw him shoot up in height, although he did not bulk out and his frame remained thin. This new-found height gave the impression he was considerably older than he actually was, leading some to think of him as 'a bit slow'.[5]

Above left: Digby's sister, Diana, on a pony. Given their mother's interest in horses, it is little wonder the Tatham Warter siblings were able riders from young.

Above right: Reverse of photo states: 'This was our transport when we were small. Mama didn't go fro prams!'

Left: Digby, seen here as a teenager riding a show pony. Digby and his siblings were very capable riders from a very early age.

Below: Digby leads a petrified-looking Ann Meredith over a hedge. Ann encountered some difficulties when spending time with the Tatham Warters, but Digby was always extremely kind to her.

John (left) and Digby (right) on horseback. The brothers were regular winners of silverware in competitions.

Digby teaching his sister, Angela, how to shoot a 28-bore shotgun.

Digby attends a race event with two female companions (date and location unknown).

After his school years, Digby followed his brother to Wellington College before moving on to Sandhurst for officer training. John attended for two years and left in 1935, just as Digby arrived. At Sandhurst John had thrived, leaving as a senior under officer with a glowing reputation. Digby left in 1937 after winning the saddle, after which he followed his brother into what would become a distinguished military career.

2

Military Life

From Sandhurst, John was commissioned into the 2nd Dragoon Guards—known as the Queen's Bays. As a cavalry regiment, the Queen's Bays were made up of experienced horsemen and John certainly fit the mould. The horses always came first and their well-being was of the greatest importance above all else. In peacetime, mounted sport was the backbone of cavalry units and morale and comradeship were sustained through these outlets. Military tournaments were held regularly and the Queen's Bays competed with much success. Between the years 1932 and 1937, they won the Champion-at-Arms every year, and a further sixteen first prizes, seven seconds, and three thirds. In other events, the regiment won prizes for fencing and the sabre, and from 1936–39, they succeeded in winning the Army Inter-Unit Command Championship at the Military Tournament four years consecutively—a feat that had never before been achieved. Countless other silver and bronze awards were also earned.

In 1935, an event held for His Majesty King George V's Silver Jubilee came with an additional reason for celebration. The year marked the 250th anniversary of the regiment's formation, and the queen issued the regiment with a bronze plaque illustrating their long history.

Later that year, however, the inspector-general of cavalry informed his regimental commanders that he no longer saw any future for horsed cavalry and was taking action to have the bulk of the regiments converted to armoured units.

Since their introduction during the First World War, the development of tanks had come on leaps and bounds—so-much-so they were seen as the natural replacement for cavalry. Many did not welcome this change, and those in the regiment feared that their tradition and identity would be lost. At the time of John's arrival in 1935, none of this was known to anyone other than those in high command, but a short time later, the transition was announced to all. Quite what John felt about this change is not known.

There was much groundwork to be laid and it would take several years for the change to be fully implemented. Officers and NCOs had to be trained as instructors,

An officer of the Queen's Bays. John Tatham Warter (front left) leads his men on horseback through the countryside.

not only in driving the tanks but in maintaining them and operating the wireless sets and new weaponry. The administration system had to be completely overhauled, and every man had to adjust accordingly, including the farriers and storemen who became fitters and mechanics.

On 12 May 1937, two days after the coronation of King George VI, it was announced that the queen had been appointed as the Queen's Bay's commander-in-chief. The following month in conjunction with the Royal Horse Artillery they put on a successful demonstration of a mechanized troop attack. In October, they departed from Aldershot for Tidworth whereupon the commander of the 1st Cavalry Brigade issued a special order:

> Before saying good-bye to the Queen's Bays I would like to take this opportunity of congratulating all ranks of the Regiment in the way in which you have maintained your great traditions during the time you have been stationed at Aldershot.
>
> During the first three years the Regiment distinguished itself as a mounted unit, winning many honours at the Royal Tournament, Aldershot Horse Show, Command Small Arms Meeting and Aldershot Races.
>
> Notable among such successes were those gained in the Aldershot Command and Army Fencing Tournaments. Unfortunately the day arrived when horses had to be replaced by machines, but the pride of the Regiment which has always inspired The Queen's Bays has enabled you to accept your conversion to mechanization

> in a whole-hearted and most efficient manner. Such spirit will ensure success in overcoming all difficulties, whether in peace or war. The zeal and energy displayed by all ranks during the last twelve months in training for your new role is worthy of the highest praise, and it is the more creditable when it is remembered that the vehicles and equipment issued to you were old or 'token' vehicles. The time spent on these temporary vehicles and equipment resulted in a standard of turn-out which equalled, if not excelled, the high standard expected of Horse Cavalry, and has called forth the admiration of all those who have come in contact with the Regiment.
>
> Such efforts are examples of the true cavalry spirit, and, while this lives, the future of The Queen's Bays is assured. The 1st Cavalry Brigade will very much miss the loyal and helpful co-operation of The Queen's Bays, and on behalf of myself and all ranks of the Brigade I wish you all Godspeed and the best of luck on your new station.[1]

Alongside the 9th Lancers and 10th Hussars, the Queen's Bays became part of the 2nd Light Armoured Brigade.

Although it is clear why John opted to join a cavalry regiment, it is not quite as clear as to why Digby chose to apply for the Indian Army. He may have been planning to join a cavalry regiment like his brother, for he too was a passionate and talented horseman and had won the saddle at Sandhurst, but their transition to armour may not have been to his taste. When Digby received his commission in 1937, he was placed on the unattached list to await a posting.

Although they were closely associated, the Indian Army and British Army were two completely separate organisations. Digby's late father had spent a lot of time in India and had many contacts there, and Digby would almost certainly have heard about his father's time in the country, particularly since their family home was adorned with evidence of his successful hunting endeavours. It may be that the great outdoors appealed to Digby's nature and joining the Indian Army—which essentially policed the Indian Empire—guaranteed the opportunity to enjoy this experience. At least one family member had served in the Indian Army, dying on active service as a lieutenant-colonel in 1889.[2]

Any officer joining the Indian Army had to first serve an obligatory period of one year on statuary attachment to a regular British regiment stationed in India. For Digby, that regiment would be the Oxford & Buckinghamshire Light Infantry, commonly abbreviated to the Ox & Bucks, whose 2nd Battalion had arrived in Rawalpindi, India, way back in 1922.

The Ox & Bucks had an overwhelming pride in their history. They also had their own set of unwritten rules, referred by one officer as their 'petty do's and don'ts'.[3] New officers had little choice but to abide by these rules or face being ostracized.

One rule was the saluting of the colonel. Unlike in other regiments where the soldiers would salute their CO every time they saw him, members of the Ox & Bucks were only expected to salute once a day, when they first met. Another quirk was they never drank a 'loyal toast', the reason being that it should be obvious that they held an unswerving loyalty to the sovereign and a toast was not required to confirm this fact. Additionally, they did not use abbreviations when referring to the ranks of fellow officers. The medical officer for example was called the medical officer, not the MO as in other regiments.

If a new addition to the mess slipped up, he could expect a few stern looks and a loss of face, but over time, these habits embedded themselves into one's memory and became second nature.

Digby joined the battalion as a fresh-faced subaltern at Mhow, India, and was posted to 'C' Company. Military life in peacetime India allowed the officers the opportunity to take part in many activities, which suited Digby's desire for exciting 'sport'. He took to the life immediately. He went tiger hunting and became a keen 'pig-sticker'—essentially riding down wild boar and 'sticking' them with a lance. He hunted with his fellow officers but also developed a tendency to hunt alone and was known for going out on one-man reconnaissance missions (something that he would do decades later when planning safaris in Kenya).

The 1938 *Ox & Bucks Chronicle* is filled with Digby's exploits and provides details on the tournaments he and his fellow officers competed in. One particular tournament—the Kadir Cup, held in March—describes an unfortunate incident involving Digby, his horse, Mandarin, and his opponent—an artillery officer by the name of Weber—that saw Digby unfairly eliminated from the tournament:

> Tatham-Warter had very bad luck indeed; he and Weber were both riding level with the pig just in front when it disappeared into a bush. As it did not come out the other side they both stuck their spears into the bush, although they could not actually see the pig. Neither of them thought his spear had gone into anything, but Weber's had definitely got blood on it so the umpire quite naturally awarded him 'first spear.' Now comes the bad luck part. When Tatham-Warter got back to camp in the evening he found that Mandarin had a small spear wound on the near side of his neck. The syce said he noticed it soon after the heat. During the hunt and just before the pig disappeared Weber had been riding on Tatham-Warter's near side and for a moment had got his spear tied up in Tatham-Warter's reins. (The latter presumably, like all good hoghunters, riding with a lose rein). It seems that quite unwittingly Weber speared Mandarin and not the pig.[4]

For the month of May, the *Chronicle* also notes:

> In May Tatham-Warter took ten day's leave which he spent hunting at Kashipur in the Teria about one hundred miles from Bareilly. Clifton joined him at the week-ends and the total bag was seven boar, three of which were killed by Tatham-Warter while hunting alone. This was a most satisfactory ten days from everyone's point of view. Here, as at Christmas, the country was quite new to the Shikaris and spears, and Tatham-Warter had to put in a lot of time reconnoitring the country. This will be of great value to the Tent Club next year as it seems a most promising place.
>
> It is to be hoped that people who have not yet tried their hand at pig-sticking will do so next year. The bag for the season was 36 boar. The average height was 29.5 inches, average weight 149 pounds. The biggest boar was 32.5 inches and the heaviest 200 pounds.

The following spears hunted from the regiment:

Tatham-Warter 43 days
Astley-Cooper 27 days
Clifton 24 days
Bray 16 days
Smythe 1 day
Hornsby-Wright 1 day
Campbell, UL.I.A 2 days[5]

The *Chronicle* went on to report that Digby's passion for pig-sticking was being overtaken by something else: 'Tatham-Warter seems to have forsaken the small band of hoghunters and become an enthusiast of "snobs-hockey"'. [6]

Snobs-hockey, as Digby called it—or polo to everyone else—was to become a life passion for Digby, and like everything else he put his mind to, he would reach a high level of excellence at his chosen sport.

Digby's reputation as a hunter was enhanced when, in 1939, shortly before the outbreak of war, he had a near-miss with a tiger that would have resulted in death or serious mauling had he not kept his cool. On that occasion, he set out on foot with some friends to prepare for the reception of a tiger at the edge of a jungle the following night, but one arrived prematurely as they were setting up. Together with some equally cautious monkeys, the party quickly scampered up the nearest trees. Later, when the monkeys descended, it was assumed the tiger had cleared out, so Digby and his pals made their way back down. But the tiger was lying in wait. Digby who was nearest, kept his composure and managed to squeeze off a shot and dropped the tiger right before it pounced.

In India, there were plenty of opportunities for friendly polo games and tournaments to be played. Digby was a great player and a valued member of the Ox & Bucks team.

Digby loved being a member of the Ox & Bucks, and as his one-year attachment drew to a close, he did not want his time with them to end. As such, he took the unusual step of applying to remain with the battalion permanently and for his commission with the Indian Army to be terminated.

Once an Indian Army cadet had passed out successfully from Sandhurst and completed his mandatory one-year attachment with a British Army regiment, he had to join the Indian Army. Having put the cadet through his training, the Indian Army wanted something for their money. They were not in the habit of funding officers only for them to join another army. Nevertheless, Digby's application to remain with the Ox & Bucks was somehow successful. There would have been complications for such a move to happen and quite how Digby managed to pull it off is something of a mystery.

On 3 September 1939, Britain and France declared war on Germany. Initially India was largely unaffected. Sporting tournaments continued as before, but training took on a new impetus in the knowledge they may soon be called upon to fight. But as the months wore on, and with no such order forthcoming, those in India began to feel frustrated at their lack of involvement. In reality, for the time being at least, not much was happening in Europe in the way of fighting either.

Digby stands (second from right) with fellow officers in India. Hunting and polo were two favourite past times.

Photograph sent home from India by Digby who wrote on the reverse: 'The only pleasant interlude in a day's training in camp'.

Digby (left) relaxes in camp with his pipe, *c*. 1940, in India while serving with the Ox & Bucks. His battalion would soon be summoned home to England to prepare for war.

The Ox & Bucks won the Mhow Polo Tournament early in 1940, closely followed by a further victory in the Indore Tournament in March. In February, the battalion had moved out on a fortnight's training made up of five exercises which, owing to a shortage of modern equipment and a lack of experience in its usage, required a fair amount of improvisation. There were, however, some positives to be taken from the exercise, the battalion recording that 'at least they served to exercise junior leaders in power of command, and kept all ranks fit'.[7]

One week's brigade training then followed, but this was also less than satisfactory and was considered to be unrealistic, mainly through a lack of involvement from other troops. The training was far from perfect but it was certainly better than nothing and helped to pass the time and keep the men occupied. Even so, it was noticed that 'there was an underlying feeling of frustration and impatience to get away from India and nearer to the battle'.[8] Things were not helped by the circulation of false rumours that they were to be shipped back to England, only for those hopes to be dashed when the rumours came to nothing.

This continued until May when the battalion received news they were to prepare to move at seventy-two hours' notice. Once more, spirits were raised and under a cloud of excitement the job of packing up their equipment and belongings began. By the end of the month, definitive orders had been received. After almost two decades on the North West Frontier, the battalion was finally heading home.

Following their declaration of war, the British Expeditionary Force (BEF) had crossed the Channel to France where, for the first eight months, no fighting had taken place. Naval blockades, bombing raids, reconnaissance missions, and other strategic moves designed to gain tactical advantages were commonplace, but other than one offensive by the French, the opposing armies themselves did little other than sit tight in their positions to await developments.

This period, known as the 'Phoney War', came to an abrupt end on 10 May with the German Army's invasion of France and the Low Countries. It was this invasion that had triggered the troops in India to be recalled.

The Ox & Bucks set off on 3 June, travelling first to Khandwa and then to Bombay where they discovered they were to form part of a convoy with seven other British battalions, all destined for England. On 16 July, after a somewhat boring and uneventful voyage with stops at Durban and Capetown, they touched down in Liverpool, England, to a rousing reception by the regimental depot that was awaiting their arrival at the docks.

Eighteen years away from home meant the returning battalions were out of date with modern tactics, weapons, equipment, and technology, and they would have to undergo rigorous training in these departments before they could be considered fit for war.

The battalion immediately joined the newly reformed 31st Independent Brigade Group consisting of regular army troops who had previously been stationed in India. The brigade additionally comprised of the 1st Borders, 2nd South Staffs, and 1st Royal Ulster Rifles, together with a field regiment of artillery, an anti-tank battery, and a field company of engineers with various support units.

Over the next few months, large-scale training exercises took place alongside smaller ones at platoon and company level. Officers and men completed countless courses and

Photograph of Digby in uniform with one of the family's many dogs.

attended demonstrations to bring them up to scratch. At this stage, rumours were rife regarding what the Germans were planning to do next, and the unfortunate Ox & Bucks were pulled pillar to post as orders and counter-orders came flooding in.

On 6 September, the brigade were given six days' notice to move to billets by Maidstone. Two days later, new orders came through that they were to go to Harpenden instead. This was in response to new information that the German Army had embarked for an invasion of Britain. An hour's notice to move was given, although this was later changed to four hours. They set out to Harpenden on the 9th, only to be diverted to Berkhamsted when part way there. They bivouacked outside the town for the night and in the morning received orders to go into billets at St Albans instead. These orders were later cancelled and they went into billets at Berkhamsted on the 11th. Frustrations were high.

Ten days later, plans for another move were underway and a reconnaissance party was sent to find suitable billets in Maidenhead. Five days later, another party headed out to Kent, but it was all for nothing. The following evening, they were sent to Wittersham, located a few miles north of the Rye where they were given the task of guarding and if need be defending the Royal Military Canal that lay on the south coast of England. Digby's 'C' Company took hold of the Stone Street area by the canal.

At this stage, the threat of a German invasion was considered to be very real. The BEF that had gone to France at the start of the war but were now back on home soil—a seemingly unstoppable German force having steamrolled its way through Europe causing France to collapse and the British to be pushed back into the sea. Desperate evacuations, notably at Dunkirk, had thrown the battered and bruised BEF a lifeline and the chance to fight another day. As Britain licked its wounds, Germany strengthened Fortress Europe.

Defensive preparations undertaken by the Ox & Bucks involved digging—lots of digging—but this laborious job came with a sweetener. The regimental journal records that they 'now occupied a seat in the front row of the stalls for the Battle of Britain and many air battles were seen'.[9]

A burst of Bren gun fire from one of Digby's company officers was thought to have caused a German plane to limp away trailing smoke, much to the delight of the men.

The urge to stop and watch the dogfights was too tempting for many to resist, and members of the battalion were dive-bombed at least once. Consequently, an order had to be issued to all ranks stating that, whether in HQ, billets, or manning the defences, every precaution at concealment had to be taken when air battles were taking place and that disciplinary procedures would be carried out for those not abiding by the rules.

In November, the former King's Shropshire Light Infantry (KSLI) regimental sergeant-major, John Howard—who would later find fame for leading the D-Day assault on Pegasus Bridge—arrived with the Ox & Bucks as a newly-commissioned officer.

Extremely conscious of his working-class roots, Howard joined the battalion with trepidation brought about by his past treatment having been previously overlooked for a commission due to his background. Because of this, he harboured a distinct dislike for the upper class and despised everything they stood for.

On his first morning, a nervous Howard edged his way into the officers' mess, fully expecting to be wholeheartedly blanked by his new colleagues—and he was, for Sandhurst tradition dictated that for his first six weeks, a new officer would be ignored in the Ox & Bucks mess. Howard, having come through the ranks instead of the military academy, was not aware of this unwritten rule and assumed he was being ignored for other reasons.

Howard was informed he would be going on a 3-inch mortar course only to be told the following morning there had been a change of plan. Another officer by the name of Capt. Digby Tatham Warter who commanded 'C' Company would be going on the course instead, and he was to take temporary command of Digby's company while he was away.

'I was all too familiar with young officers like Digby Tatham-Warter,' said Howard who referred to Digby as 'a typical "top-drawer" officer, with a Sandhurst background'.[10]

Howard made no secret of the fact that he found such upper-class men 'arrogant in the extreme', and his initial assessment of Digby was certainly rather scathing:

> Doubtless his father and likely his grandfather too, had also served as officers in the Ox & Bucks and young Digby would have been schooled from birth to leave his public school as an Army cadet, enter Sandhurst, the prestigious training college for

> Army officers in Camberley, Surrey, and graduate from there as part of the elite band of young British officers; clean-cut, 'jolly good chaps' and confident in their status in life.[11]

Howard's experience with his officers in the KSLI and being denied a pre-war commission on account of his background had amounted to class prejudice, which in turn resulted in him becoming guilty of the very same thing—something he later admitted had been the case.

He arrived with the Ox & Bucks a bitter man with a preconceived opinion of the officers:

> It made me determined to show those bastards that I would be a better officer than they could ever be in their wildest dreams. While they were off at weekends invited to shooting parties or playing golf, I would be planning my training routines and drilling the men. Damn them all to hell with their double-barrelled names and their county family forebears. It made me more aggressive and, unfortunately, inclined to be prejudiced against anyone with an upper-class name or manner...[12]

Howard, who considered Digby to be a 'blue-nosed young officer', came to realise he had been too hasty.[13]

Moreover, he discovered that Digby, unlike others he had encountered, did not judge him by his class, but by his character.

Howard later admitted his mistake:

> In the days that followed, I had a chance to get to know Digby Tatham-Warter better and realized not for the first time that I had been wrong in my initial assessment of him as a typical 'upper class pongo'. He was in fact, and easy-going chap with an attractive manner and to my surprise, I found myself liking him. So when Digby suggested that we meet up and go to the 'flicks', I readily agreed.[14]

To Howard's surprise, the two men became firm friends. Their backgrounds may have been starkly different, but they nevertheless had a lot in common. Both were solid leaders and no-nonsense men who said it as it was, and both would go on to receive the DSO for their actions in the war.

Their friendship survived an episode at an evening dance for the officers and wives where many single officers were in attendance, including Digby.

Howard related the story:

> At the officer's dance in the evening, Digby Tatham-Warter, always known to appreciate 'a good filly' rather hung his nose over Joy [Howard's wife] at the dance and caused me an unwarranted attack of jealousy. But fortunately Joy was introduced to Gil Rahr's wife, Susan, and the two young women took an instant liking to each other and fell into lively conversation. Digby sauntered away to find more responsive company.[15]

Above left: John Howard arrived with the Ox & Bucks with preconceived ideas about the upper class officers, including Digby. Yet when he got to know Digby, he found himself liking him immensely. Howard went on to lead the D-Day assault on Pegasus Bridge.

Above right: Digby as an airborne soldier. This photograph was almost certainly taken by the same photographer and at the same time as Howard's photo.

Later, when Howard was involved in a serious car accident and hospitalised, Digby would pay his friend a visit, despite the two men not having seen each other for a number of years.

Between strengthening and manning the canal defences, the battalion continued training. As they entered 1941, there was an emphasis on movement and the concealment of vehicles and on how to hunt and destroy enemy tanks and paratroopers should they invade Britain. Various scenarios were played out. In an exercise from 27–29 January, they played the part of Italians landing on the east coast heading to London while a Scottish unit was given the task of stopping them. The exercise was unsatisfactory as, beyond capturing a few prisoners through patrolling, no 'enemy' were actually seen.

Rumours of an impending move once again began to circulate. This time it was thought they would be heading to Ireland or Singapore, but these proved to be unfounded. The following month, they departed for Ross-on-Wye, Hereford, leaving Berkhamsted with some regret, 'all ranks having enjoyed great hospitality from the residents'.[16]

Constant training continued for many months, including the larger brigade exercises. Sometimes the battalion played the part of defender with the aim of repulsing an enemy invasion force, and other times they took on the role of the enemy. No stone was left unturned. In June, the brigade received orders to train for mountain warfare with pack transport. This took place in the mountains of South Wales and was described as extremely arduous work.

Between the training came times of leisure and celebration. On Waterloo Day, 18 June, an event took place in Ross, where Digby's talents as a rider were highlighted. 'Waterloo Day was celebrated at Ross with sports, mule racing', recorded the regimental journal, 'and an officers' team defeated the serjeants team in a mule race, Captain Tatham-Warter winning by a neck from Captain Favell'.[17]

Further mock battles saw the battalion representing a German force trying to capture Cardiff docks. This was carried out in conjunction with the Home Guard and was described as a 'rough ride'. The Home Guard did well in their roadblocks 'supplemented by improvised missiles which took their toll, but there were no serious casualties'.[18] Despite their rough treatment, the battalion were impressed with the Home Guard's violent and energetic performance at holding them up and surmised that in the case of a real invasion, it would be 'doubtful whether any enemy would have got as far as Cardiff'.[19]

Another exercise with the Home Guard took place at the beginning of August involving the whole brigade which was given the job of capturing Birmingham. It involved much street fighting and was thoroughly enjoyed by all as it was a welcome change from the usual open country exercises. Soon, however, the direction of the battalion was to undergo a drastic change.

3

Siblings go to War

Since the outbreak of war, the military careers of Digby and his brother, John, had taken entirely different routes. Early in the war, Digby's frustration at being stuck in India had not been helped by the fact that two of his siblings were already in the thick of the fighting: John with the Queen's Bays, and his older sister, Kit, with the Hadfield-Spears Ambulance Unit.

Kit had been the first of the siblings to go to war. The Hadfield-Spears were led by the American Mary 'May' Borden, who, following her marriage to Brig.-Gen. Edward Spears in 1918, was known as Lady Spears. In 1914, on the outbreak of the First World War, she had volunteered to serve in the French Red Cross. Despite having no nursing experience, she had been accepted because of her willingness to work in the midst of a typhoid endemic and for her ability to speak a little French. The French authorities had been reluctant to introduce British nurses into their hospitals but Lady Spears had been determined to get her way and, at her own expense, had set out to France with two nurses. Initially, things had been extremely difficult and the situation was not helped by French regulations, which Lady Spears considered to be costing the lives of her patients. On the advice of a visiting hospital inspector who promised to forward the letter with favourable recommendation, Lady Spears wrote to the commander-in-chief, Gen. Joffre, requesting her own surgical hospital consisting of 100 beds. On the understanding that the French would take it over as a military unit and provide the officers, NCOs, and orderlies, she offered to personally fund and equip it. She also requested absolute authority over all women employed in the hospital. The hospital opened its doors four months later.

The hospital was an Anglo-French affair under command of a French commanding officer with Lady Spears as British director. The surgeons, doctors, chemists, and administration team were all French and the nurses originally British and American, although by the end of the war, half of the fifty working there were French.

Lady Spears's husband and future brigadier-general was at the time a staff captain liaising between British and French troops on the Western Front. His fondness and passion for France was shared by Lady Spears. In the interwar years, he was an MP for both Loughborough and Carlisle, and his pro-French views earned him the nickname of 'The Member for Paris'.

On the outbreak of the Second World War, Lady Spears, now in her mid-fifties, had once again wanted to contribute to the war effort but having lost her wealth in the 1929 Wall Street Crash was in no position to fund a hospital. Her close friend, Lady Francis Belt Hadfield, the wife of the British steel tycoon Sir Robert Hadfield, found herself with a somewhat different dilemma.

During the First World War, Lady Hadfield had self-funded and operated one of the first Red Cross Hospitals, but by 1939, she was seventy-seven years old and unable to oversee the running of a field hospital. However, the one thing she did have was wealth, and when her husband asked her to donate £100,000 towards the war effort in any way she saw fit, her thoughts had immediately turned to her friend Lady Spears.

At the time, Lady Spears was making herself busy working with an Air Raid Precaution (ARP) unit, operating from a modest garage in Fulham. When Lady Hadfield proposed the donation, she eagerly accepted the offer. Between them, it was decided that a field hospital in France with 100 beds was achievable and that Spears would actively operate it. A letter was sent to the French commander, Gen. Gamelin, and on 30 September, a mere twenty-seven days after Britain had declared war on Germany, permission had been granted for a mobile field hospital to be formed.

Lady Hadfield promptly set up an account for the hospital into which her husband injected the funds. Lady Hadfield then handed the chequebook to Lady Spears requesting only that the unit bear both their names. Thus, the Hadfield-Spears were born.

Little time was wasted in getting things up and running. Through her contacts at the ARP, Lady Spears approached the commandant of the Mechanised Transport Corps (MTC), requesting 'twenty-five first class drivers and fifteen cars to go overseas' with her.[1] There was no shortage of volunteers.

Most if not all of these young women were from the upper echelons of society with an exclusive love of horses and Lady Spears had no trouble in gathering her team. Kit Tatham Warter, who would come to be known as T.W. by Lady Spears and the girls in the unit, had joined the MTC at the start of the war and was one of those selected by Lady Spears.

'The M.T.C was a small affair in those days,' Spears would say, 'but the war was young and London swarmed with valiant young women, eager to go overseas and ready to provide their own vehicles.'[2]

During her time with the MTC, Kit had already proven to be very capable when under a bonnet of a vehicle and more often than not could be found covered in grease with a spanner in hand.

As a mobile ambulance unit, the drivers of the Hadfield-Spears would be the core of the unit. Their vehicles included Ford station wagons, a Buick, two sunbeams, two Dodge vans, and an old Bedford fitted with benches. A limousine, donated to Lady Spears by Lady Hadfield, added a touch of class to the convoy.

The girls, like the vehicles they drove, were a varied bunch. 'Some were pretty and some were plain, some were thin and others were fat,' noted Lady Spears, 'but all were young and splendidly alive.'[3]

Spears described them as 'a motley crew' and feared they lacked elegance, but their rag-tag appearance did not worry her in the slightest. She had every confidence in their ability and considered them 'a very smart lot'.[4]

In February 1940, with the drivers dressed in khaki, and the newly recruited nurses in grey, the Hadfield-Spears departed England's shores destined for France. They were attached to the 4th French Army at Lorraine behind the Maginot Line where, for the time being, the situation remained quiet and calm.

At this time, John Tatham Warter was still in England with the Queen's Bays which, as a relatively new armoured unit, had not yet completed its mobilisation. Plans, however, had been made for them to cross the Channel to a training area where they were to become fully equipped and operational. The arranged Channel crossing had been just days away when the Germans launched their offensive and the plan had to be hastily changed.

The regiment was woefully underprepared for war, but the critical situation meant they would be seeing action much sooner than anticipated. They possessed no tools or spare parts for their newly-introduced cruiser tanks, and the guns for their light tanks were still nailed into the boxes that they had been delivered in.

The Queen's Bays disembarked at Cherbourg and by 22 May were stationed at Breval. Plans to properly equip and carry out their scheduled training regime quickly fell by the wayside. A few hours after their arrival, they found themselves heading north to meet the Germans who had crossed the Somme River and whose leading elements of armour were closing in on Rouen from the east.

Over the next few weeks, the Queen's Bays engaged in confused battle and a series of rushed northward manoeuvres. They were caught up in heavy fighting on the Somme and ordered to seize vital bridgeheads to the west of Amiens. They became divided in the process when part of the squadron responded to the order while others continued to St Leger where they had previously been told to head to as a matter of urgency; the situation not being helped by an enforced radio silence. The intended bridgeheads were not seized after advance scouting parties found nothing but Germans in the area and no sign of the French troops they were expecting to meet.

On 5 June, an urgent message was received that the German Army had broken through south of Abbeville. In response, a composite regiment consisting of the Queen's Bays, Lancers, and Hussars was ordered forward. They succeeding in holding their position, but the Germans had broken through on the right flank and they were forced to withdraw. News then came through that the Germans had broken through Amiens and the composite force rushed off once again to meet the threat, this time on the right flank of the 51st Division. The bulk of the regiment withdrew to the Andelle Valley, east of Rouen, where, together with other armoured units, they took stock of their losses. By now, many tanks had been knocked-out or lost through breakdowns and lack of spare parts. Some regiments had been reduced in strength to that of a single squadron.

For those in the north, things were not going any better. The BEF was retiring towards Dunkirk while the Queen's Bays were being pushed south with the French. By 8 June, they had become fragmented and were split into three distinct groups spread many miles apart. As the fighting withdrawal continued, German armour was regularly spotted moving behind them.

By daylight on the 9th, the bulk of their division was south of the Seine River, but the support group would soon meet their demise fighting alongside the ill-fated 51st Highland Division. Bridges along the Seine River were blown during the day, but the Germans were not to be stopped and began crossing by boat.

With the Germans pursuing the French from Rouen, the Queen's Bays continued south to an area near Le Mans where regimental workshops had been set up to enable British units to refit and reorganise before returning to the fight. The fifteen remaining tanks belonging to the Queen's Bays arrived here on the 14th. The plan was to stay for two weeks, but mere hours after their arrival, they received a visit from a brigadier who informed them of the shocking news that the French had requested an armistice and that they had to get out, now.

Leaving a skeleton crew with the tanks, the regiment set out by lorry for the coast at Brest in the hope of being evacuated. They arrived that same evening having travelled 240 miles. They managed to embark for departure shortly after, reaching Plymouth early on 17 June, minus many of their number and without a single tank to their name—their remaining fifteen having failed to make it.

John Tatham Warter was still with the regiment, unscathed after his first taste of war.

Kit's experiences during the Fall of France were not too dissimilar to those of her brother. Initially, the German offensive had done little to affect the Hadfield-Spears, but as time wore on, their situation had become more serious, and with the German Army hot on their heels, they had fled to the south-west with the French.

In June, the entire Hadfield-Spears Ambulance unit was lost without trace for two weeks. Dunkirk was cut off and little was known of their whereabouts other than they were with the French Army being routed to the south.

Newspapers in Britain ran stories about the missing unit. One, under the headline, 'Fear For 35 British Girls', published the following notice: 'Thirty-five British girls—eleven nurses and twenty-five drivers—members of the Hadfield-Spears mobile ambulance unit, who have been working day and night behind the Maginot Line since the first week in February, are feared to be missing'.[5]

Back home, with no news forthcoming, it was assumed they had been swallowed up by the German advance. However, unbeknown to those in Britain, the unit had spent two weeks in solid retreat with the German Army just a few kilometres away. Their hair-raising dash across France involved many near-misses and lucky escapes. More than once they had ran from their vehicles and jumped into ditches to dodge German dive bombers swooping down to cut them up.

Finally they reached Arachon to the south-west of Bordeaux near the border with Spain, having retreated for more than 800 miles from northern France close to the German border.

Their arrival in Plymouth on 26 June was completely unexpected and came as a great surprise to the Military Police who were overseeing disembarkations. As Lady Spears led her unit down the gangway, a sergeant, after recognising who she was, puzzlingly exclaimed, 'Mrs Spears? But you are the lost unit we've been worrying about!'[6]

'Are we?' Spears replied calmly. 'Well, you needn't worry any more. I've lost none of my girls.'[7]

The Airborne

When Digby returned from India, both John and Kit were already back in England after their unsuccessful foray to France. Frustratingly for Digby, both siblings would go on to see further active service before he himself would have the chance.

In March 1941, Kit sailed for North Africa and John followed in September with the Queen's Bays. John's departure coincided with a major development for the Ox & Bucks who, that same month, were selected to become an airborne unit.

A central landing establishment had been formed in June 1940 at Ringway Airfield, situated on what is now Manchester airport. Here, men were trained to parachute and investigations had begun on how gliders could be used to transport troops into battle.

The 1st Airborne Division, created in September 1941, were the first of their kind in Britain. Until this point, the 1st Parachute Brigade had been the only unit belonging to the airborne forces. The unit was made up of the three battalions, the 1st Battalion being the former 11 Special Air Service (SAS) that had conducted the first ever British airborne mission to destroy an Italian aqueduct, Operation Colossus, in February 1941.

Now, to compliment the paratroopers, a brigade of glider-borne troops was also required and the 2nd Ox & Bucks together with battalions from the Border Regiment, South Staffordshire Regiment, and Royal Ulster Rifles were selected to convert to airborne to fulfil this role. Together, these battalions would become part of the newly-formed 1st Airlanding Brigade.

Like the paratroopers, glider-borne troops would be considered elite. Both would fill the same essential role of landing behind enemy lines. But, while paratroopers would leap into action individually, glider troops would land in their gliders after being released from the plane towing them. Both would be an integral part of the airborne, with their own capabilities and tactical advantages to compliment the other. Gliders could carry both men and vehicles and were a good way of getting jeeps on the ground to provide instant mobility. All being well, once a glider had touched down men could emerge and instantly begin battle as a unit without having to rally. This swift method was far more difficult with paratroopers who were invariably scattered yet easier to insert into trickier areas where no adequate landing zones were available for gliders.

For the thrill-seekers like Digby, the transition from infantry to airborne was pleasing news indeed, but for others, it meant the end of their service with the Ox & Bucks. The airborne did not hold the same appeal to all, and no member of the battalion was obliged to remain if they had no desire to do so. The option to transfer into a regular infantry battalion was taken up by roughly 40 per cent of the men. Additionally there were some who wanted to stay but were unable to do so owing to their level of fitness falling below the required standard of the elite unit.

Digby's men were already at a high state of physical fitness, as were his officers who Digby had always urged to lead by example. Their fitness was confirmed in September during an all-rank cross-country march in full battle-gear. Set over 12.5 miles over varying country, the march was deliberately difficult and set to test even the fittest individuals. The names of the victors are not recorded, but it was announced that two officers from Digby's company finished first and second.

During physical training, the weak links were quickly weeded out and transferred to the regular infantry. Numbers were whittled by a further 10 per cent, but a steady stream of volunteers eagerly waited to take their place.

It was not until May 1942 that Digby's 'C' Company finally took to the air in gliders on what was their first training flight. Made from wood to preserve precious metal, the gliders were light flimsy affairs. Development of the glider had begun in 1940, the first being the Hotspur, a canvas-covered contraption capable of holding eight men. They were too small to be of any operational use so were utilised solely for training purposes. The larger Horsa, introduced in 1941, proved to be far better.

By the spring of 1942, the war had been on-going for more than two and half years. The Battle of Britain had long been won, and Britain for the time being was safe from invasion, but Hitler dominated Europe. In North Africa, the British had been pushed back by Rommel, and Britain's allies, the Russians, were under attack at Stalingrad. On the plus side, America was now in the war, although they were yet to contribute troops on the ground. Training continued, and the months rolled by.

Then, in November, Digby received some startling and devastating news from North Africa. His brother, John, was dead.

4

North Africa

Kit had been the first of the family to hear of John's death. Following their evacuation from France, the Hadfield-Spears had returned to Britain minus their vehicles and equipment. Absolutely everything, including their personal possessions, had been lost as they hopped on the last boat home.

'We started out in February with a complete hospital, all beautifully loaded onto handsome trucks; and we had lost it,' noted Lady Spears. 'The X-ray trailer and the sterilizing truck and the mobile kitchen.... And the cars the girls had given had been left on the quays at the end of the jetty in Arcachon ... such a pity. Such a waste.'[1]

Not deterred from their narrow escape, Lady Spears had set about reforming her ambulance unit the minute she had touched down on home soil. But the main issue had been the funding. Sir Hadfield had been the initial donor, but everything his money had bought had been lost and he was now very ill, shacked up in a country house near Epsom, and slowly dying. Meanwhile, Lady Hadfield was stuck in the south of France, having failed to get away during the evacuations after visiting family.

Lady Spears had written to many friends asking for contributions, but her words had fallen on deaf ears and no donor had been forthcoming. Just as it seemed all available avenues had been explored, an old acquaintance, Leslie Benson, having just returned from Washington, made contact with Lady Spears, informing her that she represented the British War Relief Society in New York and had collected a large fund to be used for the benefit of France's war effort. Now, with France out of the war, she saw no reason why some of the money should not be used for a Free French Hospital. Lady Spears duly received a cheque for £20,000 in the post.

Having escaped from France by aeroplane with Edward Spears, Gen. de Gaulle had been recognised by the British as the leader of the Free French. When Lady Spears suggested that she attach her unit to his force—the 1st Free French Brigade that was going to the Middle East—he heartily agreed.

Technically, the reformed and refitted unit was a separate entity than the Hadfield-Spears that had been put together in 1939, but Lady Spears, out of respect for Lady Hadfield and in appreciation for all she had done, felt obliged to retain the name of the original unit.

In March 1941, the Hadfield-Spears had set out for 'destination unknown', which turned out to be North Africa. After their narrow escape from France, just seven of the original girls had volunteered for further service—three nurses and four drivers, including Kit. The rest of the unit was made up of fresh volunteers from the MTC. They were hand-picked, first by Kit, who had flatly rejected half of the twenty-four volunteers when given the job of vetting them, and then by Lady Spears herself who interviewed those who had been put forward by Kit.

Kit shared a number of traits with Digby. Her language was strong and she had little patience for the weaker members of the unit who showed fear and struggled with the rigours of war. She was an exceptional driver with nerves of steel behind the wheel, even when under enemy fire. She was a good mechanic too, and always the first to get stuck into any dirty job. These skills had put the unit in good stead in France during their retreat. That all of the 'Spearrettes' made it out was in no small part down to Kit, who was often found underneath one of the vehicles carrying out some urgent maintenance to keep them moving. Her reputation preceded her, and, according to Lady Spears, when a vehicle needed fixing, the usual cry of 'T.W, we need you!' would be heard above the engines.[2]

When writing about her experiences in the war, Lady Spears described Kit as an 'outstanding driver' adding that she was undefeatable in the face of adversity and hardship.[3]

Spears wrote that Kit 'drove like a man—powerful, tireless and taciturn.... I close my eyes and see her strong shoulders and steady head behind the windscreen and know that whatever the state of the roads I needn't worry.'[4]

Lady Spears recounted one particular incident that took place on the perilous roads of North Africa:

> T.W. driving superbly could just manage by sticking to the wheel-ruts in the skiddy slush, but if she left them we were done, and when a convoy going south met a convoy coming north the thing was hopeless. A five-ton Renault would come swinging down on us, trying to pass, T.W. would shout, the juggernaut came on, a sickening lurch, a grinding noise, the sound of splintering and tearing, we both were bogged and all the great vehicles behind on both directions were brought to a stop.
>
> We spent five hours on the top of the pass among the snowy pines. The forest resounded to shouts and good-humoured curses. Dorea and I stayed huddled in our sheepskins, but T.W. was out in the slush continually with a spade. She seemed to be the only driver in the whole French army who carried one. I shall always remember her stocky khaki figure, her heavy army boots, her raw red hands, as she tramped and shouted and shovelled snow from under the army trucks.[5]

On another occasion, when it was realised she had inadvertently driven into a minefield, Kit, remaining perfectly calm, reversed back over her tracks to safety.

Kit's vehicle in North Africa was old, clapped out, and thoroughly unreliable, but having lost hers in France, it was very much a case of 'beggars can't be choosers'. 'Kit had this dreadful old thing which was a Chevrolet,' remembered one of the girls. 'It was an absolute sod to drive. It had no springs so she had to put bags of sand in it to keep it on the road at all, and it really was an awful car to drive. The steering was never right and the brakes didn't exist.'[6]

Kit cracked on regardless. She admitted to hating the vehicle, but with all its faults, she considered it better than walking.

John Joins Kit in Africa

In September 1941, after a long spell in England where they had been equipped with a new compliment of Crusader and Honey tanks, the Queen's Bays were deployed to the Middle East. Prior to departure, John married Babette Salt, his young sweetheart who was the daughter of Maj.-Gen. Harold Salt CMG, DSO.

The regiment arrived in North Africa after a nine-week voyage. Kit was thrilled to have her 'baby brother' in the same theatre of war and visited him whenever the opportunity presented itself. If an action was taking place her unit was very busy in their primary role of transportation, but in some instances, when casualties were particularly heavy, the drivers doubled-up as nurses and did whatever else they could to help. In quieter times, she drove the top brass around in a staff car.

A number of specific stories exist about Kit and her time in the desert, many testifying to her tenacity and grit. Others give an indication of her no-nonsense attitude, as discovered by a group of newly-arrived American soldiers who tried their luck with Kit and some of her friends. While the nurses were known to indulge members of the opposite sex, the transport team tended to shy away from such attention. The group of Americans got more than they bargained for when Kit and a friend shot up one of their vehicles when they had not taken the hint.

In time, owing to her frequent visits to see John, the officers and men of the Queen's Bays came to know Kit. An entry in the diary from one member of the regiment describes her pulling up in an ambulance behind the regiment's tanks one night, clad in her filthy khaki trousers, asking for her 'baby brother'.[7]

One officer, Peter Willet, who had been acquainted with the Tatham Warter family before the war and who served alongside John in the Queen's Bays, later wrote:

> John was very tough, and so were his two siblings. His younger brother, Digby, won the DSO by an extraordinary display of cool courage at Arnhem.... And his sister Kit served in a women's unit in the desert, probably driving generals. She would turn up in her staff car every few weeks. She was cheerful, self-confident and independent.[8]

Although he had nothing but kind words to say about the pluck of the Tatham Warters, Willet was compelled to write about Kit that he found 'nothing very feminine about her', adding that 'John and Digby were both good-looking in a rugged way, but what passed for good looks in a man seems out of place when transferred to a women'.[9]

Portrait photographs of the Tatham Warter brothers. John served with the Queen's Bays and Digby the Ox & Bucks prior to becoming a paratrooper.

The Queen's Bays (2nd Dragoon Guards) advance through the Gabes Gap, Tunisia, 7 April 1942.

In May 1942, the Queen's Bays took part in the Battle of Gazala, a battle in which they were rushed into various parts of the field to plug gaps as they opened. They were thrown into battle with little warning, were ill-prepared, and had no idea of the situation as a whole. During the fighting, they had no clue whether or not they were actually winning or losing overall.

By 5:30 a.m. on 29 May, the Queen's Bays had taken up their battle positions south of Knightsbridge in anticipation of a German attack which came at dawn. The Germans suffered heavily, losing three anti-tank guns, several lorries, and a number of men. Thirty-five German prisoners were also taken. Things had then quietened down, and an hour later, the men had settled down for breakfast, although this had to be hastily abandoned after the appearance of enemy tanks and the recommencement of battle.

The Queen's Bays fought in a triangular formation with the 10th Hussars and 9th Lancers. They were hemmed in and attacked repeatedly by enemy tanks, but orders were received to hold on at all costs. They did just that, and as darkness descended, they still held the field.

The battle lasted for nineteen days and the Queen's Bays were in the line the entire time, which was considered a record in the theatre. They emerged victorious, albeit battered and bruised, with many casualties.

In the engagement, John's performance under fire, particularly on 29 May, resulted in him being recommended for the Military Cross by his commanding officer, Lt-Col. Draffen.

During the battle, John's fellow officers had noticed he had taken many risks with his own life. One recorded that John, together with the CO, had 'sat out on two canvas folding chairs fixed to the back of their tank' and that he had taken no notice of the shot and shell flying in his direction.[10] After the battle, Peter Willet concluded that John 'bore a charmed life'.[11]

John's MC recommendation stated that, during the battle, they were 'very heavily engaged from three sides by German armoured units'.[12] Their orders to hold on to the position looked to be impossible. They were low on ammunition and were in urgent need of reinforcements, but as Draffen explained in the recommendation, 'neither of these could be obtained owing to the difficulty of communication and intensive gunfire'.[13] John had then volunteered to go and obtain assistance himself and to pilot the ammunition carrier to where it was so desperately needed. 'He managed to direct reinforcements up to me,' wrote Draffen, 'and also personally supervised the replenishing of every tank with ammunition, all this under intensive gunfire.'[14]

The recommendation closed by highlighting John's 'devotion to duty and total disregard of personal danger', citing he was 'entirely responsible' for them being able to hold on to their position.[15]

The MC recommendation was successful.

After the Battle of Gazala, John took command of 'A' Squadron where it was noticed he had the confidence to make decisions that other squadron leaders would not get away with nor dare to make.

The following month when John was sitting among his officers in his squadron's mess tent, he suddenly realised that every officer in his squadron was present.

He queried why they were all there and asserted that some of them should have permission to go on leave.

One who was present explained:

> Where most squadron leaders would have applied to the commanding officer, who would have threaded the application through successive layers of command until it ended up on the desk of the divisional general, for authority to send officers on leave when a great battle was imminent, John had no hesitation in making the decision for himself.[16]

The officer described John as 'one of those rare professional soldiers who knew instinctively what you could and couldn't get away with in the army'.[17] Clearly, John was not one for red tape.

John was undoubtedly brave, but his behaviour was tainted by recklessness. By a miracle, he had come through the Battle of Gazala, despite opting to go into action sitting on a deck-chair on top of his tank. In his next battle, he would go one step further, and it was here where his luck finally ran out.

John was killed on 2 November 1942 at Tel el Aqqaqir during the Second Battle of El Alamein when Rommel launched a ferocious counterattack against the British forces whose armour responded and met them head on.

In typical Tatham Warter style and in an act in keeping with his deeds of derring-do, John went into action at the head of his squadron, standing upright on top of his tank. It was bitterly cold at the time, and he was wearing a thick sheepskin coat.

They were under a murderous fire at the time of John's death. 'Every tank, every anti-tank gun, every field gun that they could muster was deployed against us,' wrote Peter Willet:

> Shot and shell rained down on us ceaselessly.... John Tatham-Warter had survived the Battle of the Gazala Line sitting with Tom [*sic*] Draffen on the back of their command tank. To expose himself in the same way to the far more concentrated fire at Tel el Aqqaqir was suicidally brave, and he was killed outright standing on the back of his tank to direct the squadron.[18]

That evening, Lady Spears was about to go to bed when the telephone in her hut began to ring. The conversation was one that she would never forget. It was an officer of the Queen's Bays, a friend of John's, asking to speak with Miss Kit Tatham Warter. Lady Spears explained that Kit was not there, but the officer was insistent and asked where he might find her. Lady Spears informed the officer that Kit was in Alex for the night and would not be back until the following day. 'Oh,' the officer had replied.

A long pause then followed before the officer somewhat nervously said that he had some news to tell Kit. Recognising the solemn tone and distress in the officer's voice, Lady Spears asked if it was bad news. 'Yes, I'm afraid it is,' replied the officer, 'I shouldn't be telephoning.'[19]

Lady Spears explained who she was and that it was okay to tell her. After a little hesitation, the officer relented and broke down, telling her that John had been killed. Lady Spears thanked him and hung up the phone.

Winston Churchill with George Draffen who, as the commanding officer of the Queen's Bays, recommended John de Grey Tatham Warter for the MC. The two men raised eyebrows and gained a lot of admiration for going into action together while sat on chairs that were fixed to their command tank.

T.W.'s baby brother was dead. 'He wasn't a baby,' wrote Lady Spears, 'He was married, but she always spoke of him like that.'[20]

Lady Spears summoned another member of the Hadfield Spears, Biddy Paterson, who was a great friend of Kit, who immediately set off to Alex to break the news.

When informed of her brother's death, Kit displayed no emotion. She returned from Alex the next morning and threw herself straight back into her work as if nothing was wrong. She did not seek out Lady Spears to thank her for letting her know, and she did not mention John's death to any of the other girls.

Later that day, Lady Spears caught a glimpse of Kit when driving past her:

> Looking out of my window before lunch I saw her at work on her car. She was in overalls and covered with grease.
>
> She didn't look up as I passed. She spent all that day and the next greasing and tinkering with the cars. I never saw her cry. She went off to find the regiment and came back again. I didn't ask for details. She didn't talk to me; nor I believe anyone, unless to Biddy, just stuck to her job and carried on. She had entered for the war and was not to be defeated. No one would have known during those days that anything had happened to her. There was no sign save her silence.[21]

Kit busy tinkering with a vehicle.

Kit (second left) stands with fellow members of the Hadfield Spears in North Africa.

Even in later years, Kit did not speak to any of her family about going to the regiment and seeing John's body, but after the war, her family would discover through the wife of an officer who was there that Kit had experienced great difficulties in recognising her brother because he had been completely decapitated by an anti-armour shell.[22] The family did not mention this to Kit and for the duration of her life she would remain unaware that they knew what she had seen.

John left behind his wife, Babette, who he had married the previous year. They had no children.

The following obituary would later appear in *The Times* newspaper:

> John Tatham-Warter was endowed with a natural gift for games and with a passion for fitness and all out-door life. He played squash rackets for Wellington and for Sandhurst and polo for the Bays, both in the subalterns' and regimental teams. He was above the average shot, and climbed mountains in Switzerland and rock faces in Cumberland and Wales. His vital personality will be sadly missed in the Cattistock and Blackmoor Vale, and by his many friends in all walks of life. His modesty, energy, and keenness in everything he undertook, whether work or play, was a delight to his older friends and an inspiration to his contemporaries.[23]

Major John Tatham Warter was twenty-seven years old when killed. He is buried in the El Alamien War Cemetery, Egypt. He is also remembered on a family memorial tablet located in the Parish Church in Hanwood, Shropshire. The memorial was installed after the war and bears the names of those members of the Warter family who gave their lives in the service of their country, spanning a number of generations. The family crest adorns the top of the tablet which bears the inscription: 'Let Those Who Come After See That Their Names Are Not Forgotten'.

The Tatham Warter siblings all had a wild streak combined with bravery. John, Kit, and Digby would all receive decorations for their gallantry in the war, although Digby's would come several years after those of his siblings.

John's MC was announced in the *London Gazette* on 13 August 1942, three months after his act of bravery at Gazala and three months before his death in action. He did not live long enough to receive the medal. His mother, Kathleen, later attended a ceremony at Buckingham Palace where the king presented her with John's award. At the ceremony, she was greatly comforted by the king's sympathetic and comforting words at the loss of her favourite son.

Kit was awarded the French Croix de Guerre for her gallantry during the Battle of Bir Hakiem (26 May–21 June 1942) which coincided with John's MC action. During the battle, the Free French defended their position in the face of overwhelming odds and as a result of their performance would be renamed 'The Fighting French'.

After the collapse of France, French decorations like Kit's were not published in the *London Gazette* and as such are notoriously difficult to confirm. French awards during this period presented a substantial problem because their government was practically non-existent. Gen. de Gaulle was recognised as the leader of the Free French, but he was not the head of state, whose job would ordinarily have been to authorise and issue the

Kit Tatham Warter with her close friend Biddy. Both women served with the Hadfield Spears Ambulance Unit during the war.

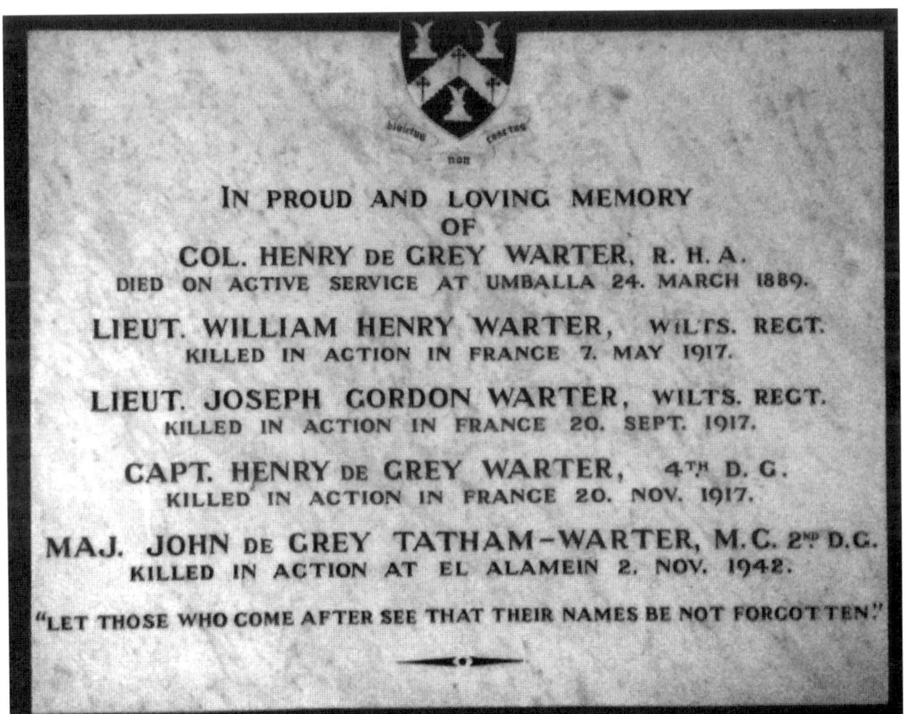

The Warter family memorial plaque was installed in the Parish Church in Hanwood after the Second World War. Digby's brother, John, was the final inscription. (*The Revd Graham D. Phillips*)

awards. The trouble was that no head of state actually existed, and there was no way of knowing whether or not any awards that were issued would be officially recognised by whatever government would eventually be put into place at the end of the war. It would be hugely embarrassing if the future French government failed to recognise the awards after they had been officially announced in Britain. This would mean a wide-scale cancelation of the awards both officially and publicly. As such, it was thought best not to publish them in the *Gazette*, despite them being granted by the French.

As it happened, the awards were indeed upheld after the war, but nothing was done retrospectively to officially publish the names of the recipients, thus creating difficulties when trying to pinpoint certain awards. In Kit's case, no difficulties exist. Her medals, mounted as worn, together with official paperwork, reside in the family and period photographs exist of Kit wearing them.

Kit never spoke about what she had done to receive her medal but contemporary paperwork describes her driving through heavy enemy fire to reach wounded Frenchmen. She served with the Hadfield-Spears for the duration of the war and was proud of her service. She became very well known in the equestrian world and by 1949 was recognised as the leading female rider in the country. She won many gold medals and competitions and represented Great Britain, winning gold in the Senior European Eventing Championship in 1957.

Kit's tough personality remained with her into old age. Several years before her death in 1999, Kit's family discovered a handgun and a box of ammunition in a

Kit Tatham Warter clears a hedge on horseback.

Above: Kit Tatham Warter, a world renowned horsewomen who won the gold in the 1957 Team Eventing European Championship.

Right: Kit Tatham Warter on Pampas Cat—'Working Hunter of the Year'.

drawer in her living room. 'It's for protection,' she exclaimed when asked what it was for. After a number of failed attempts to smuggle the firearm out of the house, her family finally succeeded in sneaking it out without her noticing. The firearm was subsequently handed over to the police during Douglas Hurd's gun amnesty, much to the amusement of the police officer on the desk who curiously asked where it had come from. Kit took the loss of her sidearm well, telling her family that she was not bothered because she still had John's old hunting rifle in the shed. 'It's a very good rifle' was her response when asked why she had kept it all those years.[24]

Kit, who never married, passed away at the age of ninety. Her medals were placed on her coffin during her funeral service.

Illustration of Digby dating from 1943.

5

The Airborne

On 23 April 1943, the War Office announced that a second airborne division—the 6th, named as such to confuse the enemy into believing there were more in existence—was to be raised to compliment the existing 1st Airborne Division. To add experience, the Ox & Bucks were among those transferred from the 1st Division to this new formation.

The first inkling that Digby was looking to leave the Ox & Bucks came several months later in July. Operation Husky, the Allied invasion of Sicily, had started. Under the codename Operation Ladbroke, the 1st Airlanding Brigade (from which the Ox & Bucks had recently been transferred) had gone in by glider to seize and capture the Ponte Grande Bridge and the harbour and urban area of Syracuse.

It is commonly thought that Digby's decision to join the paratroopers was a direct result of his brother's death and that he hoped it would speed up his entry into the war, but in reality, there was nine months between John's death and Digby's transfer. Certainly Digby's family are not aware of any connection between the two events. Besides, there was no guarantee that any move would result in a quicker deployment anyhow. In fact, by leaving the Ox & Bucks to become a paratrooper, Digby would inadvertently delay his own opportunity to see battle.

Digby's announcement that he would be leaving the Ox & Bucks came out of the blue to his friends who were genuinely shocked at his decision. John Howard was certainly very surprised that Digby had decided to 'cross over', as the airborne called it. Digby broke the news to Howard after they had been discussing the invasion of Sicily when Howard asked if he thought it was 'the beginning of the end'. 'I hope not John!' replied Digby, 'I'm transferring to the paratroops, and I want a chance to see some action!'[1]

Rivalry was a common trait among all arms of the military and this was certainly the case with the glider-borne soldiers and 'the para boys', and glider troops took great pleasure in knowing that many of them would be more than willing to take up parachuting if they were required to do so, whereas many paratroopers would not entertain the idea of pranging into action by glider.

Digby's application to transfer was successful and he soon found himself saying his goodbyes to his friends. His departure coincided with a spell of leave for John Howard. Digby approached Howard as he was about to go. 'So you're off on leave,' he said to Howard, adding with a wink, 'Be sure to give my best to your delightful wife!'[2]

'You keep your best wishes to yourself you cheeky bugger!' Howard snapped back with a smile.[3]

2nd Battalion Parachute Regiment

Digby found himself returning once again to the 1st Airborne Division, this time earmarked for the 2nd Parachute Battalion, 1st Parachute Brigade.

When the division formed in September 1941, any soldier wishing to become a paratrooper had to undergo a rigorous regime of training, including a series of 'jumps'. After three months' intense training, the initial qualifying jumps had taken place at Ringway in Manchester in January 1942.

Their first operation had taken place the following month on the night of 27–28 February, when members of the battalion launched an audacious raid against a German coastal radar system some 12 miles north-north-east of Le Havre in France. Strong coastal defences had ruled out a commando raid from the sea, so the insertion of paratroopers had been preferred. The mission, Operation Biting, had been carried out by Maj. John Frost's 'C' Company, which had been dropped several miles from the target at Bruneval. At the station, enemy guards had been overcome and essential components from the radar system successfully removed by the raiders who had then withdrawn to the beach for extraction by landing craft having captured a dozen prisoners. Among them had been a radar technician who had given up valuable information regarding radar technology. The operation put the paratroopers on the map, but a further eight months passed before the battalion got to see any further action.

On 1 November 1942, they had sailed for North Africa with John Frost as their new commanding officer. Frost, who had been awarded the MC for his part in the Bruneval Raid, had previously been the battalion's second-in-command and had all the qualities needed to run the battalion.

A plan had been drawn up to jump behind enemy lines in Tunisia where they were to destroy a number of enemy airfields. They were to drop near Pont du Fahs to wreck any aircraft found there before heading to Depienne to do the same. Then, they were to slog to Oudna located 9 miles from Tunis, where, after wreaking whatever havoc they could, they were to be reinforced by armoured units who by then would have punched through the enemy lines to join them.

Ever-changing developments on the ground were a frustrating yet common aspect of planning airborne drops. A consequence of airborne missions was that they were often rendered useless and scrapped due to change of circumstances on the ground. Sometimes they would be cancelled, and at other times hastily adjusted as new

John Frost, the commanding officer of the 2nd Battalion Parachute Regiment. Frost would end the war as a POW having been wounded and captured at Arnhem.

information came in. Such had been the case with the 2nd Battalion in Tunisia where, right before they departed, news had been received that neither Pont du Fahs nor Depienne were in use by the enemy. Instead, the battalion flew straight to Depienne, 30 miles south of Tunis, from where they marched the 14 miles to Oudna.

When dropped on 29 November, there had been no time to confirm a drop zone. Instead, they had simply flown towards the target area with peeled eyes, looking for a suitable place to jump. Once found, Frost had leapt from his plane, followed by the rest of his stick. It had been impossible to inform the whole of the battalion of the plan, but it was hoped their lack of knowledge would not matter, and after seeing their comrades from Frost's plane hurling to the ground, the rest would simply assume they were where they needed to be and follow suit. Luckily, this had proved to be the case.

Once on the ground, Frost had made his way to a small mound and rallied the men with his hunting horn. There had been some inevitable confusion among those who were expecting to be in Pont du Fahs and some considerable delays had been encountered while a quantity of weapon containers were recovered from the other side of a large gully, but eventually some semblance of order had been established.

It was a bitterly-cold night as the battalion set out on their trek to Oudna, but once reached, the local Arabs had informed them that the enemy had cleared out and were no longer in the area. Certainly there were no aircraft at the airfield and nothing to suggest any aircraft had recently been operating from the site. But contrary to what the Arabs had told them, vast numbers of Germans were still in the area and the battalion had unwittingly entered a hornets' nest.

With the battalion overlooking the airfield from a nearby hill, one company had been sent forward to investigate further, closely followed by Frost and Battalion HQ. As they got into the open, mortars and machine-gun fire erupted from the direction of the airfield and half a dozen German tanks had revved up their engines and burst out from the cover of a nearby viaduct. A group of paratroopers had made a gallant but futile attempt to grenade them, which resulted in all but one of the party being killed. The situation had grown worse with the arrival of German Messerschmitts that swooped down to attack. Luckily, the paratroopers had been well concealed among the rocks, boulders, and scrub on the hill and the shots fired were largely ineffective.

At this point a wireless signal—the only one received for the entire operation—had brought further bad news. Due to stubborn German resistance—and in a situation not dissimilar to what would later occur at Arnhem—the promised armoured support would not be arriving. As more and more enemy armour arrived, the battalion had found themselves practically surrounded. A paratrooper captured early in the fight had been sent by the Germans to request a surrender, but Frost had no intentions of giving up.

There would be no surrender and men would fight on, but the position on the hill was no place from where to do it and a difficult decision had been made regarding the wounded who could not be moved and had been left behind.

After relocating to another position to await darkness, the survivors had set off in the direction of the Allied lines some 50 miles away. On 3 December, after smashing through the German encirclement and carrying out a prolonged fighting withdrawal, what was left of the battalion had linked up with an American patrol before finally reaching the sanctuary of Medjez El Bab. They had started the operation lightly armed with just 150 rounds of ammunition per man with no reserve supply. By the time they reached safety, both ammunition and the men themselves were completely spent. The botched operation had cost the battalion sixteen officers and approximately 250 other ranks.

Following the Oudna debacle, and much to their disgust, the battalion had then been thrown straight into the line as regularly infantry. Without adequate supplies, poorly equipped, and without their own transportation, they filled the role with gritted teeth for four long months. During this period, some 250 reinforcements arrived to fill the gap left by their recent losses.

The campaign in North Africa ended successfully in May 1943. Members of the battalion were well decorated for their part, including Lt-Col. Frost who was awarded a DSO.

On top of an enhanced reputation, the 1st Airborne Division also came away with a new nickname, 'The Red Devils', which originated after 'reliable information' was received that the German forces in Tunisia had used the phrase to describe the paratroopers who they had faced in battle. Brig. Flavell, commander of the 1st Parachute Brigade, wasted no time in sending out a message, congratulating the men on their newly acquired title.

In Africa, the local Arabs referred to the paratroopers as 'Men with Tails' on account of their Denison smocks that had a 'tail' attached to the rear to assist in parachuting. Tails were fastened underneath the crotch to prevent the smock from rising over the head of the parachutist during his descent but when unfastened, they hung down like a tail. The red mud of North Africa that the paratroopers were invariably covered in, coupled with their aggressive fighting spirit, is also said to have contributed to the name. 'The Red Devils' struck a cord and the paratroopers were immensely proud of the name.

Today's airborne and those affiliated with the regiment insist their beret is maroon, not red, and a degree of frustration is often felt when it is referred to as anything other than maroon, but this has not always been the case. Likewise, the beret is a cherished—almost sacred—item among the airborne, but this too was not initially the case and a fair amount of discontent was encountered when the beret was first introduced. Many of the men much preferred to wear their old regimental headgear instead. One 2nd Battalion soldier, a tough Ulsterman, had rebuffed Frost's attempts for him to replace his 'Caubeen' with the beret, but despite Frost's efforts, the man was adamant he did not want to wear it. The man was killed in action wearing his caubeen in Tunisia.

Yet despite these early protests, the men quickly came to feel a great sense of pride in their 'red' berets. The fact that they were maroon, not red, was duly recognised, as noted by John Frost in a post-war entry in the *Pegasus Journal*:

> After we heard that the Germans were calling us 'Red Devils' no member of the Parachute Brigade would refer to his beret as anything other than being red. No one thereafter wanted any other form of headgear.[4]

And then there was the battle-cry, 'Whoa Mohammed!'[5] John Frost, in his memoir *A Drop Too Many*, offered the following explanation as to its origins:

> There has always been some controversy as to how the battle cry of the 1st Parachute Brigade came to be adopted. This was a shout of 'Wayo Mahommed'. As far as I am aware it was merely copied from the local Arabs during this phase of the campaign.
>
> These people, who lived near and sometimes within the brigade sector, were continually calling out from one hilltop to another. Like all hill people they knew how to make their voices carry and, as every Arab's name in that part of the world seemed to begin with Mahommed, all their shouted conversations to begin with:
>
> 'Waho Mahommed.'
>
> 'Waho.'
>
> 'Waho Mahommed bil Munchar,' and so on to the text of the message.
>
> It was too much to expect that the soldiers would refrain from joining in. Some became expert at imitating the more guttural sounds and, before long, as soon as our neighbours started up, the air became jammed with real and bogus Arabic. Long after the Arabs had moved and wherever the brigade went, a concerted cry of 'Waho Mahammed' brought extra spurts of energy, in action or play.[6]

American paratrooper Ross Carter, of the 504th Parachute Infantry Regiment, 82nd Division, who was serving in the same theatre of war, described a similar version of its origins. According to Carter, whilst quartered in an Arab village, the British paratroopers became familiar with a local man who would pass them each day with an overloaded donkey. The Arab would yell 'Whoa, Mohammed', or 'Wahai

Mohammed', when struggling to get the beast to move. In jest, the paratroopers took to shouting the phrase whenever the opportunity arose, and it did not take long for them to begin yelling it among themselves without provocation or reason.

Whatever the case, 'Whoa Mohammed' was here to stay and it quickly became the airborne war-cry. In future battles, it would spur them on to perform great feats of bravery.

Following the victory in North Africa, attention had turned to Sicily and the 1st Parachute Brigade, now under the command of newly promoted Brig. Gerald Lathbury, the former commander of the 3rd Battalion, were assigned the task of securing Ponte di Primosole (Primosole Bridge), the 400-foot road bridge spanning over the Simeto River. Located between Syracuse and Catania, it would provide an opening to the Catania Plain. Here, they would be pitted against an Italian Coastal Division and elite German *Fallsmchirmjäger* troops who had been sent in to harden Italian resistance.

On 7 July 1943, Frost briefed his company commanders about the operation. The three parachute battalions of the brigade together with glider troops would drop both sides of the bridge to capture it in a *coup de main*. Orders were to hold it until relieved by elements of the Eighth Army moving inland from the beaches. The brigade would jump at four separate drop zones and the gliders would land in two separate areas. The 2nd Battalion would jump south of the bridge and capture three hills codenamed Johnny I, Johnny II, and Johnny III, which offered a commanding view of the bridge and its approach. The bridge itself was to be captured by the 1st Battalion that was to drop at both sides of the river. The 3rd Battalion, meanwhile, who were to drop 1,000 yards north of the bridge, secure the area, and defend it against counterattack, thereby protecting the approach to the bridge.

Operation Fustain began on 13 July and things began to go wrong from start. Things quickly turned into a farce when over thirty aircraft strayed from their course and were fired on by an Allied convoy that had been told to stay alert in anticipation of an enemy attack. Two planes were shot down, another two collided when trying to dodge anti-aircraft fire, and a further nine were so badly damaged they had to return to the airfields of North Africa. The parachutists were badly scattered in the jump, nowhere near their intended drop zones. The glider troops later landed and came under concentrated machine-gun fire in small fields that were boxed in with solid banks and walls. Only four gliders managed to escape unscathed.

Frost was able to seize and hold his objectives, yet with less than 100 members of his battalion, and minus his second-in-command and his adjutant, he called the situation 'bitterly disappointing', made worse by the fact he had jarred his knee in the drop.[7]

At the bridge itself, some fifty men of the 1st Battalion had succeeded in capturing it. These would soon be reinforced by a further forty under Brig. Lathbury who oversaw the safe removal of demolition charges on the bridge before setting out a defensive perimeter. Stragglers and glider troops arrived later to reinforce the defence.

By 4:30 a.m. the following day, both the 1st and 2nd Battalion remained severely depleted. The badly scattered 3rd Battalion could muster only a few men who were ordered to join the 1st at the bridge. 'During the morning,' wrote Frost, 'two officers and forty other ranks had been killed and roughly the same number wounded. All through the day small numbers of stragglers continued to arrive in dribs and drabs, but the effective fighting strength remained at about sixty men.'[8]

Frost's men fought off a counterattack, but another more determined attack forced them to give up Johnny II. At 9 a.m., an observation officer attached to the battalion succeeded in making radio contact with a naval cruiser armed with 6-inch guns which opened up and caused the *Fallschirmjägers* some casualties, but a grass fire forced the paratroopers off Johnny I, leaving just Johnny III in their possession.

At 2 p.m., a force of 350 *Fallschirmjäger* troops together with an anti-aircraft battery and some anti-tank guns and light trucks attacked the bridge from the north. The attack was beaten off, but a second more determined effort supported by three 88-mm anti-aircraft guns almost gained a foothold on the bridge. This resulted in the capture of some British paratroopers, and allowed the 88-mm guns to move into a closer position to direct their fire. Pillboxes manned by the paratroopers at the north side of the bridge were soon destroyed. At 5 p.m., with ammunition running low, the paratroopers were forced to retire to the south side of the bridge. This move prompted the Germans to move closer, and when the strong-points of the south side were also destroyed, Lathbury, with mounting casualties and dwindling supplies, decided he had no alternative but to relinquish the bridge. The force moved back the best part of a mile having suffered 115 casualties from the 295 men who had reached the target. The 16th (Parachute) Field Ambulance dressing station were unable to withdraw and remained in what was now a no-man's-land where the enemy allowed them to continue treating the wounded unmolested.

The bridge was eventually captured by Allied ground forces, but things had not gone to plan for the paratroopers from the start and Frost summed it up as 'yet another humiliating disaster for airborne forces'.[9]

For the first part of August, the battalion's companies were rotated in and out of the divisional rest camp by the sea South of Tunis and given the chance to lick their wounds from their most recent disaster. The following month, they learned they would be carrying out a seaborne operation at Taranto in Italy in one week's time. Their embarkation on 11 September was followed by an unopposed and uneventful landing. At this stage, the Germans were on the run. Monty's Eighth Army was in hot pursuit, although the battalion had entered a period of training and was not involved in the offensive.

It was during this period that a new officer, fresh from England, strutted into the battalion's digs. This tall, thin, and immaculately turned out individual was full of energy, eager for action, and in no way intimidated by the hardened veterans before him.

Digby's complete self-assurance was immediately apparent to the officers, including Maj. Dover, who formed the instant impression that Digby had a thorough confidence in his own ability. But until he had experienced the acid test of battle, the jury would remain out on this new addition to the officers' mess.

6

Bitter Disappointment

For every step forward, there seemed to be two steps backwards. Delighted at finally arriving in a theatre of war, Digby's hopes of seeing action were dealt a swift blow. Shortly after his arrival, orders were received that the division, after their prolonged period of extensive fighting, were to return to England to refit and undergo a period of further training. Digby was furious and his disappointment and anger evident for all to see.

After a long period of frustration in India with the Ox & Bucks, Digby had returned to England in the hope of getting imminent active service. Instead, the battalion had undergone a period of rigorous and lengthy training. Then, in September 1941, a full two years into the war, they had become a part of the airborne. But this exciting development had meant additional training had been required. This had continued for many months before Digby became a paratrooper in the 1st Airborne Division which, at the time, had been in constant action in North Africa, which was exactly what he was yearning for. He had applied for his transfer, qualified as a paratrooper, and eagerly rushed off to war only to find he had arrived too late and had missed the fighting by a whisker.

Now, on 9 November 1943, he found himself at Taranto, boarding the troopship *Ville d'Oran* destined for a return to British shores. The division arrived home the following month and were sent to billets around the country. Frost's 2nd Battalion were sent to Grantham, Lincolnshire, which was to be their home for the foreseeable future.

After a short stint as second-in-command of the battalion, Digby was given command of 'A' Company in place of Maj. Lonsdale DSO who moved to Battalion HQ.

During a period of leave over the Christmas period, Digby visited his family, but the battalion was soon back at the billets to knuckle down on training. In the New Year, Maj. David Wallis, an old pre-war friend of John Frost, arrived from the Ox & Bucks. Frost was thrilled to have Wallis with him at headquarters as his second-in-command.

Meanwhile, Digby quickly began to forge a reputation as a something of a character.

Standing over 6 feet tall, immaculately turned-out, and with a demeanour that oozed confidence, he certainly cut an impressive figure among the airborne elite. Bad timing had denied him the opportunity to prove himself in battle, or to forge bonds that can only be established in combat, but his strong character ensured he was able to strike up immediate relations with his fellow officers and men. He had a wicked sense of humour and his eccentric behaviour was a welcome addition to the mess.

Digby, for the duration of his life, would often find himself in spots of bother when under the influence of alcohol. Although only in a theatre of war for a short period of time, it had not been long before he was engaged in booze-fuelled fist-fights, described by his brigadier, Gerald Lathbury, as 'drunken brawls'. Lathbury went on to say that Digby 'would occasionally smash up the bar room furniture and engage in wild fist fights with friends that would be forgotten next morning'.[1]

Leo Heaps, who would fight at Arnhem and who, years later, would interview Digby, noted: 'The major did not hold his liquor well, but after a night of drunken revelry he would return to his unit chastised and refreshed'.[2]

But Digby never allowed his drinking sessions to get in the way of his work, and however drunk he had been the night before, he would always be punctual and impeccably turned out the following morning, none the worse for his previous night's antics. Furthermore, there was never any ill-feeling towards anyone he had traded blows with. All was instantly forgotten.

Digby proved to be a hit with his men, who were no slouches themselves and not easily impressed. One young paratrooper recalled that Digby was not like the other officers in the battalion who would officially punish the men for any misdemeanour and have them spend time in the Glass House if the crime was deemed serious enough to warrant it. Maj. Tate of Battalion HQ was a particularly keen advocate of this form of punishment which affected his popularity among some of the men. Digby, however, preferred to deal with things his own way. 'He never put a man on a charge,' recalled Pte Morgan, a new arrival who had joined the battalion after its return to England.[3] Instead, Digby would simply approach the culprit and specify a time for them to meet in the boxing ring. Although somewhat unorthodox, Digby's methods of dealing with those who stepped out of line went down well with the men who would invariably lose the fight yet relish the opportunity to freely punch an officer without fear of repercussions or hard feelings. It was all good fun. Moreover, as far as Digby was concerned, once the fight was over, that was the end of the matter and the offence was forgotten.

Interestingly, after he had taken temporary command of Digby's company of Ox & Bucks while Digby was away on a course, Maj. Howard had described them as extremely fit yet lacking in discipline, perhaps suggesting that Digby let his men get away with more than what would be considered normal, although he could undoubtedly be stern when lines were crossed or in training.

Digby was not alone in his enthusiasm for a drink, and the paratroopers made the most of the local ale houses whenever the opportunity arose. On such occasions, the pubs in Grantham were bustling with airborne troops and their boisterous behaviour would often result in spontaneous bouts of violence. At this stage, Digby was already known for the frequent use of his fists, particularly but not exclusively while under the influence of alcohol.

The Blue Horse in Great Ponton was a favourite watering hole for the officers, and several large parties were held in the establishment, including one to celebrate Maj. Dover's twenty-fifth birthday on 25 February. For Dover, who commanded 'C' Company, it would certainly be a birthday to remember.

After a heavy night's drinking, it was custom for the officers to pile up the establishment's furniture and take running jumps over them. It was in fact a knock-out competition where those who failed to clear the pile were eliminated. As the rounds progressed, the pile got higher.

Dover described the game that was held on his birthday:

> I found myself the final competitor with Digby Tatham-Warter. He was over six feet tall whereas I was a mere five ft 8 inches. Digby cleared the obstacles with some ease, while I just caught the solid oak stool at the top of the pile with my toe. I fell on my back on the far side and watched the stool wobble. Before I could move it fell onto my mouth as I lay on the floor. What a mess![4]

Digby was crowned the champion and no doubt celebrated with another drink. Dover, meanwhile, was carted off to hospital with a deep cut that started at his mouth and extended up his face. His wound was stitched up and for the next two weeks his diet would consist only of soup.

After initially setting up his HQ at Hungerton Hall, Lt-Col. Frost had relocated to Stoke Rochford Hall, an impressive Victorian Country mansion boasting a nine-hole golf course in its grounds, which Frost made good use of. Frost was a serious golfer and very competitive, even when playing against his friends, but he soon discovered that when playing with men like Digby it was impossible to have a serious game.

Frost's regular competitors were David Wallis and Digby and they played together whenever they could, but Wallis and Digby took great pleasure in winding up their commanding officer in any way possible. Frost recalled that they were 'the most unprincipled competitors when given the slightest possible chance of winning by nefarious means', but he could not help but feel amused and accepted their pranks with good humour. 'Suddenly calling a dog, or treading on an opponents ball, were two of the least of these measures, but we all had the greatest of fun.'[5]

In an act that in hindsight would seem full of misplaced confidence, Frost's golf clubs would accompany him to Holland in the looming Arnhem operation where he hoped to grab a game or two once victory had been sealed.

In Grantham, the battalion officers ran what they called the 'Line Book'. The name derived from 'shooting a line'. In other words, it was a book of witty or humorous remarks spoken in casual conversation that were deemed too good to go unrecorded. Any officer wishing to add a line in the book had to cough up two shillings for the privilege. Several entries from the book have survived, although their context has not. An entry written by Johnny Frost read: 'Such talk makes my war wounds ache'; one from Maj. Doug Crawley, OC of 'B' Company, simply read: 'I'm the finest type of man I know'.[6]

A surviving entry from Digby portrays his trademark confidence. It reads: 'I consider it monstrous that the Brigadier should ever doubt an officer of my integrity'.[7]

But things were not always fun and games, and the battalion's leisure activities were slotted in around a gruelling training regime. Frost gave his company commanders leeway to train their men as they saw fit and generally did little to interfere. In training, Digby was known to push his men extremely hard, and in contradiction to him allowing a degree of roguish behaviour, he was described as 'a particularly severe but inspirational commander of his men.'[8]

For Digby, it was simple: they were there to do a job, and they would do it to the best of their ability no matter what. His soldiers were there to follow him and to fight, and he, above all else, was there to lead them. Following his death in 1993, it was said in an obituary that Digby's officers 'were expected to emulate his attitudes and standards'.[9]

It also claimed that he made little effort to learn the names of his men. The original source of this is not known, but it is something his family were very surprised to read in his obituary. In their opinion, this did not sound like Digby at all. This was reinforced by Arnhem veteran Albert Spring, who, upon reading the 1993 obituary, fiercely disputed this fact and asserted that it simply was not true and that Digby was a fine officer in every regard.

Digby's 'A' Company consisted of his headquarters plus three platoons, each led by an officer. His second-in-command was Capt. Tony Frank who had served with the Lancashire Fusiliers and commandos before joining the paratroopers. Capt. Frank, whose 'great qualities of leadership, initiative and gallantry' in Sicily had resulted in him being awarded the MC, was the same age as Digby and far more experienced in the art of warfare.[10]

'A' Company's Number One platoon was commanded by twenty-one-year-old Robert Vlasto, known as Robin, who had recently transferred from the King's Royal Rifle Corps. Number Two platoon was commanded by John (Jack) Grayburn who at the age of twenty-six was the oldest platoon leader in the company.[11] Taking a demotion from captain, he had transferred from the Ox & Bucks to the 7th Parachute Battalion in June 1943 before joining Frost's 2nd Battalion the following year. Now in his mid-twenties, Lt Andrew McDermont, a Scotsman known as 'Drew' by his family and 'Mac' by his comrades, was in charge of the company's Number Three platoon.

Most of Digby's officers had yet to see action, including Jack Grayburn, who, like Digby, was very excited at the prospect. Grayburn's hatred for the Germans was well-known, and he was very vocal in explaining what he intended to do to them when the time came. It was not unusual for soldiers to detest their enemy. Their fathers and other relatives had fought and died in the 'the war to end all wars' not two decades earlier, yet here they were again, facing the same enemy, and many had vowed revenge. But, while some felt hatred, there were others who felt differently. The paratroopers, between their training, were shown propaganda films and received a series of lectures designed to stir up hatred towards Germany and her soldiers, but as one paratrooper put it, it was 'an uphill task, as the average soldier appeared to have only three basic interests: football, beer and crumpet'—in reverse order.[12] To new-arrival James Sims, it seemed that members of the battalion had a 'half-admiring, half-contemptuous attitude' towards the Germans.[13]

As a form of communication between his companies, Digby decided to introduce a bugle system into his training. Wireless radios served the same purpose, but Digby distrusted their reliability, and since there was a high likelihood his platoons would be fighting within earshot of one and other, bugles could prove to be very useful. He issued two bugles to each of his platoons and HQ and every man was taught to recognise a series of specific bugle calls and what they meant. Acutely aware of the history of the Ox & Bucks, Digby likened these calls to those used by the light infantry in the Peninsular War. When sounding skirmishing orders, the light infantry had used the bugle instead of the standard infantry drum, and it was these signals that Digby decided to replicate. His decision may also have been influenced after hearing about problems the paratroopers had encountered with their radios in previous battles before his arrival.

Digby continued to cement his reputation as an eccentric, on one occasion procuring an American Dakota to whisk his company officers away to London for a night at the Ritz. Such idiosyncrasies enhanced Digby's reputation, but not every officer in the battalion enjoyed popularity. One paratrooper, in describing an episode that did little to enhance Maj. Tate's reputation, related:

> Major Tate put up a Company order on the notice board that we were to report to the parade ground early one Sunday morning and started to foot drill us. The parade ground was immediately outside the officers' quarters and within a few minutes we saw the figure of Lt Col John Frost coming down the stairs dressed in his dressing gown complete with red beret on his head. He took Major Tate a polite distance away but just near enough for the troops to hear what he said:
>
> 'Major Tate, Airborne troops do not march, they fight and soon we shall be overseas to do just that and one of these men will earn the Battalion a Victoria Cross. Quietly dismiss the men and let them go back to bed and there will be no Church parade this Sunday.'[14]

All talk was of a large-scale Allied assault involving the airborne in France. But when the time came, the battalion and division as a whole was dealt a sickening blow.

On 6 June 1944, Operation Overlord, the Allied invasion of Normandy, began. Hours before the beach landings, under the cover of darkness, paratroopers were called upon to drop into France to neutralise key objectives, disrupt enemy reinforcements, and prevent movement towards the beaches. But it was the 6th Airborne Division that was called upon to carry out the task, not the 1st Airborne Division, who remained in England in reserve.

A tense rivalry existed between the two airborne divisions. The 1st Airborne Division considered the 6th—who were a newer unit with far less experience—to be amateurs, and it was felt they did not deserve the honour of getting the D-Day drop

Stoke Rochford Hall as it looks today. This grand building was used as Battalion HQ during their stay in Lincolnshire. (*Copyright: Jonathan Thacker, via Stoke Rochford Hall © Jonathan Thacker :: Geograph Britain and Ireland*)

ahead of themselves. Rioting broke out among the 1st Airborne Division when it was discovered they would not be taking part, and only when the officers assured their men they were being left behind for 'something special' did they stop. The division would indeed get 'something special', but at the time nobody had any clue what that would be, and many of the officers themselves were disappointed in having to sit it out. For Digby, there was an added frustration; his former battalion, the 2nd Ox & Bucks, were now playing a major part in the D-Day Operation, and his old friend, Maj. John Howard, would have the honour of leading the first Allied soldiers on to French soil to kick-start the invasion. Landing by glider, Howard would carry out an audacious and very successful *coup de main* to capture what would become known as Pegasus Bridge, which he would hold until reinforcements arrived from the beach.

Following D-Day, the 2nd Ox & Bucks would be involved in subsequent battles. If Digby had remained with them, he would have got the action he so desperately craved. Unfortunately, his move had drastically backfired.

It would take several months for the promise of 'something special' to materialise, and until then there would be many further disappointments. Delayed and cancelled airborne operations were to be expected. Even so, it was a cause for annoyance for the airborne, who after becoming hyped up for action became accustomed to being let down again and again. In the follow-up to D-Day, the 1st Airborne Division had many operations planned and subsequently cancelled, some at the very last minute as they were boarding the planes.

Operation Market Garden was still more than three months away. In the meantime, rapid gains would be made at an absurd pace in the liberation of Europe. German resistance was seemingly collapsing beyond repair on a wide front and many were worried that the war would be over before they had the chance to take part in the fighting. Between the months of June and September, well over a dozen operations were planned and cancelled; the main reasons included the swift overrunning of the intended drop zones by grounds troops and through the impracticality of the flight paths to reach the target area.

Among the cancellations was Operation Comet, an audacious plan where the division was to carry out an assault to capture a series of vital bridges in Holland at Grave, Nijmegen, and Arnhem over which Allied ground forces would advance across the rivers Maas, Waal, and Lower Rhine, outflanking the Siegfried Line, thus opening the gateway into Germany. The division were told to standby for Comet on 7 September, but it was postponed three days later before eventually being cancelled altogether. All forces were warned to stand by for further operations and given five days' leave with strict orders to return on 15 September.

The operation had been ambitious—too ambitious, at least for the single division

Digby and fellow officers and men of the battalion. Others are recognisable in the group including Maj. Crawley, Capt. McLean, Lt Grayburn, and Lt McDermont. Lt-Col. John Frost is the central figure.

that had been initially earmarked to carry it out. Therefore, the staff had been busy restructuring and amending Comet to include two additional American airborne divisions. The 1st Airborne Division learned of the amended plan, named Operation Market, on 15 September, just two days before it was set to begin.

The American 101st Airborne were given the task of capturing two bridges around Eindhoven and the 82nd Division two at Nijmegen and the surrounding heights. The British 1st Airborne Division under Gen. Roy Urquhart, totalling some 10,000 men, were given the job of capturing bridges at Arnhem, including the main road bridge.

The plan, as described by the Air Ministry, was as follows:

> Main Plan
>
> The tasks for the First Allied Airborne Army were allotted as follows:
>
> (a) 1st Airborne Division with 1st Polish Parachute Brigade Group to capture bridges at Arnhem and establish a bridge-head around them, to enable land forces to move northwards.
> (b) 82nd Airborne Division to capture crossings at Nijmegen and Grave and to hold the high ground between Nijmegen and Groesbeck. The advanced headquarters of the Airborne Corps were to fly in with the first glider lift of this division.
> (c) 101st Airborne Division were to seize the bridges and defiles between Eindhoven and Grave.
> (d) 878th Aviation Engineer Battalion and 2nd Airlanding Light A.A. Battery, to land in gliders and to prepare and defend landing strips north of Arnhem.
> (e) 52nd Lowland Division to be transported in Dakotas to the landing strips provided the military situation permitted.[15]

The combined airborne and ground operation would be known as Operation Market Garden—Market being the airborne assault and Garden being the ground attack.

Of all the bridges to capture, those at Arnhem, lying 64 miles behind enemy lines, were the furthest to reach. It was the job of the 1st Parachute Brigade under Brig. Lathbury to capture these bridges and hold them for forty-eight hours until ground forces in the form of the 2nd Army's XXX Corps arrived.

The lack of available drop zones near to the target was cause for concern. Arnhem was a built-up area and this, together with dense woodland and a lack of dry open ground, ruled out a drop on or near the target area. A German airfield in nearby Deelen with flak guns added a further deterrent meaning the airborne troops would have to make their jump some distance away which was not ideal since the operation required surprise and a swift capture of the bridges. The 2nd Battalion's drop zone near Heelsum was 7 miles from the Arnhem road bridge, which meant a long slog through enemy-held territory. It would not do to become bogged down in pitched battles *en route*. Speed was essential.

In order to prevent a bottleneck, the three battalions of Lathbury's 1st Parachute

Brigade would advance to the bridge using separate routes. The 1st Battalion under Lt-Col. David Dobie would take the Leopard Route running from the rail line to the Amsterdamseweg, leading to Arnhem from the north, while Lt-Col. John Fitch's 3rd Battalion would use the Tiger Route running directly through Oosterbeek to Arnhem. Meanwhile, Frost's 2nd Battalion would take the southerly Lion Route, taking them south to Heelsum, then east to Heveadorp and Oosterbeek and on to Arnhem.

But it was not all bad news. German presence in the area was said to be both minimal and weak, consisting of old men and a number of young ill-equipped SS recruits. Luftwaffe personnel at Deelen airfield, 10 miles to the north, were also expected to make a fight of it, but on the whole there was little concern, and during their briefings, the officers were assured that there was nothing to worry about.

The Dutch Resistance had sent information warning of a strong presence of German armour in the area, but this intelligence had been disregarded as unreliable by the British High Command who suspected German infiltration within their organisation and were sceptical of their reliability. Those who dropped into action would find the information only too true, particularly since II SS Panzer Corps consisting of the 9th SS Hohenstaufen and 10th SS Frundsberg Divisions, after their battering at Normandy and subsequent battles, had recently moved into the area to re-equip and refit after escaping the Falaise Pocket. An SS Training and Reserve Battalion under SS-*Sturmbannführer* (Major) Sepp Krafft was also present and would play a major role in holding up the British airborne in early stages of the operation.

At any rate, it would not have mattered if the division had known about the opposition, such was their desperation to see action. At this stage, the men would have willingly dropped anywhere, no matter the risk. 'It didn't matter what the information was, or how difficult the plan,' remarked Frost, 'we in the division would've gone in any circumstances. We'd been waiting to go into action ever since Normandy, D-Day, and we did feel that this particular operation, if it came off, could mean the ending of the war in 1944.'[16]

Brig.-Maj. Tony Hibbert, who would soon be playing a vital role at the bridge, had similar thoughts, admitting: 'There was considerable gung-ho spirit and I'm sure that if somebody had offered to drop us in the middle of Berlin we'd have been as happy as sand boys'.[17]

Hibbert did, however, harbour some doubt about the determination of the Germans whose backs, so everyone thought, were now against the wall:

> Well my first reaction was one of enormous enthusiasm and excitement because this was the first time that anyone on our side had contemplated the proper strategic use of airborne forces *en masse*.
>
> September 17th—an enormous feeling of excitement, and I think a lot of the ones who had fought in North Africa, and realised just how tough the Germans could be, were a bit sceptical, but in the main the rest were so fed up with being buggered about after 16 cancelled operations that they said 'oh for Christ's sake let's get on with it. Let's go. Let's do it.'[18]

Lt Robin Vlasto in Digby's 'A' Company felt a mixture of excitement and trepidation

Tony Hibbert, brigade-major at Arnhem. Hibbert would later escape captivity and link up with the Dutch Resistance.

and knew who would be spearheading the thrust:

> We were pretty pleased with this job, although it did seem rather a complicated method of committing suicide. The 1st Bde. Got the best job at Arnhem and the 2nd Bn. were given the choicest task of all.... In the Colonel's own words:
>
> 'The Brig. had promised me this, that the 2nd Bn. will, without doubt, be put in the best position for taking part in the bloodiest part of any battle we may have, and believe me it will be a blood bath.'
>
> No one doubted the veracity of this statement and it was quite clear in everyone's minds exactly which Coy would be the first to dive in.[19]

On the eve of the operation, scepticism remained rife. The question on everyone's lips: would the operation be cancelled, or postponed, as had happened many time before?

Left: Digby surrounded by members of his company pre-Operation Market Garden. Lt Grayburn sits to the right of Digby with arms folded.

Below: Airborne troops board their C-47s for Operation Market Garden.

7

Sunday 17 September 1944

On the morning of 17 September, anticipation of the looming operation was high. Waking early, the men were thrilled to find that it had not been cancelled during the night. But there still remained a nagging feeling that it would be called off at the last minute.

At 6 a.m., thirty minutes before 'Reveille', Digby and his officers enjoyed a hearty breakfast whipped up by Jack Grayburn who served them two poached eggs and haddock with masses of toast and marmalade, washed down with coffee. As they devoured their breakfast, Lt Vlasto eyed the room and observed everyone was upbeat and in good form, especially Digby, who he described as having 'a continual smile on his face', which gave him the impression that Digby found the prospect of imminent action 'too good to be true'.[1]

The buzz and excitement increased further once the officers took the company out to the parade ground. Vlasto called it a 'most remarkable sight ... everyone simply dripping with packs, guns, bits of rope, etc.'[2] Things were now beginning to seem very real.

The battalion made its way to Saltby where they formed up to await boarding one of the thirty-four C-47s set to carry them into battle.

Not surprisingly given their past disappointments, doubt existed until the bitter end. The NAAFI staff turned out to see the boys off, waving and smiling yet muttering under their breath, 'they'll be back in an hour's time, with another weekend's leave!'[3]

At the aerodrome, although they dared not show it, many men were now beginning to feel seriously nervous. Some were violently sick. Others were very quiet, lost in their own thoughts. But for Digby there was no sign of nerves. As they prepared to set off, witnesses describe him being unable to contain his delight. He was observed to be in 'excellent form', when waiting to board his plane, grinning and laughing like a schoolboy.

There would be no last-minute cancellation. At 9:30 a.m., the airborne took to the sky. 'Take off!' wrote Lt Vlasto in his diary. 'What a wonderful day it is going to be, it seems quite unbelievable that we aren't going down to London for another one of those fantastic weekends. But a look around the faces assures one of the reality.'[4]

Digby was not the only man in the company whose excitement and enthusiasm was plain for all to see. Lt Jack Grayburn was just as excited and itching to get into battle. During the flight, he took great pleasure in telling his men what he was going to do to the Germans when he encountered them.

Pte Holt was sitting next to Grayburn and remembered he 'seemed calm, almost anxious to get there'.[5]

According to Holt, most of the men in Grayburn's platoon considered him a 'bit of a medal hunter'.[5] He was certainly full of bravado and had been since the start of the war, even before he had become a paratrooper. In a letter written before joining the army, Grayburn had told a friend, 'Oh, I expect it won't be long now before I sign up and then I shall be certain to get a VC or be killed.'[6]

Holt's own thoughts differed from Grayburn's. 'I kept thinking that this was the end of the war and I wanted to get out alive,' he later admitted. 'Nothing else mattered; not fame, glory or medals–I just wanted out in one piece.'[7] Words were all well and good, but whether or not Grayburn could back up his words with actions remained to be seen.

The flight to Holland and subsequent drop was successfully carried out in the early afternoon without a hitch. It was a beautiful day, bright and sunny. Better still the drop was conducted without incoming enemy fire and the few paratroopers who were lost in the jump were victims of bad landings rather than enemy bullets.

The paratroopers began to rally as soon as they hit the ground. Digby immediately set about organising lights and the release of yellow smoke upon which the battalion was to gather. Things could have gone wrong when, in the words of Frost, 'some nameless idiot released yellow smoke at the wrong end of the D.Z.'[8] Robin Vlasto was leading his stick towards the nameless idiot's signal before he spotted Frost moving off in the opposite direction, blowing his hunting horn to rally the men to put them on the right path.

For others, it ran smoother. 'The Americans had dropped us right on target and I had no difficulty in locating the yellow flare which showed where the 2nd Battalion was forming up,' explained Pte Sims. 'Everywhere order was developing out of seeming chaos as the airborne soldiers quickly organised themselves.'[9]

The battalion formed up at their rendezvous in a small wooded area a short distance from the drop zone. Capt. Frank, Lt Grayburn, and Lt Vlasto arrived with two NCOs. For a short time, they were the only ones from 'A' Company there, but then, noted Vlasto, 'Digby turns up with the rest of the coy and orders Jack and Mac to take up position on the road and me to get my pln. together and accounted for.'[10]

Thirty minutes after landing the entire battalion was prepared and ready to move. The plan was for Digby to push on as quickly as possible ahead of the rest of the battalion straight for the bridge. Frost, whose HQ would be following a short way behind Digby's 'A' Company, was distinctly aware that Digby was his only company commander who had no experience in the field, but Frost was not worried. During their time in England, Frost had formed a very good impression of Digby and considered him 'worth a bet with anyone's money'.[11]

The objective of Maj. Dover's 'C' Company was to capture the railway bridge near Oosterbeek, cross it, and head for the main bridge. 'B' Company under Doug Crawley would move at the rear of the column in reserve, ready to be deployed when needed. Later, Frost would order Crawley to thwart German interference and to cover the advance of the column into Arnhem. Once accomplished, he was to push on to a pontoon bridge less than a mile from the main road bridge to see if it was possible to cross. This pontoon had been an initial objective, but prior to Frost issuing his final orders, intelligence had been received that it had been partially dismantled. Regardless, Crawley would make his way there to check.

Shortly after 3 p.m., Frost gave Digby the nod to begin his advance. Years of pent up frustration and disappointment had been building up to this moment.

Finally, Digby was off the leash.

The Dash for the Bridge

No sooner had they set off when the leading platoon of Digby's company under Lt McDermont sighted a number of enemy reconnaissance vehicles approaching their position. Lt McDermont ordered his men to ground and as they drew nearer gave the signal to open fire. A devastating inferno resulted in the destruction of a number of lorries and motor cars. Fifteen Germans were killed and another fifteen captured with no loss to McDermont's platoon who left the prisoners behind under guard before continuing the advance.

After travelling through a wooded area of almost 3 miles and rotating who took the lead, they emerged at the other end with Grayburn out in front. At a T-junction opposite the woods, they came under enemy fire from a further wooded area. Frost had been on his way forward in his jeep to get a situation report from Digby and to put forth an *ad hoc* plan, but when the shooting started, he decided to back off and not interfere. 'The last thing a vanguard commander wants is to have his immediate superior breathing over his shoulder,' wrote Frost, 'Digby was a thruster if ever there was, and if it was possible to deal with or circumvent the enemy, I knew that we should be on the move again as soon as could be.'[12]

As the company came under fire, Digby and his officers who were not already engaged had rushed forward to see what was happening but had been forced to hit the deck after coming under concentrated fire. Meanwhile Grayburn had deployed his men in a flanking move to deal with the opposition. McDermont's platoon advanced to support Grayburn who put down some smoke and went in with the bayonet. An unseen battle ensued from beyond the trees before a bugle sounded the all-clear. Digby was 'pleased as punch'.[13]

Digby had more than one reason to be pleased. Not only had the opposition been swiftly swept aside, but his new bugle system had operated effectively in action for the very first time. Digby later admitted this gave him 'great satisfaction to see it working perfectly under enemy fire'.[14]

In contrast to Frost's account where he claimed to have held back to allow Digby to deal with the situation, Digby himself described a different version of events when relating what happened at the T-junction:

> While Jack Grayburn was working his way to the right of the enemy-machine gun, I was joined by Colonel Frost. He had been hard on the heels of my company and now came forward, impatient at the delay, to see the situation himself. But we did not have to wait long for Grayburn's bugle call signalling that he was back on the axis road, and I sounded the call to resume.[15]

The plan had been for the divisional reconnaissance squadron under Maj. Freddie Gough to rush ahead in their jeeps and carry out a *coup de main* to seize and hold the bridge until other units arrived on foot. Gough had been wary of the plan from the outset and had been worried that his force would be too vulnerable, which had proven to be correct. After clashing with Sepp Krafft's blocking line, the lead elements of his squadron had suffered heavily and Gough had been forced to withdraw behind the protection of Dobie's 1st Battalion as it made its own advance.

Having received word of Gough's failed *coup de main*, Frost had suggested to Digby that the few vehicles belonging to the battalion could be used to ferry them forward to compensate. Digby had been all for the idea and had agreed to lead them in, but the resistance at the T-Junction persuaded Frost that it would be nothing more than suicide and the idea was scrapped.

The enemy were not the only thing to cause delay. It was unrealistic to expect Dutch civilians, liberated after years of occupation, to keep calm and remain indoors at the sudden arrival of British paratroopers. Soon, they were pouring out of their homes, screaming, waving, shaking hands, and hugging the paratroopers. In the vicinity of Heveadorp and in Oosterbeek, the streets were thick with civilians thrusting cakes, milk, and a whole host of other goodies into the hands of the passing soldiers. Digby's second-in-command, Tony Frank, was impressed by 'the incredible number of orange flowers or handkerchiefs that suddenly appeared like magic', although he noticed this 'petered out when the first hold-up and sporadic firing started. There weren't so many Dutch out then, but a few stout ones stayed and watched the fun.'[16]

As had been arranged, Maj. Dover branched off with his company to take the railway bridge, but as his leading elements made their approach, they came under fire from the southern bank. Nothing daunted, they pressed on. Frost—who witnessed the assault from distance—was under the impression the bridge had been successfully rushed. He realised moments later that he had been wrong. A mighty explosion followed, sending the southern-most span crashing into the water—the Germans having rigged it with explosives. The destruction of the railway bridge rendered it uncrossable, meaning the main road bridge could not be reached directly from the south. Frost sent a message to Dover instructing him leave a party of sappers to deal with the damaged bridge and to follow the rest of the battalion.

Meanwhile, in the face of enemy sniper fire, 'A' Company were still surging forward in its advance. The appearance of an armoured car caused some casualties before it withdrew. Others were seen patrolling the streets, but Digby decided that to take them on would cause an unacceptable delay. After sending back a message for a PIAT team to be brought forward, he ordered his men off the roads—his plan being to push on through the rear gardens of the houses to bypass the enemy armour, thus saving valuable time. This improvised plan was highly effective and allowed the company to continue without being held up.

The rest of the battalion following some way behind could not see 'A' Company' but they could hear their Sten guns working away and could see the trail of destruction left in their wake. Knocked-out enemy vehicles and dead and wounded Germans lay scattered along the route. A number of German prisoners were being held by one of Digby's men who had been detailed to watch over them by the side of the road.

Frost was very happy with what he was seeing:

> Some three hundred yards beyond the railway I found a party of German prisoners guarded by one of 'A' Company's men, who wasn't sure what the situation was but had seen the company moving on fast. I surmised that Digby's garden manoeuvre had been completely successful and that he had rushed on again ...[17]

By now it was abundantly clear to Frost that his initial assessment regarding his new company commander had been correct. Digby was indeed 'a thruster'.

Arnhem Road Bridge

It was beginning to get dark by the time 'A' Company reached the north end of the bridge around 8 p.m. Grayburn's platoon were the first to arrive and took up positions on the embankment leading up to the bridge itself, a position he would keep until first light. German traffic crossed intermittently but was left alone. Things were very quiet and it seemed that the Germans were totally unaware of their presence.

Many years after the battle, Digby would describe the sight of his men moving into their positions as his proudest moment of all.[18]

More and more men began to arrive, gathering under the bridge to await instruction. Frost turned up to find Digby setting out his dispositions and could not help but notice that he was in a splendid mood. And he had every reason to be. Within seven hours of landing in Holland, Digby had spearheaded the dash for the bridge, fought through 7 miles of enemy-held territory, reached the objective, accounted for 150 enemy soldiers, capturing some thirty to forty more, and knocked-out around half a dozen vehicles for the loss of several men wounded and just one man killed. Frost called it 'a fine feat of arms'.[19]

Digby attributed his success and speed of advance to several key aspects. Firstly, they had set off from the drop zone at a time when the Germans were not very well organised, but he also gave credit to his company officers and his bugle system:

> I never had great faith in the efficiency even under training conditions of wireless communications on the company and platoon level and I had devised and continually

The embankment manned by Lt Grayburn and his platoon as they arrived at the bridge. (*Gelders Archive*)

The stairs and verge up to the bridge from the buildings that would be manned by Digby's 'A' Coy during the battle.

An aerial pre-war photo of the bridge area. (*Gelders Archive*)

> practised a system of bugle calls which combined with the normal battle drill enabled me and my platoon commanders to know exactly the state of the battle as it proceeded. Each platoon, in addition to the company headquarters, had a bugler and in outflanking movements they were able by a simple code of bugle signals to tell me whether they were held up or whether they had succeeded in outflanking the opposition and rejoining the axis of advance. This worked splendidly in the street fighting during our approach to the bridge and I am convinced that this, combined with the dash and initiative of the platoon commanders was one of the main reasons that we got through.[20]

Digby went on to explain that he and his platoon officers, who had been together throughout their training in England, had reached a high degree of efficiency and understanding. They had gelled and worked together instinctively, knowing exactly what to do and when to do it.

Lastly, Digby knew that Frost had selected him above all others to lead them, and he sure as hell was not going to let his colonel down. He later told an interviewer: 'John Frost was never far behind me and at the slightest delay was sure to be up there demanding to know what the devil was holding me up'.[21]

Paratroopers continued to arrive at the bridge, occupying the nearby buildings to prepare them for defence. It was politely explained to the occupants of the surrounding houses that it would be prudent for them to clear out. Most did, but some decided to retire to their cellars instead—a decision they almost certainly would come to regret in the coming days.

Meanwhile, Digby had deployed his men in the houses to the east and west of the bridge and had selected a building to use as his Company HQ. Frost established his

Brigade HQ post-battle.

A pre-war photograph taken from the bridge showing Brigade HQ.

Battalion HQ across the road a little further from the bridge by a large building that would soon become Brigade HQ. It had a good view of the ramp leading up to the bridge.

Worryingly, there was still no sign of the reconnaissance squadron, or of anyone else for that matter. The Lion Route taken by the 2nd Battalion would prove to be the only one to garner success, although not everyone taking this route would get there either, including Maj. Dover's 'C' Company who had become engaged in a fight from which they could not disengage. Ultimately, they would become cut off, surrounded, and forced to surrender.

The Germans had reacted quickly to the initial shock of the airborne attack and the way to Arnhem had been promptly sealed shut, but not before Digby had rushed the 2nd Battalion through the gap.

One of those gathered under the bridge before they began filtering away to man the houses was L/Sgt Bill Fulton of Lt McDermont's platoon. An unidentified officer, probably Digby, called out and asked if there was an NCO present. After replying, Fulton was ordered to move on to the bridge itself. He only had seven men with him, but was told to go anyway and that more would be sent up when they arrived.

Fulton could hear German voices as he cautiously ascended a set of stairs leading onto the bridge. Chancing a peek over the top he saw a truck at a distance of 15 yards facing south. A German officer and NCO were speaking to soldiers in the back. Fulton

The bodies of two men of Maj. Dover's 'C' Company, 2nd Parachute Battalion, lie on the Utrechtseweg in Arnhem, 17 September 1944. The company were decimated when attempting to reach the road bridge.

did not engage and after few minutes the truck moved off. The enemy still seemed unaware of their presence. Fulton began to edge forward along the side of the bridge. He could see the outlines of enemy soldiers. A few of them were lurking in the corners of some small huts and Fulton was able to stealthily take them prisoner without firing a shot. They were quickly and discretely dragged off to the rear.

Cautiously, Fulton continued forward. Spotting something out of the corner of his eye he instinctively turned and fired at a German soldier who was preparing to shoot him. The German fell, but not before squeezing off a shot that caught Fulton in the leg. A message was sent back that the bridge was heavily manned and that more troops would be needed to secure even a foothold at their own end. Fulton crawled behind an iron girder from where he would be collected and carried back on a makeshift stretcher—a door from one of the houses—an hour later.

By 9 p.m., it had become considerably darker and Digby ordered another attempt on the bridge. This time it fell to No. 2 Platoon, and Jack Grayburn would personally take the lead.

Digby emphasised the need to be as discrete as possible. 'Everything depended on stealth and surprise,' recorded Digby, 'and Jack had his men blacken their faces and bind their boots with strips of material (curtains, I think), and made sure that there was no rattling equipment or weapons.'[22]

The platoon crept to the top of the embankment and began to move quietly across in single file. Almost immediately, a machine gun opened fire from point-blank range accompanied by the fire from an armoured car situated on the south side of the bridge. Digby, who was observing their progress, described the effect as 'shattering'. Within seconds, a number of casualties had been inflicted, including Lt Grayburn who had been shot in the shoulder. In the face of heavy fire, he pushed on until ordered to withdraw owing to their heavy losses. Grayburn called for his men to fall back, but refused to personally leave until all of his men had gotten away.

It came as a huge shock to come under fire from the pillbox as its position on the bridge was almost directly adjacent to the houses manned by 'A' Company. 'We had of course, seen it and checked it out in daylight,' Digby later related, but 'we had never thought that the Germans would risk or be able to place a gun in it after dark.'[23] Digby gave credit to the German machine gunner who he considered to be 'a good soldier and certainly a brave man'.[24]

A six-pounder—one of four to reach the bridge—was reversed by jeep part way up to the bridge before being man-handled the rest of the way by its crew. From this temporary position, it opened fire on the pillbox. Meanwhile, from a nearby building manned by Lt Vlasto, a flamethrower and PIAT were also brought into action against it. The effort not only destroyed the pillbox but ignited a hut behind it containing flammables. It exploded, lighting up the area and prompted the surrender of a number of German soldiers who, according to a witness, 'came running from the bridge silhouetted against the flames from the pill box'.[25]

In the meantime, more men had turned up at the bridge having followed Frost's Lion Route. Brig.-Maj. Tony Hibbert arrived with around 300 men, including engineers from 1st Parachute Squadron, some military police, Intelligence Corps, and a platoon of RASC men, but minus Brig. Lathbury, who, while visiting the 1st and 3rd Battalions *en route*, had been caught up in the fighting with Dobie's 1st Battalion. Hibbert's arrival more than doubled the number of men at the bridge.

Maj. Freddie Gough with three jeeps from his reconnaissance squadron now also arrived via the Lion Route. Gough pulled up to find the bridge in flames and reported to Frost before parking his jeeps behind what would become Brigade HQ.

At forty-three years of age, Gough was one of the oldest officers in the division. His bright silver hair gave him a distinctive look among his fellow officers and men, many of whom were less than half his age. Gough was certainly a lively character and full of flair. Early in the war, he had commanded a provost company at Dunkirk and had played a conspicuous part in organising the perimeter defences during the beach evacuations. Back in England, he had flatly refused a desk job and had pulled strings to remain on the frontline. His gallantry in Italy had resulted in the award of a MC.

After Grayburn's failed attempt on the bridge, preparations were taking place to make another go of it when four enemy lorries came into view from across the bridge. Cautiously they began to creep forward. The paratroopers held their fire until the vehicles were level with the burning pillbox before letting loose a hail of fire that brought them to an abrupt halt. Survivors of the wreckages were pulled out and taken

Freddie Gough (far left) re-enacts his time at the bridge in the 1946 movie *Theirs is the Glory*.

Beneath the bridge, photo dated 1935. The building to the right of the image would be used as Brigade HQ during the battle. (*Gelders Archive*)

Facing away from the bridge towards Battalion HQ and the neighbouring buildings. The cluster of buildings in the centre were all manned for the majority of the battle.

A view of the bridge. Note the contrast between the large open stretch of ground on one side held by the Germans and the built-up area on the opposite end that was held by the paratroopers.

prisoner. The flames from the burning vehicles added to the already illuminated night making the bridge a death trap. As a result, plans of capturing the other side that night were duly scrapped.

The paratroopers had a good field of fire on to the bridge and could control it to a large degree, but it was important that both sides be held if at all possible. A planned drop by the 1st Polish Independent Parachute Brigade Group was scheduled to take place the following morning about a mile from the bridge on the opposite end. With this in mind, Frost pulled Freddie Gough to one side and raised the possibility of him racing across once the drop began. Gough was not particularly keen, so the idea was shelved for the time being. In the end, Frost would not have to make the decision. Owing to bad weather, but unbeknown to those at the bridge, the Polish drop would not be going ahead.

By now, a full brigade should have been at the bridge, yet just 700–750 men would arrive at the destination. There had been setbacks, but things were still looking positive with the expectation that the remainder of brigade would be arriving imminently, closely followed by XXX Corps. There were problems with the radios and communication with division could not be established, but at this stage, it was not thought to be a serious problem.

The men hunkered down in their buildings as the night set in, unsure as to the general situation and the fate of the division, yet with a confident outlook of whatever lay in store.

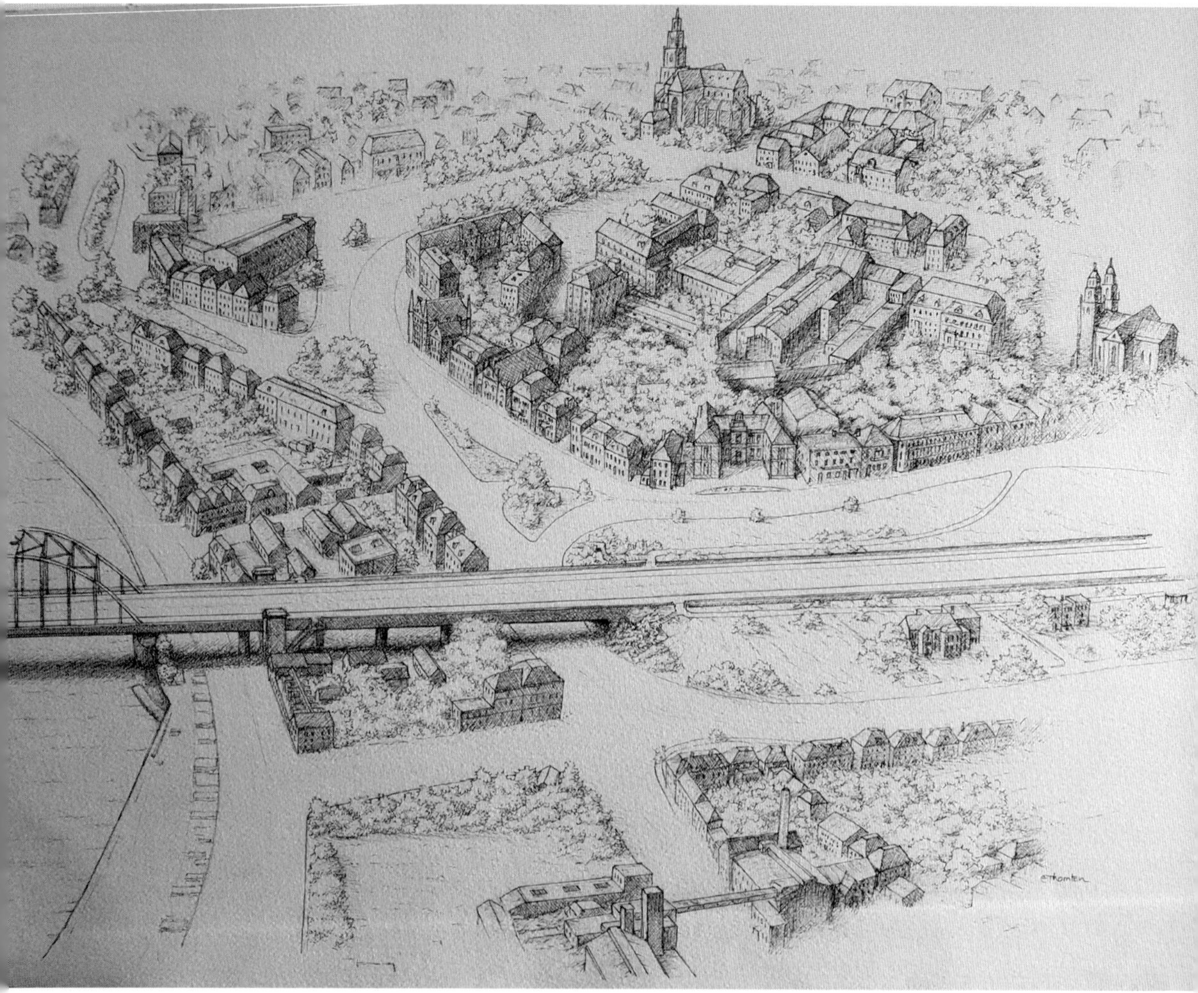

Illustration showing the bridge area and buildings. (*Artist: Eric Thornton*)

8

Monday 18 September 1944

During the night, a somewhat exposed building—the Red School that was situated alongside the eastern side of the ramp—had been abandoned by 'A' Troop, 1st Para Squadron, under Capt. Eric Mackay after it had become completely untenable. They had not long prepared it for defence when attacked by troops from a German HQ located in the next building who had poured a heavy fire into the school and thrown grenades into the rooms. Mackay and his men had relocated to the nearby Van Limberg Stirum School manned by engineers. They were later joined by Maj. Lewis and twelve men of the 3rd Battalion's C' Company who, after being detached from their unit, had fought their way through to the bridge via the railway line.

In the hours of darkness, German activity from the south side of the bridge had been practically non-existent, but in the early morning, the sound of revving engines was distinct. The tension was finally broken when, at around 9:30 a.m., a paratrooper called out that armoured cars were crossing the bridge. The 9th SS Reconnaissance Battalion was about to launch itself against their position. Leading them was the fearless *Hauptsturmführer* (Captain) Viktor Gräbner, a man known for his no-nonsense and direct battle tactics, whose bravery at Normandy had earned him the Knight's Cross.

A question mark lingers over Gräbner's intentions. His fierce nature suggests he was launching a direct attack. Alternatively, having crossed south to Nijmegen the previous night, Gräbner may have been attempting to smash straight through the British position to return to his divisional command post in Arnhem. The truth of the matter has never been fully established and more than likely never will.

Gräbner's assorted force consisting of armoured cars, half-tracks, and lorries amounted to around twenty-two vehicles. Certainly, he was aware of the presence of British paratroopers; the remnants of the lorries shot up during the night lay alongside debris from the destroyed pillbox as a stark warning that any attempt to cross would meet with determined resistance.

Initially, not all of the British, particularly those stretched back in buildings further afield, were aware Gräbner had launched his force across the bridge. Some, if they heard the approach, may have believed that XXX Corps had broken through. Regardless, five armoured cars with guns blazing sped from under the bridge arch, zigzagging through the debris and Hawkins mines that had been laid across the road during the night in expectation of such an attack. The speed of the armoured cars enabled them to pass the paratroopers in the houses adjacent to the bridge with only a few scattered shots being fired in their direction. They passed unharmed and quickly disappeared into Arnhem town, one of them minus a wheel having had it blown off by a mine.

The slower Sd. Kfz 10 and 250s (half-tracks) along with the lorries laden with SS troops that followed did not get off so lightly. Now fully alert, the paratroopers opened a murderous fire with Sten guns, Bren guns, rifles, and PIATs from all angles. A six-pounder, having blown a hole in the side of the bridge barrier from its position down in the roadway, added its own fire. Everyone who had a view of the bridge and the ramp was firing, including those in the HQ area where Frost was puzzled to hear what sounded like German machine guns being fired directly outside his building. Looking down, he discovered it was not the Germans but Freddie Gough, 'grinning like a wicked uncle' as he blazed away with the duel K-guns mounted on his jeep.[1]

In two hours, it was all over. Gräbner and a large portion of his men were dead and over half the vehicles destroyed. German prisoners taken in the aftermath of the assault brought the total number to well over 100.

After this attack, the paratroopers were subjected to an intense mortar barrage that, together with 40-mm flak gun fire, began to systematically target the buildings held by the British. The intensity of the barrage made it impossible to leave the buildings. Many were badly damaged and five were soon engulfed in flames.

An RAF Reconnaissance photograph taken after Gräbner's failed advance across the bridge on the morning of Monday 18th. The wreckages of his vehicles can be seen strewn about the bridge area. Brigade and Battalion HQ are situated towards the bottom left of the image.

Reconnaissance photographs taken by Spitfire on the morning of Monday 18 September. Wrecked German vehicles can be seen scattered on the bridge following their failed assault earlier that morning. (*Crown Copyright*)

In the afternoon, it was discovered through radio communication that the rest of the division had met fierce resistance and that Brig. Lathbury was missing. In the absence of anyone of higher rank, Maj. Hibbert asked Lt-Col. Frost to take command of the brigade. Frost moved into Brigade HQ while Maj. David Wallis took over command of the 2nd Battalion, who made up the majority of the force anyhow.

The defence was then given a boost by the arrival of Doug Crawley and seventy men of 'B' Company who, after holding the way open at Den Brink on the way in and checking out the useless pontoon bridge, had been summoned by Frost via radio to make his way to the main objective.

During the late afternoon and evening, enemy infantry supported by mortar fire and two Mk III tanks put in a strong attack along the river bank from the east. Brigade Defence platoon suffered heavily from the tanks and were forced to abandon two buildings to take up new positions. A building manned by a platoon from 'B' Company then became the focus of the assault and the occupants were forced to withdraw to another building. The attack was finally driven off with one tank being knocked out by PIAT and the other by a six-pounder.

Later, a party of sappers who had been placed under the command of 'A' Company confirmed the bridge had not been prepared for demolition by the Germans.

As darkness descended, four houses in varying parts of the perimeter had to be evacuated owing to fire and were subsequently burnt down. At this stage, Digby recorded that Brigade HQ 'narrowly escaped fire'.[2]

During the hours of darkness, extra vigilance was called for, and the close proximity of enemy soldiers moving around and manning nearby buildings meant a constant state of awareness was vital. There was little time for hesitation, and with the men's nerves at their most fragile, if a paratrooper did not reply to a challenge quick enough, he ran the risk of being mistaken for a German and shot down by a comrade.

This threat was brought home to Capt. Francis Hoyer-Millar of 'B' Company that night when he almost became a victim of friendly fire. 'B' Company had been defending the western side of the defence but had since redeployed to the eastern sector where an unoccupied house apparently had purposely been set alight to provide some useful light over this specific area. Hoyer-Millar was leading a patrol of a dozen men to watch for Germans and to protect a party of engineers who wanted to check the underside of the bridge for explosives. The patrol crossed the bridge from east to west finding in the wreckages from Gräbner's failed attack earlier in the day, a number of SS soldiers hiding among the vehicles. Hoyer-Millar, wondering if there were any more Germans over the slope leading away from the bridge, tossed a grenade to play it safe. His gamble paid off and five very scared Germans emerged with their hands up, three of them having been wounded by the grenade.

The patrol split into two groups to cover both sides of the bridge. Prior to the operation, the men had been issued with a total of six passwords to be used over several days, each with its own unique response. But when a burst of Bren gun fire spewed towards him, Hoyer-Millar gave no thought of passwords, yelling instead, 'Will the stupid bastard who is firing the fucking Bren gun cease immediately!'[3]

In unison, the rest of the patrol called out their battle-cry, 'Whoa Mohammed' and the firing stopped. Hoyer-Millar would never live the incident down. Frost for one

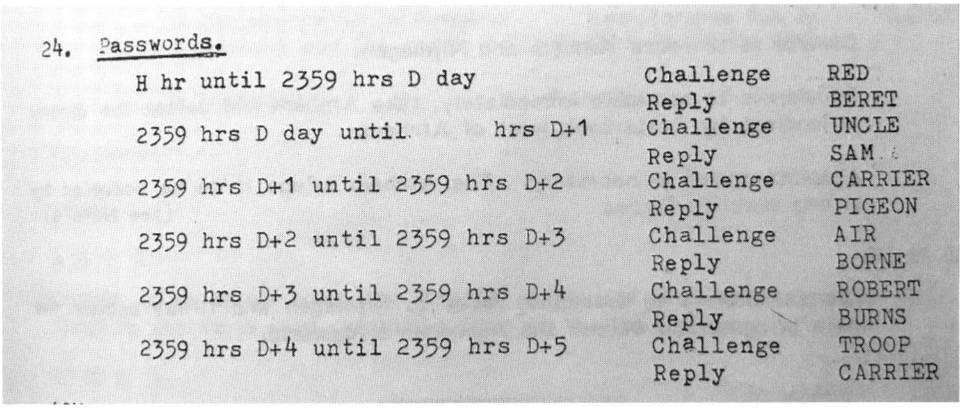

24. Passwords.

H hr until 2359 hrs D day	Challenge	RED
	Reply	BERET
2359 hrs D day until hrs D+1	Challenge	UNCLE
	Reply	SAM
2359 hrs D+1 until 2359 hrs D+2	Challenge	CARRIER
	Reply	PIGEON
2359 hrs D+2 until 2359 hrs D+3	Challenge	AIR
	Reply	BORNE
2359 hrs D+3 until 2359 hrs D+4	Challenge	ROBERT
	Reply	BURNS
2359 hrs D+4 until 2359 hrs D+5	Challenge	TROOP
	Reply	CARRIER

The passwords issued prior to the drop. In the heat of the moment, the paratroopers tended to shout the first thing that came into their head when challenged. Contrary to popular belief, Digby did not carry the umbrella due to a lack of remembering passwords. That is a myth, albeit a well-established one.

ribbed him mercilessly about it. Years later during a reunion in 1991, a paratrooper who had been on the patrol with Hoyer-Millar relished the chance to bring it up, but it was all in good humour.

Passwords were all well and good, but in reality, when challenged, a man was more likely to shout out whatever instinctively came into his head, and more often than not it was not a password.

The consequence of confused close-quarter street-fighting was rammed home that night after two of Digby's forward outposts had been overrun by German infantry under the cover of darkness. Digby in his HQ received a visit from Maj. Wallis who had been conducting a tour of the perimeter, but as Wallis left the building, a burst of Bren gun fire rang out and he dropped dead—killed instantly after being struck in the chest by one of his own. The man responsible, a sapper, belonged to the 9th Field Company, but nobody blamed him for the mishap. He had shouted a warning, but Wallis either did not respond or responded too quietly to be heard. 'It was at a time when the next shape in a doorway could be the enemy, such was the proximity of the fighting,' explained one witness. 'Response time was very short, and a German grenade had a short fuse.'[4]

Nevertheless, the man who had pulled the trigger was completely inconsolable and full of remorse. Later, in a railway car on the way to a POW camp, the sapper would sit sobbing in the corner of the wagon. 'This poor lad was devastated,' a comrade would write. 'He didn't look up or talk to anybody, even when his friends were trying to comfort him.'[5]

Digby, when later writing his report on the battle, opted not to mention the circumstances surrounding the death of his close friend, nor did he mention it to Wallis's parents when writing to them. Wallis's death hit Frost hard, for they had been very good friends before the war. When Frost came to write his book, *A Drop Too Many*, he too failed to describe the manner in which Wallis had met his end, although

Digby's 'A' Company HQ can be seen in the centre of the three buildings in this pre-war photograph. All three were manned by his men as they arrived at the bridge. (*Gelders Archive*)

he certainly knew what had happened. Both men undoubtedly concluded that nothing would be gained by describing the specific circumstances.

Frost now handed command of the battalion to Digby. This decision caused a degree of tension, for in giving Digby command, Frost had gone over the head of more experienced seasoned veteran Maj. Doug Crawley who was senior to Digby. Frost was acutely aware of Crawley's displeasure, but he considered it to be the best decision given the circumstances. Digby had been first on the scene and had a greater understanding of the dispositions and situation as a whole, and the bulk of the battalion at the bridge belonged to his 'A' Company anyhow. More importantly, Digby's performance so far had been nothing short of spectacular and Frost had full confidence in him commanding the battalion.

The unfortunate Crawley had been similarly let down previously when in North Africa after locking horns with Maj. Dover about who would lead an attack. Both officers had argued their case to Frost, who had had no particular preference. A coin had been tossed to settle the matter and Crawley, much to his disappointment, had lost the flip.

Before making his way to Battalion HQ, Digby handed over command of 'A' Company to Capt. Frank.

Three buildings manned by 'A' Coy. The centre building with the white trim was Company HQ. (*Gelders Archive*)

Above left: Maj. David Wallis, KIA on 18 September. Wallis had just left Digby's HQ when he was struck by a burst of fire from a Bren gunner.

Above right: Major Tatham Warter, photo taken prior to Operation Market Garden.

The Umbrella

Contrary to popular belief, Digby did not take the umbrella with him into Holland. He picked it up from one of the houses after Wallis's death. In his book *The Grey Goose of Arnhem*, Leo Heaps, who personally interviewed Digby when gathering his information, recorded that Digby plucked it from a pile of rubble.[6]

It is widely believed that Digby carried the umbrella because he struggled to remember passwords and he thought it would help to identify him as British. A supposed quote along the lines of, 'Only a bloody fool of an Englishman would carry an umbrella into battle' is often attributed to Digby—the belief being that no German would carry one and therefore he would be identified by his comrades as a friendly. It is a nice quote, but its authenticity is highly questionable. Certainly, no evidence is forthcoming to suggest that Digby ever said it and the origin (primary source) of that quote is mysteriously unknown.

Post-war, a newspaper quoting Digby's own reasons for carrying the umbrella referred to it as 'a totem of British resistance', while Digby himself said, 'I suppose it was good for morale but there was more to it than that. I wanted my troops to recognise me at all times and to be conscious of my presence.'[7]

Digby spoke of his reasons for carrying the umbrella with a number of people, yet not once did he mention anything about remembering passwords. In post-war years, particularly after the release of the movie *A Bridge Too Far*, Digby's family enquired as to why he had carried it. He told his niece, Jane Randle, it was for identification purposes. He did not elaborate, but Jane took this to mean that he wanted to stand out to his men and to be instantly recognisable, which tallies with the newspaper quotation. In the early 1990s, when his daughter, Jo, was assisting him to write his privately published short memoir *Dutch Courage & Pegasus*, Digby told her the same thing but this time he added that the second-in-command of the battalion had been shot by a comrade and he did not want the same thing to happen to him. Digby also told Jo that the second-in-command (Wallis) had in fact answered the challenge from the Bren-gunner who pulled the trigger and that his final words when identifying himself had been 'second-in-command' but the Bren-gunner mistook the word 'command' for '*kamarad*!', thus giving the impression he was German, which prompted the man to open fire.

In conclusion, Digby in his own words stated he carried it to stand out to his men who would no doubt feel heartened by his presence. It also reduced the chances of him being shot down by friendly fire, as had happened to David Wallis.

As the newly appointed battalion CO, Digby's responsibilities had widened considerably, as had the number of men under his direct command. The buildings populated by the battalion were widely spread and from this point on, Digby would make regular visits to every inch of the ground held by the battalion to check on the wellbeing of his men.

Later that night, Digby watched in alarm as the fires spread through the buildings where the paratroopers were stationed. The inferno presented a worrying sight. Flames from the buildings set alight by enemy mortar fire had taken hold from the top floors and were spreading downwards. As each floor became untenable, the men inside descended to the next floor until being finally forced out to find new places to defend.

At 1 a.m., hope was briefly injected when cries of 'Wayo Mohammed' were heard from somewhere outside the perimeter. It was hoped that the rest of the brigade or at least a portion of it had finally managed to break through, but this was not the case. Gradually, the shouts and gunfire that accompanied it faded to nothing. It had been a single platoon from 3rd Battalion who, having made a gallant attempt at reaching their beleaguered comrades at the bridge, had been cut up and repulsed. The war cry had signalled their last stand.

Other familiar sounds began to echo through the night. At Brigade HQ, Hibbert's ears caught the occasional note of a bugle. Once sounded, the call would echo around the perimeter as others from 'A' Company responded. One man described these calls as coming 'from the rubble of a house', noting that as soon as one sounded it was 'answered by another nearby'.[8]

An officer described it as an 'ingenious method of communication' amid the houses. 'The platoon buglers sounded their clear clarion calls to the incomprehensible astonishment of the enemy. They were always heard above the din and roar of the guns.'[9]

Despite their ever-decreasing perimeter and worsening situation, the morale and fighting spirit of the paratroopers remained unbroken.

A German photograph of the bridge, taken after the battle.

Above the din of battle, Digby's bugle calls could often be heard sounding out. The calls were said to have originated from 'from the rubble of a house'. When a bugle sounded, the call was taken up by those in others buildings. They served to identify which buildings were held by the paratroopers and which had been lost or abandoned.

9

Tuesday 19 September 1944

Daylight brought a series of further determined attacks against the holed-up paratroopers. Furthermore, the planned Polish parachute drop expected to take place a mile or so from the south side of the bridge failed to materialise owing to poor weather in England that prevented the flight. In a way, Gough was relieved as it meant he would not be called upon by Frost to make what he considered to be a suicidal attack across the bridge to coincide.

From this point forward, Frost admitted to having very few decisions to make for the remainder of the battle. It was simply a case of the occupants of each building holding on as best they could, with the officers on the spot reacting to threats as and when they came.

Through the day, anyone leaving a building instantly became a prime target for snipers and machine-gun fire, meaning movement from one area to another was strictly limited. Witnesses, however, describe Digby moving around the streets regardless. Many accounts from those who were present feature anecdotes of Digby and his umbrella, which can be pinned down as occurring on this day.

The padre of the 2nd Battalion, Father Bernard Egan, was no slouch under fire; his MC, awarded for his devotion to the wounded in Tunisia, testified to his courage. But even for old hands like Egan, the severity of the German barrage was becoming unbearable. Egan had been keeping busy doing all he could for the wounded, mainly at Battalion HQ, but his spiritual comforts were required elsewhere in other buildings. This came with a problem since the increasing enemy fire made it almost impossible. Egan had little enthusiasm of venturing out into the streets.

Digby was out on a walk when he spied Father Egan, cowering sheepishly in a doorway, trying, unsuccessfully, to pluck up the courage to make a run across the street. Having recognised Egan's intention and nervous apprehension, Digby strolled over to him, opened his umbrella above the padre's head, and said in a calm tone, 'Come along padre.' Somewhat taken aback, Egan pointed out that enemy mortars were exploding in the street, but Digby told him not to worry as he had an umbrella.

The absurdity of the situation was not lost on Egan who found himself stepping out under the 'protection' of Digby's brolly.

Egan later described the episode to author and historian Cornelius Ryan, who noted:

> Father Egan remembers on one of his trips across the street to where some of the rest of the Battalion occupied houses, he came out at the beginning of a fairly heavy mortar bombardment, intending to make his way to Battalion HQ.[1]

Father Egan described the incident:

> Outside, strolling up the street was Major Digby Tatham Warter, one of the Colonel's Company commanders. He saw me and started walking over to me. In his hand was an umbrella. As he came up to me, he opened it and held it over my head. 'Come along, padre,' he said, and taking me by the arm, began to lead me along. When I showed signs of reluctance, he said, 'Don't worry—I've got an umbrella.' It must have looked like he was helping some old lady across the street. He acted as if he was just out for a stroll, but I know I was wishing he'd hurry up!
>
> He was just on his way over to the bridge to see Tony Frank's platoon which was dug in on the bank and I had no choice but to remain with him till he finished there and walked me back to Battalion with the umbrella up and over our heads. I remember distinctly seeing the sun was shining then. It started to cloud up by midday and by the afternoon was quite overcast. But it certainly wasn't raining during our stroll.[2]

It may have been around this time that Lt Pat Barnett of the brigade's defence platoon—who, like Gough, was the wrong side of forty—was sprinting over an open stretch of road when he caught sight of Digby strolling down the street with his umbrella raised over his head. The strange sight stopped Barnett dead in his tracks and prompted him to yell out to Digby that his umbrella would not do him much good. Digby, with an exaggerated expression of mock surprise, replied 'Oh my goodness Pat, but what if it rains?'[3]

On Tuesday, in the words of Digby: 'The attack East of the bridge was resumed with heavy mortaring and attempted infiltrations throughout the morning'.[4] The German mortar barrage had prevented their own armour and infantry from attacking, but once it had ceased, 'A' Company came under a series of attacks from both. At midday, three tanks moved into position by the river and began to target the building manned by Lt McDermont whose location was key to the perimeter but vulnerable and exposed. The tanks, firing at close range, were soon reinforced by two more. Without anti-tank weapons and in spite of heavy casualties, McDermont held his ground.

From his position under the bridge, Capt. Frank rushed forward with one or two men armed with PIATs. After ordering McDermont to retire from the house, he set out to stalk the tanks. In the words of his Silver Star citation, awarded for his part in the battle:

> Captain Frank at once organised a party of two P.I.A.Ts which he himself led under heavy fire to a position on the flank from which he could engage the Tanks. Meanwhile, two more Tanks appeared. Altogether, three Tanks were hit and all of them withdrew. The situation was restored and the platoon enabled to re-occupy the house.[5]

Frank's citation says that his actions enabled the platoon to reoccupy the house, but there was much more to it than simply walking in and retaking possession. Under the cover of the tanks, some twenty to thirty Germans had occupied the building. Now, with the tanks having backed off, the Germans inside were unsupported by their armour.

After returning from his foray, Capt. Frank was under the bridge with a cluster of 'A' Company men who had been blasted out of their buildings. Lt McDermont and Lt Grayburn were there with their platoons. Incoming fire was very heavy.

Over in Battalion HQ, Digby had gotten wind that something was amiss and that the enemy were infiltrating a portion of his perimeter. After collecting some men, he set out to see for himself.

Capt. Frank, still under the bridge, saw Digby coming:

> Digby Tatham-Warter came walking calmly across from Battalion HQ with his brolly, quite unconcerned about any danger. He was very angry with me for letting McDermont's platoon come back and ordered me to retake the house.[6]

From an upstairs window of a nearby building, Pte Morgan, who had a good view of proceedings, noticed that Digby was furious. He also noticed that Digby had acquired a new accessory to compliment his umbrella—a bowler, which was now perched on his head in place of his beret that he had been wearing instead of his helmet.[7]

From Brigade HQ, Freddie Gough had observed Digby leaving the neighbouring building of Battalion HQ. Gough had started the battle in fine fettle, laughing and smiling behind his jeep's K-guns as he ploughed bullets into the Germans on the bridge during Gräbner's attack. But now was a different matter, and even the most steadfast men like Gough were beginning to feel the pressure. The appearance of the German armour had horrified him and he admitted that his heart sank when he saw what he described as 'huge Mark IV's thundering down the street', firing into the buildings at point-blank range.[8] But Gough's spirits were instantly raised when he saw Digby heading outside. 'I looked and then looked again,' said Gough, 'There, out on the street, was Tatham-Warter, leading his men. He had found an old bowler someplace and he was walking along, twirling a battered umbrella, looking for all the world like Charlie Chaplin.'[9]

The sight of Digby in the bowler hat was too much for Gough, who, despite the seriousness of the situation, 'roared with laughter and went off to find John Frost'. 'When I mentioned it to him,' noted Gough, 'John just smiled and said, "Oh, yes. Digby's quite a leader."'[10]

Perhaps not surprisingly, Digby's use of the bowler hat was short-lived and he had soon switched back to wearing his beret.

Amusing incidents aside, things were about to get very serious very quickly. Digby gave Frank some strong words for losing the house and ordered for it to be recaptured immediately. In turn, Frank conveyed the order to McDermont, telling him he would need to launch a counterattack to win it back. McDermont's platoon had endured prolonged close-range shelling and Frank could see they were 'all very tired', but they did not grumble, they simply shrugged their shoulders and began to prepare for the task at hand. Capt. Frank was impressed by their spirit.

Pte Morgan and several others who were still watching from the windows of their building were spotted by Digby who ordered them down to lend a hand in the assault.

From under the bridge, McDermont led the attack on the house from the front. As the first man to enter, he charged in through the back door. Firing from the hip, he ran up the stairs, but was cut down by a burst of fire as he turned onto the first floor landing. Another man, directly behind him, was also hit before the German responsible was killed. The melee turned hand-to-hand, and bayonets were used freely before the house was secured. Those Germans who were not killed leapt from the windows in an attempt to escape, only to be shot down by paratroopers from other buildings.

Tony Frank arrived to find McDermont propped up on a chair in the hallway being attended to. He was bleeding profusely having been shot through the lower stomach and, according to one witness, the head. The tops of his fingers that had been clutching his Sten as he stormed up the stairs had also been shot off. He was conscious and in a lot of pain, so Frank jabbed him with morphine and had him carried away.

Hand-to-hand fights like the one to recapture McDermont's house were commonplace around the perimeter as the men fought for ownership of the buildings.

With McDermont's allotted building secured, Jack Grayburn led an audacious assault to retake another building further afield that would have considerably expanded their

The building directly east of the bridge—a tram office—held by Lt McDermont. McDermont was mortally wounded storming the building from his position under the bridge in order to retake it.

perimeter. It was a bold move made under the cover of smoke, but in the face of overwhelming fire, they were repulsed not long after forcing an entry.

When two armoured cars penetrated along the river and opened fire on 'A' Company's positions, one was knocked-out by a PIAT and the other retired, but the buildings were being destroyed at an alarming rate and were fast becoming untenable. Frost noted at this stage, 'It became increasingly difficult to find new positions while keeping the bridge under our control.'[10] Worrying too was the fact that PIAT ammunition was beginning to run low, and nothing could be done to prevent enemy armour from approaching their position.

Around this time, Capt. Frank was wounded by shrapnel that embedded itself deep into his ankle and could not be extracted. Frank continued until it began to get dark before handing over command to Lt Grayburn to have it attended to. He would resume command the following day.

As darkness approached, enemy tanks rolled up in force and many other men were wounded, including Digby. A tank appeared at Brigade HQ and worked its way down the road sending shells into each building.

Frost recalled:

> Towards evening heavy tanks appeared, incredibly menacing and sinister in the half-light, as their guns swung from target to target. Shells burst through our walls. The dust and settled debris following their explosions filled the passages and rooms. The acrid reek and smell of burning together with the noise bemused us. We had to stay prepared to meet the rush of infantry I knew would follow if we wavered for a moment. The battalion Headquarters building suffered badly. Digby, Father Egan and others were hit.[11]

A knocked-out German tank, destroyed during the fighting at the bridge.

Enemy vehicles knocked-out by the bridge.

Moving with impunity, the tank responsible was able to negotiate the street unhindered, blasting methodically into each building at point-blank range. Approaching from the north, the tank first put a few rounds into Brigade HQ before continuing its journey of destruction. The next target was Digby's Battalion HQ. Frost believed it was here where Digby was wounded, but an account from Digby himself suggests he may have been wounded in another building closer to the bridge:

> I was visiting one of the houses held by our chaps near the bridge when a German heavy tank—I think it was a Tiger, which was methodically firing into every house in the road—connected three times at point-blank range with the house that I was in.
>
> I was knocked about a bit by pieces of masonry and was so dazed by the blast that I was placed with the wounded in a cellar, and I remained there for a few hours—I can't remember how long—before I was able to resume command.[12]

It is not known whether it was here or elsewhere during another incident that same day where Digby had part of his trousers 'whipped out by a blast', the result of which was said to have given him 'a vaguely scarecrow-like appearance instead of his normally immaculate turnout'.[13]

Leo Heaps described:

> A particularly brutal assault on the third afternoon by Mark IV tanks barely beaten back with Piat bombs and anti-tank grenades, left the dwindling garrison at the bridge badly mauled. Tatham-Warter had been hit by shrapnel splinters and the seat of his pants blown off. But he did not feel amused.[14]

Digby was badly concussed and unable to think straight. Semi-conscious, he was placed in the small cellar of Battalion HQ—nowhere near as large as the cellar belonging to Brigade HQ that now held a couple of hundred casualties.

Other members of the battalion were in the cellar with Digby, including Father Egan who had been severely wounded in his legs and back. All but one of the casualties lay directly on the concrete floor. Lt McDermont, lying on a stretcher, was the exception. A wounded patient—a paratrooper with a broken femur—was sickened by the sight of McDermont, whose face he described as having been 'blown away'. He also noticed McDermont's severe stomach wounds and marvelled at how he was still alive.

Not only was McDermont alive, he was still very much conscious and aware of his surroundings, as described by the wounded paratrooper, who never forgot the moment:

> Then occurred an incident that has forever lived in my mind. He began to shout for the medical orderly and in a fine voice with thick Army language, eventually we got one to him. We expected the worse, but no, it was his shirt that had rolled up his back and was making him uncomfortable, despite those terrible wounds, and he worried only about his shirt making him uncomfortable. Such is a man's endurance.[15]

Digby unconscious after a Tiger tank fired point-blank into his building.

Battered and bruised, Digby gradually began to come round and regain his composure, albeit with his arm now in a sling and his trousers torn right down the rear.

'Major Tatham-Warter was wounded in several places, he was in a room that received an 88MM,' related the man with the broken femur.[16] But Digby 'concluded that he had had enough of laying on his back and took off to take command of the battalion again.'[17]

Digby went to the attic to assess the scene outside. He was horrified. The entire area was ablaze. He watched flaming roofs collapsing 'into their own hollowed-out graves' and thought the town burned both 'sadly and magnificently'.[18]

Illuminated by the burning buildings, the streets were as bright as day. Observing the direction of the wind, Digby hoped it did not shift to the west. If it did, they stood a good chance of been burnt out by the flames. His mind also turned to the plight of the civilians hiding in their cellars.

As a light rain began to fall, Digby decided to visit his men.

Signalman George Lawson was braving the streets in order to find some ammunition for the men in his building. He was dashing down the road with a shopping basket slung over his arm worried about becoming a target for the enemy when Digby spotted him:

> I ran through the street—I broke all Olympic records, but then I saw Major Tatham-Warter; he was the coolest chap I ever saw, walking about with his red beret, with one arm in a sling, with his umbrella hooked over it and his right hand holding a revolver, directing operations. He asked me what I wanted and, when I told him, he said, 'Hurry up and get some and get back to your post, soldier, there are snipers about.'[19]

Since buildings were being regularly evacuated due to flames or enemy assault, it had become very difficult to establish just who was where. Ordinance man Ted Mordecai was settling down to rest behind his makeshift barricade at an upper-floor window when he heard movement in the street below. Looking out, he glimpsed a shadowy figure approaching the house with an umbrella. The man's tall, gangly figure coupled with his commanding and authoritative voice and demeanour led Mordecai to believe the man was Brig. Lathbury. It was not until later that he discovered it was Maj. Digby Tatham Warter.

There were indeed a number of similarities between the two men. A fellow officer in the 1st Division wrote:

> Superficially Lathbury and Tatham-Warter had many qualities in common. Both were tall, lean men who paid excessive attention to their personal turnout. Equally determined soldiers, they could endure great hardship and had considerable powers of endurance. But Lathbury was a diplomat more than a soldier. Tatham-Warter was a soldier first and never very diplomatic.[20]

Digby shouted up and asked for six volunteers from Mordecai's building to accompany him further down the street to establish which buildings contained friendly troops. Mordecai and five others promptly joined him outside. Slowly and cautiously, they made their way along the road, alert and ready, with their weapons poised. Digby's intention was to reach one particular building and to ascertain who was in it, but his method of doing so was not particularly popular with the men that accompanied him. As they neared the house, Digby casually strolled up to the door and shouted into it, demanding to know who was inside.

Mordecai related:

> Personally, I thought it was stupid, because if Jerry had been in the house we would have been in for a rough time out there in the open. Fortunately for us, the reply came back that it was occupied by some of our gunners and sappers. This evidently satisfied the major and he strolled off into the darkness, still directing operations with his brolly.[21]

The goal complete and with Digby gone, Mordecai and his companions turned to return to their position. The danger they were in was brought home to Mordecai's party as they returned to their position:

> We started to make our way back to the house we had occupied, but Jerry must have heard the voices and spotted us in the half light as a machine gun opened up from the far end of the street and bullets came whistling at us through the air.[22]

By timing their runs between bursts of fire, the six men made it back, but with such danger lurking, it is little wonder they considered Digby's stroll down the middle of the road to be a risky enterprise.

Such actions undoubtedly contributed to Digby's reputation. Sgt Neville Ashley called Digby 'a nutter', but added, he was 'a good bloke, him, as brave as could be'.[23] John Mills who went to Wellington with Digby and was a member of Waterloo Company at Sandhurst with him related that he was 'marvellously mad and very brave!'[24] Steve Morgan agreed. During an interview, I asked him to sum Digby up, he grinned and told me, 'He was as mad as a hatter.'[25]

Digby's nonchalant behaviour brought a mix of admiration and bewilderment, particularly from those who did not know who he was or were not familiar with his eccentricities.

Capt. Arvian Llewellyn-Jones of the 1st Airlanding Anti-Tank Battery, RA, was with several men in a house. The upper floor was blazing furiously, the flames were rapidly spreading, and in a short space of time the building would be completely untenable. Llewellyn-Jones and his men were crouched at the entrance, discussing where they should run to next.

'Only the Bde. HQ seemed to be not on fire at the time,' remembered Llewellyn-Jones. 'It was agreed that each man should run zig-zag across the square at ten second intervals, and make for Bde. HQ.'[26]

But, as related by Llewellyn-Jones, 'Just as the first man was set to go across the square came a lone figure':

> It was raining slightly. He had a black umbrella. Under it was a discerning figure, but only as he came closer did we realise it was a Parachute Battalion officer. His smock was undone, and hung down between his legs like a raped skirt. He came to us at the door and said, 'How are you chaps getting on—XXX Corps are on the way, and should be with us tomorrow, in fact we could hear their guns from the south of the bridge earlier today. So we just have to hang on through tomorrow and then we should be OK. Glad to see you are in good heart. Keep up the good work!'
>
> He turned away from the door and walked quietly and methodically back over the square. He was not shot at, though this did not diminish our appreciation of his quiet bravery.[27]

Llewellyn-Jones had his own theory as to why Digby did not attract enemy fire. It certainly was not because the enemy were not alert, as he and his men discovered just moments later when trying to cross the very same space:

> I have always been convinced that the Germans thought he was an eccentric old women, and that is what the silhouette looked like. But we were greatly encouraged by this act of quiet bravery.[28]

Llewellyn-Jones, who referred to Digby as 'The remarkable Major', likened his impromptu visit to that of a spiritual apparition. But Digby's calm bravery had given them added confidence to get out into the streets themselves:

Llewellyn-Jones continued:

> Encouraged by the short somewhat ghostly visitation, the first man was sent off across the square. Troop Sgt. Quinn, a tough Glaswegian with a short but colourful vocabulary, stuck his head out to see if any sniper or machine gunner was readily visible. A quick tap on the shoulder, and the first man was off, running a series of aide-stepping junks, to occupy his mind, over the next hundred yards. A bullet hit the pavement in front of Sgt Quinn's well-polished boots.... Out of 5, three got to Bde. HQ.[29]

The day's fighting had taken a heavy toll. In his report written after the battle, Digby recorded that, by this stage, the number of casualties had reached serious proportions. Their only hope lay in the arrival of XXX Corps which was never going to happen.

The Armoured Car Incident

Through thorough cross-referencing and a close examination of the sources, it is possible to ascertain when the majority of Digby's specific actions took place. The often told 'armoured car incident' is the exception.

It is said that Digby neutralised an enemy vehicle by poking the driver in the eye through the observation slit with his rolled-up umbrella, thereby incapacitating him. The vehicle in question changes in its telling. Sometimes it is an armoured car and other times a half-track, or tank. The incident has featured in books, articles, blogs, and just about everywhere else, but where did this story come from?

An extensive search of primary sources and a desire to find the truth has proved frustrating. Information is murky, although the possibility of the vehicle being a tank can, I think, be categorically ruled out.

Digby did not speak of Arnhem to his family, the only exception being when he came to write his memoir in 1991 when he related events to his daughter, Jo. But even then, he did not go into detail about his own actions at the bridge, focusing instead on his time with the Dutch Underground after the battle. But two sources do exist that describe Digby's personal encounter with a vehicle. Only one of them, until now, has been published.

In his book *The Grey Goose of Arnhem,* Leo Heaps wrote:

> Tatham-Warter walked calmly around the battered positions quite unconcerned about his personally safety, cheering the wounded and organising his men in shelled houses. Once, in anger, he poked his rolled-up umbrella—which he had picked up in a rubble heap—through a slit in a passing German armoured car, immobilizing the driver.[30]

Unfortunately, since Heaps's narrative jumps from one event to the next without sequence or chronology, it is impossible to know just when this incident is said to have occurred, or indeed where.

In October 2018, I sat with Pte Steve Morgan, who, as a member of the 2nd Battalion's Medium Machine Gun Platoon, supported Digby's 'A' Company during the battle. Morgan explained that, from a building overlooking the bridge, he had personally witnessed Digby 'jabbing his umbrella at a German half track' on the bridge itself.[31] Steve was busy firing at enemy soldiers at the time and admitted to only seeing Digby for a split-second as he glanced back, but it was evident to him that Digby was attempting to break through a 'window' without actually managing to do so. Morgan was also abundantly clear that the vehicle had already been knocked-out and was not moving at the time. This does not fit with Heaps's version of events, in which he says Digby jabbed 'through the slit of a passing German armoured car'.

Assuming the vehicle was stationary, as stated by Morgan, quite what Digby was hoping to achieve by jabbing at the vehicle will sadly never be known. He may have been prompting a hidden German to come out, but equally there could have been any number of other reasons. Morgan did not see Digby approach the vehicle and he did not see him leave it, but the sight struck him as particularly surreal, and remained fresh in his memory until he passed away in 2019.

When asked by his niece if he could remember what day this occurred, Morgan said he thought it was on the Tuesday. This fits nicely with other episodes and would make sense since this was almost certainly the day he acquired the umbrella. Quite what Digby would be doing on the bridge on the Tuesday is unclear, but it seems the more likely of the two scenarios we are presented with. We know that others had also ventured onto the bridge following Gräbner's attack, after which a good number of Germans remained hidden on and around the structure. Some of them remained in their wrecked vehicles, not daring to move in fear of attracting fire, as discovered by members of Capt. Hoyer-Millar's patrol. One member of this patrol, Don Smith, found a German officer cowering under an armoured car who promptly surrendered by waving a white handkerchief to make his intentions clear. Around a dozen prisoners were taken in that one patrol alone.

So what is the truth?

It is highly unlikely that Digby was involved in two separate incidents with enemy vehicles, meaning both Morgan and Heaps are describing the same event with slight differences in the detail. The account from Heaps is at best a second-hand anecdote, which leaves more room for error than in Morgan's first-hand account. It may be that the incident was explained to Heaps by another person who did not get it quite right and it became muddled along the way. It is doubtful that the story came from Digby himself since he seems not to have related any other aspects of his personal battle to Heaps or to anyone else. Alternatively, Heaps could have embellished what he was told, either by mistake or design. It is worth noting that other errors regarding Digby did make their way into his book. For example, Heaps describes Digby as having fought in North Africa and Italy where 'he had always found good defensive positions in the stony rubble of houses'.[32] Digby, however, did not see any action in either of these theatres.

Twenty-one-year-old Canadian Lt Leo Heaps, who parachuted into Holland with the 1st Parachute Battalion HQ during Operation Market Garden, admitted he 'should not have been here' adding that he had 'come only because the Canadian Army was so anxious to see the last of [him]'.[32] Heaps had in fact been discharged from the

Canadian Army having been deemed 'not officer material'. Not to be defeated, he had then joined the British Army with whom he had fought at Normandy on D-Day. Now with the 1st Airborne Division, Arnhem was his first jump. For his bravery during and after the battle, he would be awarded the MC.

During his research for his book, published in 1976, Heaps carried out extensive interviews with those who were there, including Digby. Since Digby was very much alive and involved in providing information for the book, would Heaps really have embellished or exaggerated Digby's actions, knowing full well he would read them when the book was released?

As frustrating as it is, there simply is not any clear-cut evidence to nail down the story with any certainty. Frustratingly, we are left with more questions than answers and the exact specifics of what happened remain a mystery.

Digby with umbrella.
(*Artist: Eric Thornton*)

10

Wednesday 20 September 1944

By Wednesday morning, the buildings either side of the bridge had completely burnt down. Enemy shell fire began early, targeting the remaining houses. Over the coming hours, the situation would go from bad to worse, and by the day's end, the paratroopers' grip on the bridge would cease to exist.

Radio contact had been established with the rest of the division in the early hours, but the news was far from promising, with Frost being informed by Gen. Urquhart that the division was practically surrounded at Oosterbeek and unable to move. It was now clear to those at the bridge that no support from the division would be coming. It had also become apparent during the radio call that Urquhart did not quite appreciate the severity of the situation at the bridge. Frost had informed him of their critical supply of ammunition, and their lack of medical supplies and water. In response, Urquhart had suggested they send civilians out to collect additional water and supplies. This idea was completely impractical since stepping foot in the streets meant almost certain death. Besides, by now, civilians were very much conspicuous by their absence.

Digby, in his HQ, had just returned from a tour of the perimeter when he heard a series of explosions in the street. Moments later, a breathless runner came bursting in to tell him that John Frost was lying out in the cobbled road badly wounded. Frost had been with Doug Crawley outside 'B' Company HQ discussing plans to send out a fighting patrol when an explosion had tossed him into the air. Frost had hit the ground hard with shrapnel wounds to the legs and was lying where he had landed, dazed, shaken, and unable to move. Stunned and bemused, he was carried to the makeshift Regimental Aid Post in the Brigade HQ cellar along with Doug Crawley who had also been wounded.

It was a blow to lose Frost, but other capable men were on hand to fill his boots. Maj. Freddie Gough now stepped up to take overall command.

In Digby's area, things were getting more and more desperate by the minute. German attempts to infiltrate were taking their toll on his men down by the bridge.

Casualties were stacking and many men were now carrying more than one wound, but they carried on fighting nonetheless. Through a lack of available defensive positions, members of 'A' Company, some engineers, and elements from other units had gathered underneath the bridge itself. They numbered around thirty. Capt. Frank and Lt Vlasto were there, the latter having fought from three separate buildings with his platoon before each had been systematically destroyed or set alight. The wounded Lt Grayburn was there too, backing up his words with actions. By now, he was carrying multiple wounds, the first having occurred on the Sunday night when hit by machine-gun fire from the pillbox on the bridge. He had been wounded again, more than once. His head was heavily bandaged, his right arm was in a sling, and his leg was also bandaged. As a right-handed man, he was now firing his pistol with his left.

At least one of these wounds had been inflicted leading assaults against German infantry who were covering their engineers attempting to lay charges on the bridge supports. Under the cover of Grayburn and his men, British engineers had removed the charges from the pillars.

The desperate nature of the fight now made it impossible to move the wounded from the bridge area to Divisional HQ. Instead they had been placed in a recess under the bridge. Lt Vlasto described it as 'a hole-like thing, with steps down into a pitch dark cavern'.[1]

A large stock of building materials was stacked under the bridge consisting of cobblestones, flags and slabs, and mounds of gravel, which offered the paratroopers some degree of cover, but casualties continued to mount and it was clear the position could not be defended for any length of time.

At some point, Digby ordered the men to withdraw to the Battalion and Brigade HQ area. The move would have to be carried out with caution and the men were to move in small groups. Capt. Frank took stock of what they had between them before ordering Robin Vlasto to recce some buildings to the west to see if they were held by Germans. With a couple of men, Vlasto dashed out towards the buildings but they soon came under fire and were forced to split off in their own directions to avoid being shot down. From his hiding place, Vlasto looked back towards the bridge to find his comrades had gone.

After knocking out a tank with gammon bombs, Capt. Frank had asked for volunteers to assist him in a breakout. With the remaining Bren guns, he had charged off with his party. Vlasto, who could not help but wonder if he had been used as a sacrificial lamb to draw the enemy's attention, would be captured by a German patrol while trying to sneak away after dark. He would be the only officer of Digby's company to avoid being killed or wounded in the battle.

Not everyone from the bridge had accompanied Frank in his breakout. Lt Grayburn was now in charge of the handful of remaining men, holding the position for as long as humanly possible. An enemy tank, brought forward to cover their engineers, sat just 30–40 yards away keeping a watchful eye for any movement. Hunkered down behind the building materials, the paratroopers attracted machine-gun and sniper fire the second they strayed from cover. Frustrated in its lack of clear targets, the tank began to fire at the bridge itself, specifically the thick concrete beams directly above where

Robin Vlasto.

the men were hiding. It was an effective method of fire. Soon, very few men were left on their feet and Grayburn decided the time had come to leave the position.

Looking around, Steve Morgan saw that nobody else was left. 'Little by little we were being whittled down until there were only two of us left which was Lieutenant Grayburn and myself,' remembered the private. 'Most men were badly wounded and couldn't take part and had no ammunition left and Lieutenant Grayburn tapped me on the shoulder behind a heap of gravel and he said, "It's time to go lad!"'[2]

The aim was to reach a row of crumbled houses nearby. Morgan was the first to go, followed closely by Grayburn who became an instant target for the tank's machine gun. Morgan reached the remains of the houses and turned to see Grayburn badly wounded, but still alive, lying on his side in the road, riddled with bullets. A voice then called out from the ruins of a nearby building and asked Grayburn how badly he was hit. The identity of this man had never been established, but Morgan could tell from the 'cultured tone' that it was an officer.[3]

Grayburn, who was still conscious and able to respond, shouted to the officer, 'Leave me! Leave me!'[4]

After a slight pause, as if struggling to know what to say, the officer responded with the heartfelt words, 'Goodbye dear boy.'[5]

Although the identity of this officer can never be known for sure, it is distinctly possible that it was Digby. As Grayburn's company commander, this would certainly account for the sincerity of those last words that hint at a personal and fatherly connection between the two men. We know that Digby was down by the bridge at this time as he is documented as having personally ordered the men to withdraw to the HQ area. Additionally, Digby's family have related that this is exactly the kind of thing he would have said.

The sight of Grayburn lying in the road was too much for Pte Morgan, who, despite Grayburn's proclamations and being in full view of the tank, crawled back out to him. But other than hold Grayburn's hand, there was nothing he could do. Grayburn was dying and he knew it. Grayburn ordered Morgan to leave him, which the young private begrudgingly did. Returning to the destroyed houses, Morgan was thankful that the machine gunner in the tank had not shot him down when he clearly could have done so. Perhaps the sight of the young private crawling to his stricken comrade was too much for the tank crew who chose compassion over killing. After moving along the buildings in the direction of the HQ area, Morgan hid in a cellar where he found three others doing the same. Soon, German soldiers could be heard moving around above them, evidently in some strength, and German tanks were cruising up and down the road safe in the knowledge the British paratroopers had nothing with which they could knock them out.

At this stage, 'A' Company were all but destroyed. As for the officers, McDermont was slowly dying in a cellar, Vlasto was hiding and would later be captured, and Grayburn lay dying or was already dead in the roadway down by the bridge. The wounded Capt. Frank had succeeded in reaching HQ, as had various others from around the perimeter. Digby estimated around fifteen men from 'A' Company, and a further twenty-five from other units, succeeded in getting away from the bridge and other locations nearby. The HQ buildings were now the final hub of resistance.

Above left: Lt McDermont died of wounds received when he stormed a building that had been previously lost. He was cut down when running up the stairs and passed away several days later whilst in German captivity.

Above right: Lt Grayburn had been eager to get into the war and be in the thick of battle. He got his wish at Arnhem where, wounded multiple times, he led his men with remarkable gallantry.

Above left: Private Steve Morgan fought at Arnhem with the 2nd Battalion's Medium Machine Gun Platoon. Ordered down from his building by Digby, he took part in Lt McDermont's charge to retake one of the houses previously held by 'A' Coy. Morgan was with Lt Grayburn as the latter was mortally wounded. He was later captured and spent the rest of the war as a prisoner. (*Photograph signed by Pte Morgan for the author*)

Above right: Digby with bowler hat, umbrella, and arm in a sling. One witness described him hooking the brolly on his sling during the battle. (*Artist: Eric Thornton*)

After the withdrawal from the bridge, Digby visited John Frost in the cellar of Brigade HQ to give him an update. He told Frost of the fate of Grayburn and explained that in his opinion they could not hold out through the following day. During the conversation, Digby, who was fighting his first battle, asked Frost if it was worse than previous battles or not as bad. Ever the diplomat, Frost told him it was rather difficult to compare because in some ways it was worse, but in others it was better. The 'worse' was the intensity and the increasingly hopeless nature of their predicament; the 'better' being that, unlike their experiences in the desert, they still had a little food and some water—the latter having been recently found in one of the houses, despite the Germans shutting off the water supply.

Frost was given another dose of morphine to help deal with the pain and soon drifted off to sleep. When he woke, Digby was gone. By now Frost realised that the bridge was lost and that the battle could only end one way. Even so, he knew that Digby and the others, 'would fight on til all hope had gone'.[7] Sadly, this scenario seemed to be drawing nearer and nearer by the minute.

During the day, Brig.-Maj. Tony Hibbert had still hoped they would be relieved: 'We had by this time about 300 wounded in the cellars, but I still believed that 30 Corps would be coming up certainly up to the south bank within a matter of almost hours', he remarked. 'And damn it we could hear them!'[8]

But as the day wore on, he finally accepted the game was up:

> At 8 O'clock I realised that our little battle was finished. We just didn't have the ammunition. When the other side can run tanks right up to your front window with no chance of you retaliating, there comes a moment where you can't go on.[9]

The point-blank fire from tanks had a bad effect on the wounded in the cellar, one of whom, Pte Sims, could hear a mixture of British and German voices outside as the fighting progressed. When asking for an update on the situation, the wounded were told that a Tiger tank had parked itself directly outside their building. Sims hobbled upstairs and heard Freddie Gough pleading into the radio set: 'We cannot hold out much longer. Our position is desperate. Please hurry'.[10]

The Truce

Brigade HQ was set ablaze and soon became untenable. The hundreds of wounded in the cellar were hastily dragged out of the rear of the building out of sight of the tank to be transferred into another building nearby, but that too was set ablaze as this move was taking place. The only houses in the immediate area that were not on fire were in German hands and there was nowhere for the wounded to be taken. The case was now hopeless.

Begrudgingly, Frost gave his approval for a ceasefire and for the wounded, including himself, to be given up to the Germans. After agreeing to a ceasefire and temporary truce, enemy infantry moved in to accept the British wounded.

The truce was conducted with the greatest of respect by the SS who were very polite and complimentary, heaping praise on the paratroopers for their fighting spirit.

His battalion it tatters, Frost remained upbeat:

> No living enemy had beaten us. The battalion was unbeaten yet, but they could not have much chance with no ammunition, no rest and with no positions from which to fight. No body of men could have fought more courageously and tenaciously than the officers and men of the 1st Parachute Brigade at Arnhem.[11]

Maj. Gough's jeeps were needed to help transport the wounded, and at the request of the SS, he had little choice but to hand them over.

Strict orders were issued to those set to carry on the fight that they were not to fire until all the wounded had been removed and the truce had ended. It would take two hours, but approximately 300 wounded paratroopers together with many enemy prisoners were handed over. Frost locked eyes with Maj. Crawley as he was being carried away: 'Well Doug, I'm afraid we haven't got way with it this time'. Crawley smiled: 'No sir, but we gave 'em a damn good run for their money'.[12]

'The battalion was unbeaten yet' is what went through Frost's mind as he began life as a prisoner of war, and this was indeed the case. Digby had gathered the remaining men in the open garden behind Brigade HQ out of reach of the tanks at the front. The truce presented an awkward situation for the non-wounded paratroopers. During the ceasefire, the Germans were able to move freely around the British position. An SS officer with some men walked among the paratroopers' slit trenches in the garden and demanded that they assist in removing the wounded. The officer handed them cigarettes while telling them they did not stand a chance and that they were 'silly bastards to carry on fighting'. After telling them they should just all surrender, the officer was told quite bluntly to 'piss off!'[13]

Digby was concerned by the enemy infantry moving freely around his position and even further disturbed to see them using the ceasefire to move their own positions closer to where he was now located. In fact, Digby was furious, but he knew he had to tread carefully in what was a very delicate situation. He decided to send Capt. Hoyer-Millar who could speak German to protest.

Hoyer-Millar approached an officer in a long leather coat: 'He spoke good English,' noted Hoyer-Millar. 'I warned him that if his men continued, we might have to open fire. He, in turn, kept stressing that there was no hope for us and that we should surrender. I told him there was no chance of that…'[14]

In reality, Hoyer-Millar's threat of opening fire was an empty one, and the Germans knew it. It was impossible to open fire during the truce while the wounded were being evacuated.

In a couple of hours, the truce was over and battle quickly resumed, although it was a one-sided affair from the onset. The paratroopers in the garden immediately found themselves under attack from enemy grenades. With burning buildings on three sides, and the enemy on the other side, it quickly became apparent to the survivors that they were completely hemmed in.

From his cellar down towards the bridge and with no knowledge of the truce, Pte Morgan had wondered what was happening: 'All the firing had stopped. Even 2nd Battalion Headquarters on the other side of the road had been overrun. There were one or two shots being fired—what exactly that was I don't know…'[15]

A little later, Morgan heard a familiar sound: 'I remember somebody from what had been 2nd Battalion Headquarters shouted out our battle-cry, "Wayo Mohammed!", and it echoed through the buildings'.[16]

Throughout the battle, any war cry had resulted in multiple responses from comrades around the perimeter, but this time there was no reply, just a single solitary voice. It was an ominous sign.

It may have been around this time that the final radio message from the bridge was sent—a message, sent from Digby's position, is often described as coming from Digby himself, though in reality there is no evidence for this. The message was not picked up by friendly troops but was heard by the Germans on their own radio. The message ended with the words: 'Out of ammo. God save the King!'

A concentrated barrage was directed on Digby's position. Sgt Wallace recalled: 'At 2300 hrs on Wednesday 20th September after Major Tatham-Warter had refused to surrender, the Germans opened up a terrific barrage of shells, moaning minnies and mortars'.[17] Digby conferred with Maj. Gough, who had joined Digby's party after abandoning Brigade HQ during the truce, and the two men agreed they could no longer remain where they were.

A nearby warehouse became their target. It was held by the Germans, so Digby told his men that they would take it by force, selecting his own 'A' Company to lead the charge. At around midnight, they stormed headlong at the building, capturing it at the point of the bayonet. However, the warehouse soon proved to be just as precarious as their previous position, and Digby soon realised that they were virtually surrounded and the place could not be defended.

Digby decided to split the force into two smaller parties, surmising they would stand a better chance. One group would be led by Digby himself, and the other by Maj. Tate. The plan was for the two parties to go their separate ways and find a place to hide for the night before returning to their original position at 5:15 a.m., just before daybreak, to resume the fight. It was a gutsy plan—particularly since they had little ammunition—and one that encapsulated the stoic determination and spirit of the paratroopers who had resolved to cling on to a position by the bridge for as long as possible.

Several hours after taking possession of the warehouse, the two parties went their separate ways, but both were subjected to a murderous close-range machine-gun fire the moment they set out. Digby's group quickly became fragmented. Around half managed to reach a building some 200 yards away while the other half was scattered. Maj. Tate's party did not fare any better, and a number of men, including Tate himself,

Under the (modern) Arnhem road Bridge where the paratroopers fought so desperately. (*Alex de Groot*)

were killed. Others were captured, including Lt Tom Ainslie, HQ Coy, who, as their case became hopeless, called out to the Germans, 'Don't shoot. There are wounded here.'[19]

Ainslie was politely greeted by his captors and complimented by a German NCO who wished him a 'good evening', and told him it had been a 'lovely battle, a really lovely battle'.[20] Ainsle and his comrades were then offered cigars before discussing the battle with their SS adversaries who, only moments before, had been mowing them down with machine guns.

Meanwhile, Digby was among those to reach the building a couple of hundred yards away. A small cluster of RASC men under Capt. Gill arrived shortly after. They had been part of a larger force of around 120 men who had abandoned Brigade HQ during the truce with the intention of finding another location, but had failed to do so. Instead, they had split into smaller groups of ten and tried to make their way out of the town, but this had proven impossible. Most of the group had already been killed or captured.

No organised body of men remained and resistance was finally over. Small groups, pairs, and lone individuals were scattered around the area with no hope of reforming as a fighting force. The best they could hope for was to reach the rest of the division at Oosterbeek. Accepting the inevitable, Digby gave one final order, telling his men there was nothing else they could do and it was now a case of every man for himself.

L/Cpl Harold Back, 2nd Battalion Intelligence Section, related:

> We were told it was 'every man for himself'. We didn't know what to do or where to go. We had no idea where we were or where the rest of the division was. Three or four of us wandered around for a while and found some trenches that had been dug sometime before and laid in them for the night. There were 60 or so British around our general area, I would guess, and some wounded because I could hear them groaning in the dark.
>
> One of the chaps with me had a wound in the foot and we couldn't move fast with him. I had a Sten gun with me, but it was useless. It didn't have any ammunition and I didn't have any grenades left. I could hear the German patrols moving around us in the dark.[21]

Harold Back and his comrades crept back to the warehouse where he found Freddie Gough and several others hiding. After a pep talk from Gough, they left the building to try to escape but instead walked straight into a German patrol. Gough himself was captured shortly after.

Meanwhile, Digby had paired up with 2nd Battalion adjutant Duncan McLean and together they had taken refuge in a culvert under a roadway. It was far from ideal, but German troops were swarming over the area in a vigorous and methodical sweep, hunting down the last of the paratroopers. Digby hoped that they could remain undetected until nightfall the following day—for it was now beginning to get light—at which point they would attempt to sneak away, but it was not to be. They were discovered during the morning and, in the words of Digby, were unceremoniously 'winkled out at the points of several bayonets with a lot of rather rude shouts'.[22]

For Digby, the war was over—for now at least.

Members of the 1st Airborne Division—many of them wounded—help each other along as POWs after the failed operation.

Arnhem Bridge, post-battle following an Allied bombing run.

Opposite above: The location of Brigade HQ. The floor space was vast. During the battle, some hundreds of casualties were placed in its cellar.

Opposite below: The ruins of Arnhem.

11

Escape and Evasion

Resistance at the bridge had finally come to an end. There had been no official surrender and no precise time can be placed on when the fighting actually ceased. It had simply fizzled out with the men falling into the enemy hands piecemeal as they tried to get away or hide.

For Digby, his first and only battle of the war was over. Five years of training had amounted to little more than four intense days of action. Digby and his company had been the first to arrive at the bridge and he had been among the few remaining men at the very end. Now in the hands of the SS, he was a prisoner of war. On the plus side, he still had his revolver, which he had managed to conceal from his captors when pulled from his hiding place. Digby was taken to a nearby church that was being used as a dressing station and a collecting point for prisoners. Looking round, Digby realised that almost everyone from the bridge was present, including those who had tried to get out after he had given the 'every man for himself' order. Clearly the breakout had been completely unsuccessful.

Later that afternoon, the Germans began separating the wounded and unwounded paratroopers with a view to moving the non-wounded to POW camps and the wounded to hospital. Digby did not consider himself to be a casualty, but he did think he would stand a better chance of escape if he was placed with them and taken to a hospital. His battered appearance certainly gave the impression of being wounded, and although he had shrugged them off, he did have several minor shrapnel wounds.

As a part of their training, it was drilled into paratroopers that if captured, their chance of escaping diminishes as time goes by. This is because the enemy will become more and more organised, which in turn will make it more difficult to slip away. Therefore, if a man was to attempt an escape, the sooner he tried it, the better chance he would have.

Digby noted:

> In the late afternoon the wounded were separated from the other prisoners and taken to a small hospital in the Northern suburbs of Arnhem. I thought that if I could include myself among the wounded, there would be a rather better, if remote, chance

> of escaping. I was lucky to achieve this as, although knocked out for some hours during the battle and battered in appearance, I had in fact suffered nothing which could be called a wound.[1]

During the battle, Digby had been knocked unconscious by shell fire, struck by falling masonry, had the rear of his trousers ripped out by an explosion, sustained a shoulder wound from shell splinters that necessitated a temporary sling, and was generally battered and bruised. He may not have considered himself to be wounded, but he was certainly a far cry from his usual immaculate appearance.

It was fellow prisoner Maj. Freddie Gough who came up with the plan to get Digby out. At the church, a number of the more serious cases had already succumbed to their wounds and the pile of bodies outside was steadily growing. Several of the more recently deceased lay inside on stretchers with blankets drawn over their faces. Some empty stretchers had been brought back in after the previous and now deceased occupants had been carried out. Local Dutch boys acting as stretcher-bearers were busy carting around the dead and wounded.

With wounded paratroopers being loaded on to trucks, Gough approached Digby with his plan. His idea was this: Digby would lie on one of the empty stretchers in the church, play dead, and be carried outside by the Dutch lads where he would then blend in as one of the wounded to be loaded on to a truck and taken away as a serious casualty. Digby was all for it and asked Gough to accompany him, but Gough laughed and refused the offer, telling him, 'Digby, do you see this white hair of mine? I'm the only one around here with white hair and they'd spot me immediately.'[2]

German soldiers in church watch over British paratroopers captured at Arnhem.

Paratroopers captured around Arnhem Bridge. A German guard stands to the right looking at the camera. (*Gelders Archive*)

Others would escape using the same method as Digby, while Gough, the instigator, remained behind as a prisoner. He would escape from his POW camp a few months later.

Slipping discreetly and undetected on to one of the stretchers, Digby set the wheels in motion. The Dutch boys re-entered the building and Gough gave them a wink and glanced down at Digby lying still on the stretcher. The boys smiled and winked back, instinctively grasping what needed to be done. After covering Digby's face to avoid him being recognised by an observant guard, the boys scooped up the stretcher and carried him out where he was successfully placed with the wounded to await transportation.

Digby soon found himself being taken to St Elisabeth Hospital in the northern suburbs of Arnhem. Capt. Tony Frank, who had been captured during the final attempt to break out, did not have to fake or exaggerate his wounds to earn his place on the hospital truck. The shrapnel was still firmly lodged in his ankle and the wound had stiffened so he could hardly walk. Digby sat beside him and made it clear to Frank that he had no intention of hanging around any longer than was necessary. Despite his wound, Frank also expressed an interest in escape, and Digby promised to stick by him if the opportunity arose.

St Elisabeth Hospital was a place of utter chaos and confusion. It had exchanged hands several times during the fighting, but the Germans now held firm possession. Medical teams from both sides were busy treating the numerous casualties. One wounded paratrooper, Sgt Eric Hall, described it as 'a rather sickening sight'.[3]

Amid this hell, the Dutch Red Cross did all they could for the wounded, but the hospital was close to bursting. Many casualties lay in extreme agony. Their groans and screams echoed through the corridors.

Civilian medical services at work around St Elisabeth Hospital.

'I didn't go very far into the hospital,' Sgt Hall related. 'I was only in the hall. Everywhere you could see, the halls and the stairs, and the wards that I could see into were chocker-block with wounded. They were everywhere. There was blood in all directions. The place was like a mad house really.'[4]

A mad house was just the sort of place Digby had hoped for. German guards were placed in and around the hospital, but they had their hands full with everything that was going on and had little hope of maintaining tight security. Escape attempts at this point were rife.

Sgt Hall for one did not stay long before making his own escape with the help of Hans and Bert Kuik, two Dutch brothers who were members of the resistance doubling up as hospital workers with the Red Cross. Both would later be executed after being caught aiding paratroopers.

Meanwhile, Digby and Frank managed to get into a small room on the ground floor with one other occupant, a paratrooper, who was in much distress with a very serious head wound. The officers were ordered to strip and to get into bed, which they did, Digby concealing his pistol in his clothing as he shoved them under his bed.

The overstretched hospital staff were busy tending to the most urgent cases, meaning Digby and Frank were left alone. Their roommate, however, whose wound was causing him to drift in and out of consciousness, was kept under close observation.

Digby quickly formulated a very basic plan of escape. They would wait until dark, get dressed, jump out of the window, and crawl away into the shrubs. Despite its simplicity, there were a number of risks to be considered. Were there any German sentries in the immediate vicinity outside? Would they be shot if caught? Would it be possible to get away with Frank's wound? These questions were impossible to answer, but they considered it worth a punt.

Once darkness had descended, Digby set the plan into motion:

> I first had to move a small table under the rather high-set window so that Tony [Frank], handicapped as he was, could use it to climb out. He was to go out first and wait for me in the laurels. If all went well I would first return the table to its proper place and then follow Tony. If I had not joined him within ten minutes it would mean that something had gone wrong and he was to go on alone. As it happened something did go very wrong. When Tony was half way out of the window, he kicked over the table with a horrible crash. This seemed to disturb out room-mate and caused him to have one of his fits, screaming and throwing himself about. I could only lie in my bed watching while a doctor and orderlies rushed in to control the poor man. I imagine that they thought he had knocked over the table himself as they soon departed without apparently noticing Tony's absence, leaving me to follow through the window. We made out departure from the hospital grounds with great caution and without further incident and began our long slow walk towards the West and the sound of gunfire.[5]

The above version of events, described by Digby in 1991, differs slightly from an earlier narrative he gave when discussing the event with Leo Heaps—the difference being on that occasion he related that both he and Frank had already jumped from the window by the time the hospital staff entered the room to calm their roommate down and that they had heard the staff chatting in the room from outside the window where they hoped their absence would not be noticed. But such minor discrepancies are perhaps understandable given the passage of time. In his later account, Digby also mentioned they stuffed their hospital clothes in the bed sheets to make it look like they were sleeping.

Digby and his wounded deputy remained undetected as they hit the ground. Cautiously they moved away, disappearing quietly into the night with high hopes of escape.

As had been expected, Frank's ankle slowed them down greatly and proved to be an immense hindrance. Frank experienced a lot of pain, but Digby helped him along as best he could. The going was also slowed by the presence of German positions and bivouacs scattered throughout the area. At times, they were so close that the distinct sound of chatting and snoring could be heard. Occasionally they would hear the sound of Germans on the move, ferrying equipment with horses which would send them scurrying for cover. But according to Digby, 'the clearest warning of all came from their smell':

> I am not suggesting that they were any dirtier than any of us in similar conditions. It was almost certainly the spiced food, such as sausages, that they ate and the ersatz tobacco they smoked. Whatever the cause, it was a very distinctive and unattractive smell and this helped us enormously.[6]

As dawn approached, they had finally broken through the suburbs into open country, having travelled perhaps 4–5 miles. By now, they were completely exhausted and feeling the effects of five days without sleep. Fatigue was setting in, and their rumbling stomachs were long empty.

At the end of their endurance, they spotted an isolated house in the moonlight and in sheer desperation, approached it and knocked on the door. It was a big risk, but one that they felt worth taking.

Tony Frank, Digby's second-in-command who was wounded by shrapnel at the bridge. Capt. Frank made his escape from St Elisabeth Hospital with Digby, his company commander.

A 'little middle-aged' lady answered. At first it looked as though she was about to usher them away in panic, but she hesitated and seemed to have a change of heart. Stepping from her house, she led them across to a cow-stall and guided them up some ladders into the loft space. She left them briefly and returned with a much-welcome meal of bread, eggs, cheese, and milk, which was quickly devoured. Later, when she came to retrieve the plates, she informed them through hand gestures that they needed to be careful as there were Germans nearby. It did not matter, for they were in no fit state to do anything more without resting first. The exhausted officers buried themselves in the straw and were soon fast sleep.

Digby stirred from his slumber to find pair of beady eyes peering over the top of the ladder towards him. The sight of this strange man gave Digby the shock of his life, but he need not have worried. It turned out to be a 'little Dutchman' who had been summoned by the lady to assist. The man was Lodewijk Van den Ven, a painter by trade who spoke fairly good English. Van den Ven had brought with him a set of razors which he handed over with the suggestion that they shave and smarten themselves up. Before he left, Van den Ven advised them not to venture outside as a German artillery unit was stationed in the next field. He said his goodbyes and promised to return.

When Van den Ven came back, he had with him two sets of paint-splattered overalls and some tins of paint. They were to change their clothes and go with him; if stopped, Van den Ven would tell the Germans they were his sons and that they worked for the family business. Things would get tricky if Digby or Frank were questioned directly, but Van den Ven knew the location of the German positions and, with a slight detour of a couple of miles, he was confident they could make their way past without being stopped. Frank's wound restricted him to nothing more than a slow hobble and added considerable time to the journey. Nevertheless, they succeeded in reaching Van den Ven's residence without incident.

Van den Ven directed the two men to an orchard towards the rear of his land, unobtrusive, secluded, and not visible from any road. He ushered them into an old van which was to be their temporary home and gave them food and bedding. Their future was now in the hands of their new Dutch friend. All they could do was wait to see how things played out.

That evening, a doctor arrived to check them over. He was concerned about Frank's ankle and concluded it needed some considerable care and attention. After cleaning it as best he could, he left, telling them he would come back tomorrow.

The following morning, Digby and Frank found themselves with little to do. With the excitement of the past days now subsided, Digby was able to look back on his experiences and concluded he had been remarkably lucky—not only to get through the battle, but also in finding his way into the hands of the Dutch.

Digby noted:

> The escape from the hospital, in spite of one close shave, had gone according to our plan. We had avoided colliding with the enemy on a number of occasions during our night walk and, when just about at the end of our endurance, had found a very brave lone Dutch women willing to take us in and hide us. Then had come Mr. Van den Ven to whom we owed our new refuge, sustenance and medical care. But we had no right to expect this sort of luck to hold out forever. Nevertheless we could possibly be forgiven for thinking that the worst could be over and that the future held a fair chance of final escape. For the time being we could only wait to see what our Dutch friends were going to do about us.[7]

Digby's mind turned to his comrades and of their final break-out attempt from the bridge. He knew from those he had seen in captivity that very few, if any, had made it out and that it would be some months before an accurate report could be written up. He also knew that he was the highest-ranking officer from the bridge not in enemy hands, and so, with the assistance of Frank, he decided to write a report on the action while it was fresh in his mind.

The gallantry of certain individuals from the company was also discussed and Digby wrote up those who he thought deserved recognition. Jack Grayburn, whose bravery had a profound effect of Digby, was top of the list.

Digby addressed the report to his divisional commander, Gen. Roy Urquhart, and would hand it over to the Dutch for safe-keeping. For the time being, however, it was impossible to get the report to Urquhart who, with the remnants of his division, was still holding out in the final pocket of resistance around the Hartenstein Hotel at Oosterbeek. They would continue to hold out until the night of 25 September when, under the cover of darkness, Urquhart, with less than 2,000 of the original 10,000 members of the division, would withdraw across the Rhine.

Since the drop, Digby had seen nothing of his brigadier, Gerald Lathbury, and knew nothing of his fate. Lathbury's battle had in fact been closely associated with Gen. Urquhart's. Early in the operation when attempting to rectify some confusion, and after failing to establish radio contact with units of his division, Urquhart had set out by jeep to find Lathbury to inform him of Freddie Gough's failed *coup de main*. Lathbury at the time had been with the 3rd Battalion, which had encountered fierce resistance. Urquhart caught up with Lathbury there, but the situation had then rapidly deteriorated. Urquhart's jeep was destroyed by enemy mortar fire and German infantry began to counter-attack their position leaving them unable to disengage. By morning, they were trapped with 'B' Company, some way ahead of the rest of the battalion on the outskirts of Arnhem, isolated in a few houses. Frustratingly for Urquhart and Lathbury, the situation had remained unchanged throughout the morning and into the afternoon until, through sheer desperation and under the cover of a smoke grenade, they had attempted to break-out with two other officers. Lathbury had been cut down in his tracks by machine-gun fire during this manoeuvre and dragged into a house, paralysed. He had begged his comrades to leave him and get to Divisional HQ, which they did—Urquhart having first shot a German soldier who appeared at the window as they discussed the situation. Lathbury had been left in the care of the home-owners who had promised to get him to a hospital as soon as it was safe to do so.

At around 7:30 a.m., after being forced to hide in the loft of another house overnight, Urquhart had finally reached Divisional HQ. He had then established contact with John Frost and it was at this point the men at the bridge were told there was no immediate hope of them being reinforced.

Digby and Frank remained confined to their van in the orchard. Daily visits by the doctor helped to break the monotony, where the only thing to look forward to was the delivery of a meal. Van den Ven kept them well-supplied with dried tobacco sourced from the leaves of plants in his garden and they were able to roll something that vaguely resembled cigarettes to smoke.

On 3 October, they received a visit from two members of the Dutch Resistance who had come from neighbouring Ede a few miles north-west of Oosterbeek. These men, Digby was soon to discover, were Derk Wildeboer, the leader of the Ede Resistance, who was known as 'Bill', and his right-hand man, Menno de Nooy, alias 'Tonny' on account of his middle name being Antonie.

After a series of questions to establish if Digby and Frank were legitimate British paratroopers, Bill and Tonny departed with the promise to return the next day to collect Digby. For the time being, Frank, owing to his wound, would regretfully have to remain behind.

Van den Ven had done a tremendous job of looking after his two guests, and he would continue to care for Frank for as long as was needed. It was not until later that Digby discovered Van den Ven was not actually a fully-fledged member of the resistance and with the area rife with pro-German spies had not been fully trusted by Bill and Tonny at the time. But now there was no doubt as to where the little Dutchman's loyalties lay. He had proved himself to be solid, dependable, and completely devoted to the cause.

The following morning, Digby said his farewells, and with a feeling of deep gratitude, set off on a bicycle with his new friends.

12

The Deaf and Dumb Son of a Lawyer

Over the coming weeks, Digby would come to form a great appreciation for the steadfast devotion of the Dutch Resistance who, during their years of German occupation, had performed many feats of extraordinary courage. Not only did they take huge risks with their own lives, but they also risked the lives of their families who stood a high chance of execution or imprisonment if a person's true loyalties were discovered.

After sweeping through Holland in 1940, Germany had set up a puppet government of Dutch Nazis who tracked down, tortured, and executed their fellow countrymen. They were utterly detested and considered 'the lowest of the low'. With military garrisons spread the length and breadth of the country, the Germany Army did their utmost to maintain discipline and proactively sought to eradicate the resistance.

As the war had progressed, the underground network had expanded, becoming more and more calculated in its endeavours. They gathered valuable intelligence and relayed the information to London, and they also carried out acts of sabotage. Their command structure was complicated and was one that Digby never fully understood. He knew that Bill had recently taken command of the resistance in the Ede district after various factors had merged to form one organisation, and he knew that many members of Tonny's large family were involved and doing sterling work.

Now in his early forties, Bill Wildeboer had taken command of the Ede Resistance just two weeks before Operation Market Garden. He had resided in Ede since the age of seventeen and was a former warrant officer in the Dutch Army, having served with the mounted artillery and later with their school of reserve officers. He had been with the resistance from the start of the war and in August 1941 had sheltered a downed English pilot in his home.

Since setting out from Van den Ven's orchard, Digby, together with Bill and Tonny, had cycled many miles, or at least that was what it seemed like to Digby, whose legs ached immensely as he tried to keep pace. There was a system in place where one man rode 200–300 yards ahead of Digby to check the route was clear while the other man cycled alongside him. They eventually reached a large and rather impressive property situated in a wooded area set discreetly within its own grounds. At the house, Digby was introduced to its owner, a young lady by the name of Miss Lambert, who he considered both elegant and attractive.

With introductions complete, Digby was ushered into the sitting room where he received a very pleasant surprise. Sat before him in a comfortable chair was Brig. Lathbury.

The two men greeting each other heartily and over some light refreshments, which, to Digby's delight, included some sherry, they traded war stories and discussed their current situation.

After Lathbury had been wounded, the Dutch couple had been true to their word and got him to hospital where it was found a bullet had chipped his spine. Luckily the paralysis had only been temporary and movement had soon started to return. To hide his rank, Lathbury had donned the uniform of a lance-corporal that he hoped would give him a better chance of escape should the opportunity arise and help prevent any unwanted attention his true rank may bring. He had been placed with the 'other ranks' in the hospital, and although recognised by his men, not once did they do anything that could jeopardise his true identity.

Lathbury's eventual escape made Digby's own successful endeavour of climbing out of a window seem like a highly complex accomplishment. Lathbury had made good progress in recovering from his wound, and after a week in the hospital, although in a lot of pain, the paralysis had worn off to such an extent that he was able to walk unaided.

When Gen. Urquhart and the remnants of the division had retired across the Rhine, a huge bombardment had taken place to disrupt the Germans and disguise the withdrawal. The patients in the hospital, including Lathbury, had mistakenly believed the barrage to be a precursor to an advance by the 2nd Army and they expected the Germans would be forced into a hasty withdrawal. Lathbury surmised that they would first move the wounded out of the area, meaning it would be much more difficult to escape. As such, he had concluded it was now or never. That night, with assistance from the resistance and a Dutch doctor who sketched him a plan of the hospital to aid his escape, Lathbury had hobbled straight out of the front door before being whisked away by a waiting car. He had been hidden by the Dutch before being moved to the elegant Lambert residence where he now sat, relaxing in his chair, drinking sherry, chin-wagging with Digby.

Digby learned that a number of other airborne troops were in hiding and scattered for many miles and that the resistance were doing all they could to ensure they remained undiscovered. But the sheer quantity of paratroopers was putting intolerable pressure on the resistance who were at great risk of being overwhelmed.

Lathbury's stay at the Lambert household was a temporary measure. On 6 October, he would be moved to a safe house in Ede to continue his recovery, as would Tony Frank who would relocate to a separate house nearby.

At the Lambert residence, Bill and Tonny explained to Digby exactly who they were and what they were all about. Digby was told he would be staying with Bill

Brigadier Gerald Lathbury, commander of the 1st Para Brigade, 1st Airborne Division at Arnhem.

at his family home with his wife and two daughters. During their discussion, Bill immediately formed a high opinion of Digby and considered him to be the ideal man to help ease the burden put on the resistance and to assist in maintaining order. 'It seemed that he needed someone to visit and coordinate activities of the considerable number of airborne evaders in the district,' Digby later explained, 'and to act as liaison between the resistance and the allies across the Rhine. He seemed to consider me suitable for this job.'[1]

When the time came for them to leave, the same system of one man in front and one alongside him was used. In the coming weeks, this was to be the standard method of travel. It was a strange feeling for Digby as he rode past units of German soldiers and he could not help but feel particularly vulnerable. But they were not stopped. The only excitement came when Tonny, who was acting as forward scout, came hurrying back to report that there was a checkpoint dead ahead, but it was nothing that a detour could not solve.

At Bill's residence, 32 Lunterseweg, on the outskirts of Ede, Digby was introduced to Bill's wife, Hil Wildeboer-Voskuil, and their two daughters—eleven-year-old Hilly and one-year-old Dicky. Back in August 1941, when the Wildeboers had given shelter to a downed RAF pilot, Guy Conran, the family, in keeping with their use of pseudonyms, had christened him 'Peter'. Digby now became 'Peter the Second', and would be known as 'Peter' throughout his stay.

With introductions complete, Digby was whisked away by Tonny and another man affiliated with the resistance. He was taken to a clothing emporium and fitted with a change of clothes, 'a sort of dark cheap grey suit' that seemed to be made of string.[2]

Next they rode to a place where a fake identification could be forged. Digby had his photo taken and they were told that a passport would be ready for collection the following day. Upon acquiring it, Digby discovered that his new name was Peter Jansen and that he was a deaf and dumb son of a lawyer from The Hague. Should he be stopped, the passport would give a good chance of passing as authentic, but Digby's acting skills would also have to be convincing.

Quite worn out from his day's cycling, Digby returned to Bill's house where he sat with the family to have supper. Bill liked what he saw in Digby, and recognised that this cool customer would be a valuable link between the resistance and the evaders. The feeling was mutual, for Digby had quickly formed a very good impression of Bill whom he found to be both physically and mentally tough. Little did the two men realise that at this early stage in their partnership, a life-long friendship was beginning to bloom.

In the garden, Bill pushed away a pile of logs to reveal a hidden bunker that was to be Digby's sleeping quarters. Four or five steps descended into the bunker, which measured a modest 7 by 5 feet. Rough timbers lined the walls and roof, and the construction was solid. The bunker was around 6 feet high, meaning Digby at 6 feet 1 inch had to stoop slightly when standing up. There was a narrow bed with a small table and a chair and a couple of hooks on which to hang clothing. It had ventilation, a light source, and a bucket for toilet purposes. It was not the Ritz, but Digby found it more than adequate.

In describing what would become his daily routine, Digby noted:

> I spent the nights in an underground sort of dug-out (shelter) which was concealed under a wood pile, and Bill used to tuck me in there after supper every night. He had built this thing himself to hide when he was on the run, when the Germans had information that he was a member of the underground and were after him, and it was a very well-constructed affair with quite a comfortable bed, a bit damp, but very adequate.
>
> In the early morning he used to let me out of this shelter when he could see that the coast was clear. Then I would have a shave in the sink, and breakfast with the family and then I would spend usually virtually the whole of the day bicycling round with either Bill or one or more of his underground chaps, visiting various people who had been put in hiding by the underground, sometimes in houses, sometimes in a barn, and the idea was to go around and kind of reassure them that they were being looked after and that steps were being taken for their future.[3]

Breakfast usually consisted of a variety of smoked meats, cheese, and bread. Digby spoke no Dutch whatsoever, Bill spoke only a little English, and his wife, Hil, virtually no English at all, making conversation a little tricky, but they got on as best they could. As time went by, Digby would begin to pick up bits of Dutch, and Bill's English steadily improved. Over the course of his stay, Digby would learn of some stories of close-calls experienced by the Wildeboers.[4] These stories led to Digby developed a huge amount of admiration towards not only Bill but also his wife, who he referred to as 'an exceptional women' and 'a very gallant lady indeed'.[5]

Digby soon had his routine running smoothly. He would rise early each morning and after washing, shaving, and having breakfast would set off on his trusty bicycle to attend daily 8 a.m. conferences with the resistance. Over the next few days, he cycled

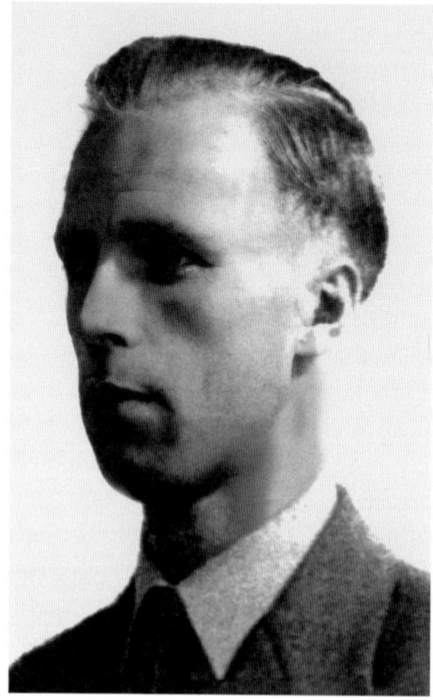

Above left: The redoubtable Bill Willdeboer, leader of the Ede Resistance.

Above right: 'Tonny' de Nooj—a brave, daring, and dependable member of the Ede Resistance and 'Bill' Wildeboer's 'right-hand man'.

many miles to establish contact with scattered evaders who had been placed in various hideouts. Most were within a 10-mile radius, concealed in barns, farms, forests, and houses. For one not accustomed to riding a bicycle, it was initially a tough graft, but Digby later admitted that 'after a day or two, when the early discomfort had worn off, I began to enjoy these often long, and sometimes exciting rides around the countryside.'[6]

Digby's days were extremely busy and he met with many people, both Dutch and British. His aim was to check on the well-being of the evaders, give them hope, and to reassure them that they had not been forgotten. Digby often rode past units of Germans in and around the areas he travelled to, but they generally paid him little attention. Nevertheless, it was a very risky endeavour. He was dressed in civilian clothing, and as such was not covered by the Geneva Convention. If caught, he could quite easily find himself being lined up against a wall by the *Gestapo* and shot as a spy. Yet his confident nature enabled him to ride around with no outward sign of nervousness that could have brought suspicion. Bill was always very busy and often unable to accompany Digby on his sojourns, but Tonny or other members of his family regularly did so, and so too did 'Flip' Van den Pol, who Digby described as a 'prominent and daring member of the Ede Resistance'.[7]

On one occasion, just prior to the execution of Operation Pegasus, Digby, Flip, and an unnamed female member of the resistance would cycle past a German staff car that had veered off the road and was stuck in a ditch. Seeing their plight, Digby—or rather, the deaf and dumb Dutchman 'Peter Jansen', for he was firmly 'in character'—would stop to help push it out before riding away in fits off laughter.

Digby related:

> There was an attractive girl who often came with me, usually acting as a forward scout. She was with me one day when an amusing incident occurred. A German staff car overtook us at high speed and then skidded off the muddy road into the ditch. As the officers seemed to be in an excitable state, we thought it wise to help push their car out. They were gracious enough to thank us for our help and went on their way, leaving my Dutch friend and me to have a good laugh.[8]

Digby had discovered that another group of evaders were hiding nearer to Arnhem and he was thrilled to learn that they were being looked after by Brig.-Maj. Tony Hibbert who had been captured but had escaped by jumping from the back of the lorry transporting him to a POW camp. It would later transpire that Hibbert's escape had prompted a nervous German soldier to open fire not only on Hibbert but also on the other POWs in the lorry, resulting in men being killed, which was something that troubled Hibbert for the rest of his life.

Hibbert had been fortunate to make contact with the resistance and would now embark on a mission similar to Digby's by organising and looking after the evaders in his area, although it was noted that his methods were more refrained and cautious than those deployed by Digby.

At the bridge, Digby had strutted around with little concern for his own safety. His carefree manner continued in Ede. But on one occasion, it became a serious concern for the Dutch who were prompted to have a quiet word in his ear.

The occasion involved Brig. 'Shan' Hackett of the 4th Parachute Brigade, who would arrive in Ede to stay with Tonny's family. During the battle, Hackett's brigade had suffered severe losses holding the eastern side of the divisional perimeter. Hackett had been wounded early in the fighting, and on 24 September, he had been transported under the protection of the Red Cross through the German lines to receive better treatment. His life had hung in the balance, but an operation by a skilled surgeon to remove a piece of shrapnel from his small intestine had saved his life. This, and a painful leg wound, was the cause of great discomfort and it would take many months for him to recover.

Shortly after his operation in St Elisabeth Hospital, Hackett's morale had been raised by the appearance of a familiar face at his door. It was a fellow prisoner, 'the tall angular figure of Gerald Lathbury, the other parachuting brigadier in the Division, Commander of the 1st Parachute Brigade'.[9]

'It pleased me enormously to see him,' noted Hackett, 'for there was a warm and special friendship between us':

> He had a fine sense of the ridiculous, with an appearance that suggested arrogance. This was misleading. Those who got to know him well found (often to their

> surprise) that this highly intelligent and courageous professional soldier was also a compassionate and modest man.[10]

The two brigadiers had been delighted to see each other, but their time together had only lasted minutes, for Lathbury had been about to make his escape.

At this time, Hackett had been one of only thirty or forty British patients remaining in the hospital, the majority having been relocated to POW camps or sent for treatment in other hospitals away from the frontline. As Hackett had begun to show signs of improvement, he received a visit from a hitherto unknown Dutchman wearing a Red Cross armband who promised to help him. The Dutchman, who introduced himself as Piet, persuaded Hackett of his credentials by producing a handwritten letter from recent escapee, Gerald Lathbury. The letter stated that the man who brought the letter could be completely trusted. That was good enough for Hackett.

Piet Kruyff, known as Piet Van Arnhem, headed the resistance in the Arnhem district and had played a hand in Lathbury's escape. Once free from the hospital, Lathbury had asked if anything could be done for his friend. Piet had agreed to help and his visit was to inform Hackett that plans were being made to get him out. This came to fruition somewhat suddenly four days later. Hackett had been dozing in his bed when he had a sudden sense of being watched. On looking up, he saw Piet who asked if he could walk. 'I expect so. I haven't tried yet,' Hackett had replied.[12] Piet then told him that if he could walk out of the hospital within fifteen minutes he could get him away. If not, he may not be able to get him out at all.

Hackett changed into civilian clothing and a blood-soaked gauze and bandage were produced and wrapped around his head. He was then led out of the hospital in the guise of a civilian, bundled into a car, and taken to Ede. They had passed German checkpoints, and were stopped and questioned, but Hackett had been told to lie still with his eyes closed and do nothing. He was, so Piet told the Germans, a civilian victim of a British air raid who needed urgent medical attention.

At Ede, Hackett was taken to a house belonging to Tonny de Nooj's brave family. Tonny did not live there himself, but his four aunts and a niece and nephew did. It was the first time they had taken in an evader and they were considerably nervous about doing so. The matter was not helped by the German Military Police base situated at the end of the road, or by the many German soldiers who were constantly walking by. Some were billeted in the house directly behind the de Noojs' abode and the two properties had adjoining gardens. Every precaution was taken to avoid Hackett's location becoming compromised and they operated with the utmost secrecy.

Shortly after Hackett had been taken in, there was a knock on the door. The de Noojs cautiously opened it to find a stranger on a bicycle. He was tall and thin and wearing a cheap grey suit. Their initial alarm was magnified when this individual casually asked to speak with 'Brigadier Hackett'.

By now Digby was riding around Ede in broad daylight like he owned the place, and he did not consider the swarms of German soldiers to be a deterrent. But the de Noojs were horrified. After recovering from their initial shock, they surmised that the stranger stood before them could only be an Englishman. Their minds were put at rest when Hackett confirmed the man's identity as Maj. Digby Tatham Warter.

After hearing Hackett had been brought in, Digby had taken it upon himself to include him on his rounds. Hackett, who was still very much bedridden, related that Digby's impromptu visit 'put the household into something of a flutter'.[13] 'Miss Ann', Tonny's aunt, was particularly horrified.

Of the incident, Hackett later related:

> He turned up at the front door one day, unknown and unannounced, and asked for 'Brigadier Hackett' by name. He had heard from Gerald where I was and it cheered me up enormously to see him but Miss Ann took a rather grave view of the way he had arrived.[14]

Miss Ann informed Hackett of her concerns, telling him they had to be very prudent. It was agreed that in the future people could only visit when accompanied by a member of the family, and that the number of visits must be limited to avoid suspicion from any nosey neighbours. Hackett had a quiet word with Digby and the problem was sorted. His subsequent visits were in strict accordance with the rules set out by Miss Ann.

Bold and risky ventures aside, Shan Hackett—who, when the time came, would not be well enough to take part in Operation Pegasus but would escape later—held Digby in very high regard. He described Digby as 'a brave and engaging person with a rather special mixture of eccentricity and panache'.[15]

During their time in England prior to Operation Market Garden, Hackett had got to know Digby rather well and his only regret was that Digby was not in his own brigade.

13

Developing Plans

Digby had been with Bill for about a week when asked if he would like to meet with a Belgian SAS officer who was operating nearby and liaising with the resistance.

Gilbert Sadi-Kirschen, known as Capt. Fabian King, or simply 'King'—his codename—had parachuted in near Utrecht on 15 September with his small team of three Belgian SAS on what should have been a five-day mission to seek out the location of the German V-2 rocket bases firing on London and to supply intelligence for Operation Market Garden.

Under the cover of darkness, with twenty-four containers of supplies, a wireless set, and a generator, the team had dropped unopposed in the middle of a meadow. As soon as they hit the ground the resistance had emerged from the darkness, carried away the containers, buried the parachutes and whisked the SAS men away in a car.

King's original mission had evolved into something else entirely and he was now feeding back information such as German troop movements, as well as assisting airborne evaders.

Digby was extremely impressed by the set up that the SAS had established and also by King himself who he described as having an 'air of efficiency and quiet confidence' about him.[1]

They were operating from a small post in one of three chicken coops located in a clearing in some wooded farmland to the west of Ede where it was extremely unlikely they would be discovered. Better still, they had a direct link to London via radio.

Prior to Operation Market Garden when the continuous stream of dejected Germans had been retiring through Holland, the underground had been busy recording their movements. At the time, elements of the underground had wanted to launch an attack against the Germans while they were in a state of disorganisation. Tonny had been particularly keen on the idea and had wanted to retake Ede by force. He had pressed Bill to give the nod, but the ex-soldier did not think the time was right and had vetoed any such action. The urge to do something had not gone away and they had considered timing an attack to coincide with the Allied airborne drops, but the Allied top brass had firmly rejected the idea.

The airborne invasion had failed, but the Allied offensive was expected to continue and friendly troops would be crossing the Rhine in the very near future to liberate the areas in which the evaders were hiding. Discussions within the underground took place on the best course of action. Digby told them he would be willing to attack the Germans with his evaders and carry out sabotage missions when the time was right. 'Certainly we were all getting very excited about it,' Digby remarked, 'and [I] used to discuss plans with Gerald Lathbury and of course the Underground and we were just very keen to have a go when the opportunity arose.'[2]

Bill had agreed that an attack planned to coincide with the Allied advance would be an opportune time to strike. King agreed to arrange a weapons drop to ensure the paratroopers were well-armed for the occasion.

A plan was put in place that would begin once the Allies had formed a bridgehead. It was decided they would operate in small ten-man teams made up of five resistance members and five paratroopers. In addition to weapons, a supply of uniforms would also be dropped so the evaders could go into action as legitimate paratroopers.

The acts of sabotage would render all roads from Ede to Arnhem and as far north as Apeldoorn impassable for the Germans and would cause considerable disruption at the vital moment. Tony Hibbert was to take charge of the Arnhem evaders who would also play a part, while Digby would lead those around Ede and coordinate the whole operation. Digby explained their intention was to carry out guerrilla warfare: 'We hoped to make road movement, by night at any rate, impossible without a strong escort. The country was ideal as most of it was thickly wooded'.[3]

The supply drop took place on the night of 7 October, 'some way to the North', and consisted of weapons, food, and a good stock of cigarettes that had been specifically requested, though the quantity turned out to be less than expected.

Digby had his suspicions as to the reason:

> Four years of war and home grown tobacco got the better of our Dutch friends' sense of honesty and very few cigarettes survived transit. We couldn't grumble as they kept us very well supplied out of their meagre stock of home grown tobacco.[4]

The weapons were taken away and concealed in a farm near Ede to be collected when needed. Further drops would take place in the coming days for uniforms and other essentials.

The Ede Resistance were in fact already sabotaging specific carefully chosen targets. Digby described that Bill 'very wisely refrained from all sabotage except for cutting the railway when required':

> It is of interest that he received orders from his 'Brigade' Commander to carry out wholesale sabotage and slaughter of Boche officers. If he had done this Ede would have ceased to exist and both the Intelligence System and our safety would have been compromised. His prompt action on the railway was on one occasion directly responsible for the destruction of quite a number of light tanks. These were parked in sidings North of EDE. Bill cut the lines North and South and then asked the RAF

> to complete the job. The result was quite good. The line was cut on three other occasions and only four trains passed through during my stay in EDE.[5]

Around this time, Digby was asked to take part in a sabotage mission to blow up a train on an important line some 20 miles to the north. He would have liked the job, but in a rare moment of restraint, he begrudgingly turned it down; his reason being that with more experience in such activities and better facilities at their disposal, the underground were in a much better position to make it a success.

The Power Station

Following his capture at Calais in May 1940, Airey Neave had become the first British officer to escape front the notorious Colditz POW camp. He had gone on to join the intelligence service and since the beginning of October had been operating from his headquarters on the outskirts of Nijmegen. Well aware of the situation with the airborne evaders, Neave had recognised an opportunity to establish direct communication.

In his first days at Nijmegen, Neave discovered the existence of a power station located near to Nijmegen Bridge with a direct telephone link across the Waal and Rhine to transformers in German-held territory. 'One of these was at Ede, twenty miles from the Nijmegen power station and about six miles from the German bank of the Rhine,' related Neave.[6]

The power stations 'in Nijmegen on the Waal and at Ede on the northern bank of the Rhine were linked by private telephone lines which remained intact as the battle raged', noted Neave. 'The exchanges were controlled by the resistance and they gave us the information that in the houses and forests of Ede were hidden nearly one hundred and forty men, among them Major Digby Tatham-Warter…'[7]

The Dutch Underground assured Neave that the line was secure and could be used with confidence. In fact, they were already using it to communicate with members of their own organisation. Neave's superiors, however, were sceptical of the suggestion of direct communication using the telephone exchange:

> When they heard of this plan the 'cold feet department' were horror struck. The idea of telephoning across the enemy lines was regarded as lunacy. But I was assured by the power station engineers and staff that it was safe and there was no reason to think that the enemy could tap it.[8]

Neave persisted and was finally granted authorisation to give it a go.

The telephone exchange in Ede was located quite close to Bill's house. Digby had previously been aware of its existence and had known that the underground were using it, but given the risks of communicating over an open telephone line he had not thought it possible to utilise for his own needs. When told that 2nd Army was willing to give it a try, Digby readily agreed to use it to contact them.

At times, the station was guarded by 'Dutch Home Guard chaps' whose loyalties supposedly lay with the Germans, but were quite the opposite. The exchange staff had been infiltrated by the resistance and those members, including Alex Hartmann, were able to inform Bill what times their own men were on duty.

Digby and Bill travelled to the telephone at night by hopping over a fence to the rear of Bill's property and sneaking along a railway line. This always took place shortly after the 9 p.m. curfew, once it was dark. Digby found this a heart-thumping experience, more so than when he was riding round in plain sight on his bicycle.

At the station, Digby was able to speak directly with those awaiting his call. During the conversations with Neave, Digby reeled off lists of evaders who he had made contact with and provided the names of known casualties from the battle.

Neave explained:

> At first, it was simply a question of waiting each night for the telephone to ring, and hearing a British officer's voice reading a long list of names. In this way, reports of casualties and the names of those who were still in hiding were reported back to their families. It was a strange sensation to hear 'The Voice' from behind enemy lines...[9]

In his book *They Have Their Exits*, Neave provided a further account:

> I sat every evening in the gaunt power station with Major Hugh Fraser, M.B.E., of the S.A.S. listening for the telephone bell. It seemed that we were waiting for a signal from another world. The shells from the enemy batteries at Arnhem crashed around Nijmegen Bridge, shaking the power house. Beside us sat technical officials, their staunch Dutch faces betraying no emotion. We would wait with beating hearts for a faint ring on the telephone and Tatham-Warter's voice.[10]

When describing Digby, Neave would say:

> This officer, a man of calm and ingenuity, conducted the conversations that followed between the two power stations. Despite the risk of capture he came from his hiding place each evening between nine and ten to the terminal house at Ede and there spoke to the rescue organisations at Nijmegen.[11]

Digby met with King a couple of times a week to discuss their options, and by 10 October, a detailed plan for a series of ambushes against the enemy had been made. An elaborate plan to evacuate Shan Hackett whose severe wounds needed more attention than they were getting in Ede was also drawn up. The plan, however, was scuppered.

Digby noted:

> We made a detailed plan for a strip out in the country to be prepared and lit up and that night a small aeroplane was going to come in and whisk him off.... This plan was made together with these SAS chaps. Anyhow, the whole things was laid on, but on the night when we were going to take Shan Hackett out—these underground

> chaps, and I was going along with them—were going to take him out by car to the appointed place where he was going to be taken off, but the whole thing was blown; the information had leaked, and the field in fact was surrounded by Germans and we had to call the operation off.[12]

From here on in, Digby sauntered out after curfew to use the telephone exchange every night, but not all incoming news was positive. Days later, word was received that there was now no question of the Allied offensive resuming in the area any time soon. They could not say when it would come, but, certainly, it would not be taking place during the winter months, meaning the evaders would have to remain hidden for the foreseeable future.

Somewhere in the region of eighty evaders were located in and around Ede. In addition, Tony Hibbert had a further thirty to forty men in his sector around Arnhem and others were known to be hiding much further afield. In total, it was estimated that at least 200 men were in hiding and it would be decidedly difficult to keep them concealed throughout the winter. The strain on the resistance would be too much and one slip could bring the whole thing crashing down. 'It would have imposed an intolerable strain on them and their families,' acknowledged Digby.[13] If caught, the consequences for their plucky Dutch hosts did not bear thinking about.

The morning after receiving this bad news, Digby visited Brig. Lathbury and he too was not keen on the prospect of a prolonged concealment. Guerrilla warfare, however, still held some appeal.

The question was what to do.

Towards the middle of October, after escaping from captivity and going through his own series of adventures, Lt-Col. David Dobie unexpectedly arrived in Ede. As the commanding officer of the 1st Parachute Battalion, Dobie had been captured on Tuesday 19 September and taken to hospital to have wounds to his head and arm treated. He had escaped while his German guard was flirting with a nurse, proudly showing off a watch that he had snatched from Dobie. With his guard temporarily distracted, Dobie had seized the opportunity to slip away and conceal himself in some bushes. Under the cover of darkness, he had moved away and taken refuge in a bombed-out house where he had met with a Dutch doctor who provided further treatment to his wounds and a place to hide. He had then been smuggled to Ede.

Dobie was surprised yet overjoyed to find his comrades had set up a secret organisation. Arriving at a time where plans for sabotage were being arranged, Dobie was taken to the Underground HQ, 'where Major Tatham-Warter, Capt. Brian [*sic*] Franks and two or three more officers were having their morning coffee'.

Dobie noted:

> It seems quite incredible, but during their short stay, under Major Tatham-Warter's command and in liaison with the Underground, they had managed to plan an operation to coincide with any crossing of the River Rhine by General Dempsey. This plan entailed the ambushing of all roads leading from any bridgehead that was established by the 2nd Army. A proportion of airborne personnel and Underground

Lt-Col. Dobie who commanded the 1st Battalion worked closely with Digby in planning Operation Pegasus.

> would be in each ambush party, and they would be fully equipped with Bren-guns, PIATs, anti-tank mines and all necessary small arms.[14]

Dobie's unexpected appearance was perfectly timed. The situation at this point was very much 'up in the air', and the planned sabotage missions were all well and good, but on the flip side they could not remain hidden for the time it would take 2nd Army to renew the offensive. It was also thought that the Germans suspected something was amiss in Ede. 'By the 15th October things in Ede became rather difficult,' wrote Dobie in his after-action report, 'as the Green Police had been drafted into the district. The Underground were quite certain that the Germans realised that something was very peculiar was happening.'[15]

Instead of communicating solely with the intelligence service, Brig. Lathbury decided that somebody had to get across the river to explain the situation directly to 2nd Army HQ and to inform them of their 'organisation and proposed plan for the ambushing of roads'.[16]

Digby's crucial role with the underground ruled him out, but the ideal candidate had landed at their feet in the form of Dobie, whose rank and 'resourcefulness and determination' would ensure he was taken seriously by those across the river. Furthermore, he could personally hand over paperwork and provide concise first-hand knowledge of the situation.

Before Dobie's departure, Digby and the resistance gave him a detailed briefing on every aspect of their situation as it stood and of the dilemmas they faced. In his report written later, Dobie recorded: 'Went to underground HQ and saw Major Tatham-Warter, and went through plan of ambushing roads when 2nd Army cross the Rijn. All arrangements and communications fixed before I left'.[17]

Dobie also wrote in his diary:

> At Bill's I talked to Digby (Tatham-Warter) and we fixed up the taking of the documents and the possibility of getting the remainder of our chaps out should the

> road plan not work out. By now we had some hundred Airborne organised and ready for the fray. Digby had certainly done his stuff.[18]

It was arranged that Dobie, following his departure, would call Digby on the underground telephone on the second night. If the call did not come, Digby was to assume Dobie's mission to cross the Rhine had been unsuccessful.

On 16 October, guided by the underground, Dobie set out on his journey. After an exciting and somewhat perilous adventure with several very near-misses along the way, he reached Eindhoven where he came face-to-face with the 2nd Army Commander, Lt-Gen. Dempsey.

It took Dobie a full hour to fill the general in on the situation. He spoke of their plans for sabotage, of the two wounded brigadiers, of the men in hiding, of the assistance from the Dutch Resistance, and of the fact that they did not think it possible to remain undetected through the winter. Dempsey listened intently, absorbing everything. When Dobie had finished, there was a silence that lasted several seconds. The general then turned to his staff and uttered three words: 'Get them out'.[19]

On the second night after Dobie's departure, Digby and Bill crept out to the telephone exchange. The phone began to ring and Bill answered. A few words were spoken in Dutch before he handed the receiver to Digby:

> There to my relief and delight was David's voice as clear as if he had sitting in the room beside me. He did not waste words in describing his many adventures crossing the Rhine, but did say that everyone over there seemed enthusiastic about getting us back. He had not had time to discuss a plan with XXX Corps and suggested we talk again the following night.[20]

The next morning, Digby mounted his trusty bicycle and set out to visit the evaders to inform them of this latest development. By this time, Digby had come to notice that the morale of the men was very low so he did his utmost to cheer them up and raise their spirits.

That night, when Digby once again spoke to Dobie, he was delighted to learn that things were moving very quickly and a plan had already been drawn up to get them out. The plan—for which the finer details were still to be finalised—would see the evaders make their way to the river at a prearranged spot codenamed 'DIGBY'. The whole operation had been given the codename of Operation Pegasus, the exact time and date for which would be arranged later.

From the banks of the river, boats would be sent across to collect the evaders. They would be guided to 'DIGBY' by Bofor guns that would fire bursts of tracer shells. Digby was informed his main contact on the telephone would be Neave's second-in-command, Maj. Hugh Fraser of the SAS, who Gen. Horrocks, the corps commander, had assigned to the operation.

After this latest development, one of the first places Digby visited was an old barn (sometimes referred to as a sheep pen or sheep cage) way out in the countryside. Located in a wooded area by a series of dykes and only accessible on foot or bicycle path, the place was relatively secure for those hiding inside. Digby was taken there by the farmer, Gijs Janssen, who owned it. Hidden in the barn were around thirty weary men who, save for a lone Russian, belonged exclusively to the Royal Army Medical Corps under the command of a young officer of the 133rd Parachute Field Ambulance by the name of Lt Donald Olliff. The group, having missed their drop zone by 18 km, had received help from the resistance, specifically Tonny, who oversaw more than one change of location for them during their time evading capture.

Olliff, who, according to Leo Heaps, had not met Digby until now, was not quite sure what to think of this eccentric officer stood before him.

Heaps noted:

> One day as he made his rounds towards the middle of October, Tatham-Warter rode up to the sheep pen at Jagersveld, parked his bicycle against the wall and approached the British doctor. Neither man had met before. Tatham-Warter, attired in a white mackintosh and dark glasses, introduced himself to the suspicious officer. After a small chat during which the major reassured the doctor that his credentials were in order, he climbed onto a table in the shed and addressed the astounded medical orderlies and the uncomprehending Russian. He told them they were all going to escape.[21]

Digby told them that 'a bold plan was now being prepared by the airborne headquarters in Ede in cooperation with the Allied Army on the South side of the Rhine'.

> Olliff did not feel entirely confident that the man standing on the table with dark glasses could lead them all out of this wilderness. But Olliff did not know Tatham-Warter very well. In the following week he visited Olliff once again and the doctor grew increasingly confident that the major might just do what he said he would.[22]

Although portraying a confident exterior, Digby inwardly recognised the great risk involved in achieving a successful evacuation and knew he would 'need a great deal more than ordinary good luck', admitting that he began to pray very hard for a successful outcome in his dug-out each night.[23]

With such large numbers, the crossing point would have to be carefully selected. Downstream, some evaders had already made successful crossings as individuals or in small groups, including Leo Heaps who was now working alongside Neave and Fraser in the intelligence team.

A couple of established routes existed 'many miles down stream to the West', but these were described as Digby as 'very fragile' and at best they could handle only one or two men at a time.[24] 'Route W', as Digby called it (see Evasion Report), was never really satisfactory. The route involved the crossing of two rivers—the Waal and the Rhine. Eleven men had been sent at different times to use the route, three of whom had been captured. 'Later,' noted Digby, 'we sent an officer, Lt. Adams, to establish a post North of the WAAL with a view to speeding up the process. He was replaced by an 'I' officer from 2nd Army who was caught and the route was finally blown'.[25] This route had been looked into prior to knowing the sheer amount of evaders currently in hiding.

There was another route, 'Route R', to the south of Ede, which was much shorter in distance and involved only one river crossing. An American pilot had previously been sent to try it, but it had been 'blown' just before he reached it. The 'established escape route' used by Dobie had since been discovered by the Germans and could no longer be used. At any rate, it would not have been possible to get this quantity of men through it. Their only hope, Digby concluded, lay directly South of Ede, but this might mean they would have to fight their way through the German frontline river defences. On the plus side, the nearby wooded country would provide some degree of cover.

After much deliberation a route near Renkum was decided upon. The plan was very simple. Digby would make his own arrangements in getting the evaders to the river where, 'at midnight and every hour after that a Bofors would fire a burst over "DIGBY". When we were ready we would flash a red Vic[tory] and ten boats, with flank protection, would come across. Col Dobie guaranteed the fullest support from the South bank if we should get into trouble'.[26]

As yet, the date for the operation was not set, but would soon be confirmed for the night of 23–24 October. With a plan now firmly established, there was a lot to do in order to pull the operation together. Neave, Fraser, and their small team together with Dobie would all play their own part from over the Rhine and would keep in close contact with Digby.

During the time the evaders were in hiding, a number of developments to their plight took place. Realising there was no immediate threat of attack, German soldiers, referred to by Digby as 'the back room boys', began to return to Ede and the surrounding areas, having previously cleared out when the fighting had started.[27]

Due to an increase of *Gestapo*, Green Police, and Dutch SS, rumours began to further circulate that the Germans were aware of the evaders' presence. As had been happening elsewhere along the river, the Germans began to strengthen their defences in preparation of any attempted offensive against them in the future.

The increase in enemy soldiers meant the need for additional billets, and Dutch residents soon found themselves under pressure to house enemy soldiers. More than one attempt was made to enter the temporary home of Brig. Lathbury, among others.

Hiltje Van Eck, who resided with her family next door to the Wildeboers, was just a young girl at the time but she remembers with some hilarity a story related by her mother, Tine, where a number of German soldiers knocked on the door of the Wildeboers' home at a time when Digby was inside. Digby, after getting out the back door and jumping the fence in the rear garden, knocked on Van Eck's back door. Tine quickly let him in. But just as he gained an entrance, Tine, upon seeing the soldiers approaching, called out, 'there coming here now!' As they knocked on the door, Digby muttered, 'Oh for God's sake' under his breath before turning around and walking out the back door again. Hiltje's mother, Tine, remembered Digby as 'a very cool and calm man around the Germans, and something of a character'.[28]

Another development was a call up of all bicycles by the Germans. They set up roadblocks and carried out searches of the houses and farms for any bicycles that had been hidden. Fortunately, this was only temporary.

Eventually, the Wildeboers had to open their home to the enemy in the form of four members of a *panzer* unit who decided to take up residence in their household. Digby at this point was spending much of his time in the house planning Operation Pegasus so was obliged to remain firmly in character as Peter Jansen. The Germans soon came to recognise Digby and began to stand aside for him when they met on entering and leaving the house, occasionally giving him a friendly pat on the back as he passed. Having the enemy give way to him was both pleasing and amusing to Digby, who could not help but feel he was securing a small victory over his unwitting foe. Brig. Lathbury would provide the following short description with mention of one of these encounters:

> It was Tatham-Warter more than anyone else who helped co-ordinate our efforts. He did a magnificent job moving about the district freely, and was so cool that on one occasion he arrived at the door at a house simultaneously with two German soldiers—and allowed them to stand back to let him go in first.[29]

In more detail, Leo Heaps wrote:

> While the Germans stepped up their search for the evaders, Tatham-Warter went about his business unconcerned. However, at the house of Bill Wildeboer certain incidents for Tatham-Warter were becoming distinctly embarrassing. The major had a problem that occupied him every evening and whose resolution had now become a question of principle. When he returned before curfew from his long bicycle tours he would often find the doorway blocked by the simultaneous arrival of German officers billeted at the house. At the beginning he made way for them, but his attitude gradually changed. A discreet individual would unquestionably have allowed the Germans to pass first. But the major decided otherwise. He thought the moment had come to assert his pride. The first time he tried to cut off the enemy in the battle of the doorway a brief jostling took place and then stopped. To his surprise, the Germans reacted with unexpected courtesy and allowed Tatham-Warter to go in ahead. Eventually the Englishman developed a nodding acquaintance with the officers billeted in the big room upstairs, some of the Germans actually giving the major a friendly pat on the back at their frequent meetings on the front doorstep.[30]

In his privately published booklet, Digby actually referred to the four German soldiers as 'decent fellows'.[31] Years later in Kenya during the Mau Mau Rebellion, Digby, when in the bush with his men, would joke about once having dined with several Germans. He did not go into detail or elaborate, but it is highly probable he was referring to members of this *panzer* unit.

As the date of Operation Pegasus drew nearer, Digby and the evaders were about to get the huge dose of the luck Digby had been praying for.

14

A Golden Opportunity

Digby Tatham-Warter had carried out a brilliant reconnaissance the night before and had mapped out a route that led down to the river, avoiding all German troop positions. Without Digby's reconnaissance the whole plan would have failed.[1]

Maj. Tony Deane-Drummond (evader).

On 20 October, a meeting took place at the Wildeboer residence between Bill, Digby, Flip, Tonny, and another Dutchman called Max. As they discussed the route to the river news came in that the Germans had called for a mass evacuation of the area. This was a stunning development indeed.

Since the failure of Operation Market Garden, the Germans had been strengthening their river defences. In doing so, local inhabitants residing in the towns and villages close to the river had been evacuated. Now, it was the turn of Bennekom and the immediate surroundings on the Rhine. The inhabitants were informed they had to be out by Sunday 22nd.

While undoubtedly terrible news for the residents who would be forced to leave their homes indefinitely, the evacuation presented a golden opportunity for the evaders to make the most of the chaos it would undoubtedly create. Civilians would soon fill the streets with all manner of transportation as they moved along with their families and possessions. The German had unwittingly created the perfect cover for the evaders.

Everyone was in agreement that the operation had to happen sooner than had been planned. It was not ideal since preparations still had to be finalised, but, if they waited, it would be impossible to transport all of the men through an area that had been evacuated. It was now or never. The operation had to go head the following night.

Digby noted:

> Sadly, the short time left to us meant that a number of evaders, who were in hiding too far afield could not, as had been originally intended, now be included in 'Pegasus'. However

Digby's fake identification was forged by members of the Dutch Resistance. Digby was given the name of Peter Jansen—the deaf and dumb son of a lawyer.

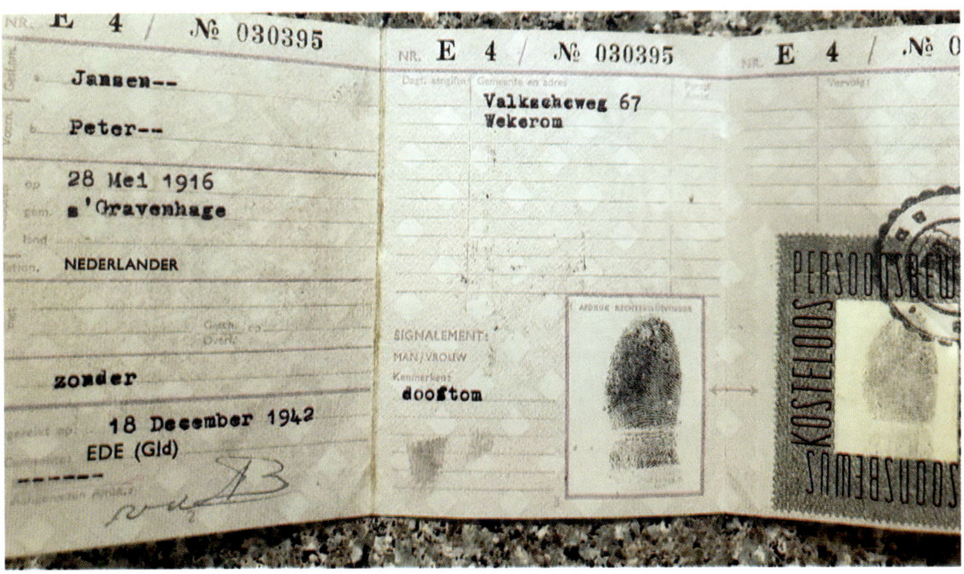

The inside of Digby's fake identification, complete with false name, date of birth, and fingerprint.

Digby and Jane. Digby's seventieth birthday.

Above left: During the Battle of Arnhem, Digby approached the battalion padre Father Egan who was hesitating to cross the street under mortar fire, but Digby assured him it would be okay because he had an umbrella. (*Artist: Eric Thornton*)

Above right: Jane Tatham Warter and the author (Neil Thornton) outside the Tatham Warter family home, January 2020.

The point where Digby led his evaders across the river to safety during Operations Pegasus. (*Ruud Slangen*)

Digby's miniature medals. Together with his para wings, original DSO citation, and various other items, Digby's miniature medals remain with the family. Much to Jane's annoyance, he sold his full-size medal group in the 1960s for next to nothing. His DSO can be seen on the far left of the group.

Above left: Digby.

Above right: Kit Tatham Water.

Digby sits alongside his close friend and best man at his wedding, Bobby Hornsby-Wright. Bobby served in India with Digby, a fellow officer of the Ox & Bucks.

Digby with Jane and his mother.

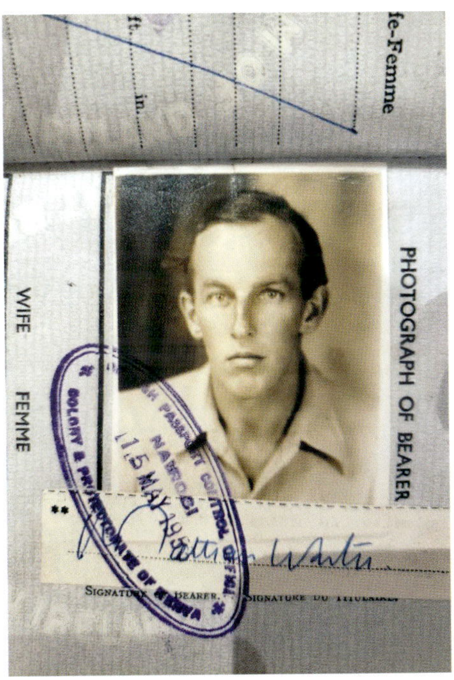

Above left: Digby's passport.

Above right: The headstone for Digby's final resting place. Located on 'Digby's Hill' the rarely visited spot offers fantastic views over the Lewa Downs Conservancy.

Escape From Arnhen by Brian Sanders.

Operation Pegasus. The route taken by Digby and the evaders took them down through the wooded area and across the open stretch of ground towards the river.

Above: The umbrella marks the crossing point. (*Ruud Slangen*)

Below: A page from one of Digby's many photo albums from his safaris.

Digby was presented with a beautiful album of watercolour paintings in 1982. The artist—a happy customer of Digby's safaris—was Caroline Blunden. The album contains many humorous illustrations of her party's time with Digby and Jane.

BAGS OF CHEERIO!
AFRICA AIR
DUTY FREE
DUTY FREE
DUTY FREE
DUTY FREE
DUTY FREE
DUTY FREE

UP YOURS
SHOULD'NT BOTHER ABOUT THAT BLOODY, BORING BIRD.
I SAY DIGBY WHATS THAT

GRRRR
DID'NT SEE A F...ING THING ALL DAY!

WELL DARLING WHAT DO YOU THINK OF THIS LOT?
NOT QUITE AS BAD AS PETE THE BUGGER — BUT "BOOZY CROWD" TAKES ON A NEW MEANING !!
(THINKS) HOPE THERE'S ENOUGH FOR ME!

IGBY YOU SAID THAT OUGHT ASSUMPTION IS THE MOTHER OF FUCK-UPS" !!!
I ASSUME IT'S THE UP-HILL TRACK
MAP
MAP READING EN ROUTE TO CRESCENT ISLAND.

WELL IF YOU MUST KNOW — ITS THAT BOY ACROSS THE RIVER WITH A BOTTOM LIKE A PEACH !!!! — SO TAKE A RUNNING JUMP THE LOT OF YOU !!
"JUST ONE LAST QUESTION DIGBY "WHAT MAKES THE LION ROAR" !!?
GO WILD IN KENYA

FOR CHRIST'S SAKE PASS THE GNAT'S PISS !!
CSB

THIS MUST BE THE BEST BOOK IN THE WORLD!
TRASH!

← COMPLAINTS FROM MANAGEMENT
THE ARK
ONE FOR A DICK-DICK!
QUIET PLEASE!
ORDER ORDER
THREE FOR A BONGO!
AND SIX FOR A GANG BANG!!
HA! HA! HA!
BEST OF ORDER
BANG BANG
BZZ BZZ BZZ BZZ BZZ BZ
CSB '82

Above left: A totem of resistance.

Above right: John de Grey Tatham Warter Digby's brother was a man of reckless bravery. His actions in North Africa earned him the MC.

Akropolis, Athens. April 1973.

Above: The author (centre) sits with Digby's daughters at their father's grave. Jo sits to the left and Caroline the right.

Left: Hell's Highway—as the airborne fought for possession of the bridges, the ground elements advanced along 'Hell's Highway'—named as such because of the deadly nature of the route. Those taking this narrow route would face a murderous fire from all sides and suffer dearly.

Right: Digby & Jane.

Below: Digby introduces his Kenya team to his imperial majesty the emperor of Ethiopia, 1956. Team members (L-R) Digby, Robert Foster, Jeremy Allen, Donald Rooken-Smith, Francis Foster.

The place where Digby and the evaders awaited their rescue was hidden from view to those on the opposite bank. The snaking curves blocked their 'V' for Victory signals from Dobie and the others awaiting the signal.

Arnhem Bridge, by artist David Shepherd. Digby owned a framed print of this classic painting. It hung proudly in his family home for many years. Indeed, it was still adorned the wall of his family home when I visited in January 2020. (*Published with kind permission of the family of David Shepherd*)

As resistance under the bridge itself crumbled, Digby ordered the survivors to pull back to his HQ area. Wounded multiple times, Lt Grayburn told Pte Morgan that it was time to go. After dashing across the road directly in front of a Tiger Tank, Morgan would see Grayburn fall, riddled with bullets. (*Artist: Steve Noon*)

Above left: An artist's impression of Digby during the 'armoured car incident'. Details are sketchy about what actually took place. There are but two accounts of the episode and the particulars differ somewhat, although both agree that he was jabbing and thrusting his umbrella at the enemy vehicle. (*Artist: Eric Thornton*)

Above right: Digby's medal ribbon, wings, and first page of the lengthy citation for his DSO, awarded for his actions at Arnhem and its aftermath.

Above: When word reached him that one of his buildings had been lost by the bridge, Digby marched across to see for himself. At this point, as related by Maj. Gough who witnessed the scene, Digby was wearing a bowler hat, 'looking for all the world like Charlie Chaplin'.

Left: Digby leads his men forward with bowler hat and brolly. The bowler proved to be impractical and was soon discarded, but not before he had turned a few heads with this unusual choice of headwear. (*Artist: Eric Thornton*)

> there were eighty to ninety in the vicinity of Ede and another forty or fifty near Arnhem, and this was really enough to handle. The Resistance plan was to concentrate the evaders scattered around the Arnhem district in some woods at Oud-Reemst, several miles to the East of Ede and some twenty miles by road from the rendez-vous. Here Hibbert was to take charge of them and they would be equipped with arms and uniforms brought there by the Dutch. From there Piet undertook to bring them by night on the finals stage to the rendez-vous in his lorries. Meanwhile the Ede contingent would move by foot, bicycle and horse drawn carts on Sunday morning, with the whole party hopefully assembling at the rendez-vous soon after dark that night.[2]

For the plan to work, all evaders would have to be in place at the main gathering zone at the edge of the woods in Renkum on the night of the 21st. From here, they would move through a wooded area before crossing a stretch of open ground spanning several hundred yards between two German posts to reach the river. Then all they had to do was move along the bank a short distance to reach the point where the boats would be waiting.

The evaders would now have to be contacted and made aware of the change of date. After penning a brief operational plan to circulate among the evaders, Digby hopped on to his trusty bicycle to put out the word. Members of the resistance got to work doing the same.

Later that night, Digby spoke with David Dobie on the telephone and informed him of this latest development. Dobie had been busy making his own plans to get the evaders to safety. His report, dated 20 October, stated:

> Friday 20 Oct 44
>
> Two crossings were decided on:
>
> 1. For personnel North of Arnhem at area OOSTERBEEK 6975.
> 2. S.E. of WAGENINGEN - 604759.
>
> the date to be night 23/24 October.
>
> 1. to be carried out by 50th Div.
> 2. To be carried out by 101 U.S. Airborne Div.
>
> Rough outline plan completed, and I passed plan by telephone to Major Tatham-Warter at EDE. Was informed by him that they had to get out night 21/22 October and could only go by the western crossing.[3]

Dobie's plan fell by the wayside. The two crossings now became one and the date was duly brought forward. The rest remained the same.

Easy Company, 2nd Battalion, 506th Parachute Infantry Regiment, under First Lt 'Moose' Heyliger had been selected to row across in twenty-three boats to bring the evaders back.

After a series of reconnaissance patrols probing for weak spots in the German lines, the exact route to the river would soon be set. Both Capt. Wainwright of the 156 Parachute Battalion and CSM Grainger, 10th Parachute Battalion, were of great assistance to Digby who gave them much credit for their energy and keenness both prior to and during Pegasus. Their patrol the night before the evacuation, described by Digby as 'very bold', was particularly crucial in learning of the enemy dispositions.[4]

As the day broke, paratroopers in hiding scattered for miles were busy preparing for their journey to the rendezvous point. After an emotional farewell to Bill's family, Digby set out with Bill and Tonny to collect Brig. Lathbury, who had, after a month of inactivity coupled with his wounds, become 'very unfit', according to Digby.[5] Digby also had his doubts about his brigadier's attire. 'I remember being somewhat doubtful about Gerald's similarity to a Dutchman,' remembered Digby. 'He was abnormally tall and, looking a bit seedy in a dark clerical suit, did not quite fit into the landscape. He didn't look too happy on a bicycle either.'[6]

Unlike Digby, Lathbury was not accustomed to cycling around a town that was swarming with Germans and his heart pounded as he cycled passed them. Quite what these two men looked like to passers-by is difficult to imagine. Lathbury agreed with Digby's assessment of his appearance and admitted to looking like a 'seedy don'.[7]

'I shall never forget the journey to the RV,' Lathbury later recalled:

> Digby and I cycled along the road side by side, and every time we saw a German–and we passed at least 200, some in groups, some in platoons marching along–I expected to be challenged, but nothing untoward happened. We had chosen for a RV a large wood, which seemed to be filled with German gun positions, but it was thick enough to give us a chance of concealment...[8]

'The peaceful Dutch countryside became the scene of abnormal activity,' wrote Digby when describing his journey to the RV:

> There were many people on the move, some on foot and others on bicycles and some with horse drawn carts. Among them we recognised several evaders with their resistance guides and we also passed German troops on the march, or resting by the wayside. More than once we came upon emergency first-aid posts that had been established by the Dutch Red Cross, ostensibly to provide help and refreshment to tired refugees from Bennekom. But it so happened that all the nurses, some of them quite young girls, were members of the Resistance and had been positioned and briefed to give warning of unusual enemy activity and point evaders in a safe direction. Bill and Toni [*sic*] had a brief word with them as we passed by.[9]

A number of evaders had already arrived at the RV by the time Digby, Lathbury, Bill, and Tonny arrived. 'Bill had other arrangements to make and had to leave us now,' remembered Digby. 'It was a sad moment for me, as I had grown to like him enormously during the few weeks we had been working together.'[10]

Tonny and one or two others remained with the group. The evaders discarded their civilian clothing and changed into uniforms, thus becoming *bona fide* paratroopers once again. Many of them managed to catch some sleep while waiting for others to arrive.

Piet Kruyff had arranged for Red Cross lorries to transport Tony Hibbert's lot through German checkpoints from their destinations further afield. They had changed into their uniforms *en route*.

From the start, Brig. Lathbury knew that Digby was best placed to lead the operation and that nothing would be gained by him taking over at this late stage. Instead, he delegated overall command to Digby who decided he must carry out one final reconnaissance to ensure the way to the river remained open. Setting out with his guide, Maarten van den Bent, he returned at 9 p.m. having approached to within a few hundred yards of the Rhine without being challenged. Digby now felt much better and was more confident that the evacuation could succeed.

Once everyone had arrived, Digby organised the men into small platoons, each under the command of an officer or NCO. Owing to a shortage of weapons, only the front group of paratroopers—the fittest fighting men—were armed, although it was hoped they would not have to use them. A running battle was something Digby dearly wanted to avoid. The success of the mission relied on stealth and guile as opposed to all-out battle, regardless of how tempting the proposition may be.

He addressed the evaders: 'Now, you have got to hold onto the coat, or whatever, of the man in front,' he told them, 'and don't for God's sake let go. The important thing is to be absolutely silent—the Germans are only a few yards on either side and there are 130 of us to get through.'[11]

Digby finished his pep-talk and took a deep breath.

It was time to go.

Operation Pegasus

The evaders were in single file, spread over a considerable distance. Lathbury was somewhere in the middle, worrying about just how dark it was. He could not see the man stood directly in front of him, although he knew he was there and he wondered how they would stick together.

At the head of the party, Digby raised his hand and pointed forward, signalling the start of their journey. Contrary to his earlier pep-talk about the need for silence, Digby was horrified about the noise being created behind him. Twigs snapped, bushes rustled, and men stumbled into one and other, tripping over roots and falling into unseen holes and ditches. The men cursed and complained, ignoring their leader's pleas for quiet.

Digby noted:

> Although the importance of moving silently was obvious, and I had stressed this at the briefing, we were soon making far too much noise, and the further we went the worse it got. The morale of these men was low anyhow after several weeks of

> confinement to one place, and most of them had never set eyes on the officers and NCOs appointed to command them. And, of course, many were totally untrained and unsuited to this kind of adventure.[12]

The column was likened to a large caterpillar, travelling very slowly. A rope was passed back to keep some semblance of unity as the men wound their way cautiously between the trees. Of course, besides a few at the front, nobody had any idea where they were going.

For the first two miles, through the woods, Digby ordered the men to double-up instead of moving in single file to minimise the chances of separation, and frequent stops were made to ensure nobody was left behind or lost. The silence of the night seemed to enhance every sound and Digby likened the noise to a herd of stampeding elephants. Despite this, the edge of the wood was reached without incident. Here, with heartfelt handshakes, Digby bid farewell to his Dutch friends. The time was 11 p.m. An open distance of several hundred yards now had to be covered before they reached the river bank. Lathbury had moved up alongside Digby, as had Tony Hibbert, while Tony Frank, who had recovered sufficiently from his wound to take part in the evacuation, brought up the rear.

The wooded area used by the evaders on their way to the river. (*Ruud Slangen*)

Now came the most dangerous section of the journey, the crossing of the open field. Luckily, a series of drainage ditches ran part way towards the river, which offered some little degree of cover should they come under fire. 'But for the last 200 yards or so,' recalled Digby, 'we had to crawl across a completely open meadow in full view of the enemy.'[13]

Digby thought it a miracle but, just before midnight, they had succeeded in reaching the river without a shot being fired. Turning west, they set off downstream towards the crossing point 'DIGBY'. 'The going was better now,' Digby related, 'and we were making much less noise':

> I think that everyone appreciated the danger of our situation, out in the open and only about 300 yards from the German defences. And luckily there was now some cloud cover, and the night had become appreciably darker. We could just make out the far side of the river, here some 300 yards wide.[14]

Shortly after starting along the river bank, the unthinkable happened. Several bursts of machine-gun fire erupted from a short distance in front. 'Our advance guard returned the fire,' recorded Digby, 'and we all went down ready to defend ourselves, expecting at any moment to be lit up by star shells and plastered by mortar and machine gun fire.'[15] But nothing of the sort happened. A few Very lights were sent up over the German posts and the silence resumed.

Digby's version of the firing may not necessarily be completely accurate, and it is likely that owing to the darkness and confusing nature of the situation, Digby and those with him, including Lathbury who gave a similar account, mistook exactly what had happened. In fact, Capt. Wainwright, who was leading the very tip of the advance guard, had shouted 'Get the bastards!' and had been the first to open fire after he and his men ran into a German patrol. One enemy soldier was killed and the rest, having seen the large number of soldiers before them and no doubt fearing they were under attack by a sizeable force from across the river, retreated without firing a shot.

Point 'DIGBY' was reached without a single casualty, but no boats were to be found. The leaders discussed the situation and agreed they were at the right spot. All they could do was wait, but half an hour passed without sight or sound of the rescue party. Torch signals—the 'V' for Victory flashed across the river—met with no response. Digby began to think something had gone seriously wrong.

From his position across the river, David Dobie was equally worried. Heaps recounted:

> All day Dobie had been in a mood of nervous anticipation, of high tension and purpose. If devotion to friends could bring the men back, they would return.[16]

The members of Easy Company under 'Moose' Heyliger were fully aware of the job at hand and were thrilled at the chance to be involved in the rescue. 'Their enthusiasm for the operation was quite unbounded,' wrote Dobie:

> The thought of rescuing British airborne personnel some 5 weeks after our combined operation together appealed to them, and it was with the greatest difficulty that the

> commanding officer, Colonel Strayer of the 2nd Btn., 506th Parachute Regiment, was able to pick the necessary men for the operation, as every man in his battalion wished to cross the river for the task.[17]

Looking out across the river, Dobie could see no sign of the evaders. From their position on the forward slopes of the dyke, Majors Hugh Fraser and Airey Neave were also deeply frustrated and nervous. There was no sign from across the river whatsoever. From his position at the river by the boats, an equally concerned Leo Heaps then spotted something:

> West of Arnhem the Rhine curves north and south in a series of bends. From our sector of shoreline on the south an advancing column of men could easily be lost from view if they hugged the far bank. No one had thought of this possibility, nor did anyone anticipate it. Nor did Tatham-Warter realized the poor visibility of his signal light. By chance, about half an hour after midnight, I looked in the direction of the bridge for the first time. I thought I saw a tiny light flicker on and off. I raced down to Dobie to tell him.[18]

Canadian Leo Heaps took part in Operation Market Garden. After escaping across the Rhine, he worked with the intelligence teams to co-ordinate the rescue of paratroopers in hiding who were stranded on the wrong side of the river.

Heaps and Dobie watched again together. At first there was nothing, but 'after a few minutes a faint, red pinpoint of light signalled the "V" for victory symbol.'[19] It was hard to tell the distance, but they surmised it could be as much as several miles east of their prearranged rendezvous. 'Dobie did not wait any longer,' recorded Heaps. 'He and the Moose excitedly pushed off and with a weird cry vanished from sight on the river.'[20] Heaps set to work ordering the men to drag their boats along the shore in the direction of the light before plunging in after them.

Meanwhile, all kinds of thoughts were racing through Digby's mind. Why was there no response? Had something gone wrong? If so, what? Had the whole thing been called off? Were they in the wrong place? Why had the boats failed to show?

Whatever happened, there was no way back, and if they remained where they were, they would be finished. The only viable option was the river itself, but it was freezing cold, wide, deep, and fast-flowing and would spell death for many.

Over four decades later, when thinking back on the episode, Digby related:

> It can be imagined what a very worrying time this was for us all, especially for me, as I had agreed the plan with Dobie and Fraser on the telephone and so felt that the responsibility for our situation was largely mine. Were all our efforts and the bravery of the Dutch to be wasted at the last minute?[21]

But Digby was able to breathe a huge sigh of relief:

> And then out of the night came what must have been the most welcome words I ever heard, 'Are you people by any chance looking for some boats?' Had I been a modern footballer I feel sure that I would have hugged and kissed the owner of this voice, such was my joy. As it was, I am reputed to have said something like 'Well, actually we are rather.'[22]

Leo Heaps was the man who had asked the question. No doubt brought on by sheer relief, Heaps laughed at Digby's calm response, so too did Tony Hibbert who gave his own version of the event:

> I was up front with Digby Tatham Warter and Gerald Lathbury and we'd waited for a bit but were a couple of hundred yards too short because the signal was firing the Bofors over the crossing point. We thought we'd found the right place and were waiting and suddenly a figure loomed out of the mist—because luckily there was a mist—and he said, 'Are you guys expecting some Americans to pick you up?' and Digby said, 'Well, as a matter of fact old boy, yes we are.'[23]

Heaps led them a short way down the river to where Dobie was waiting impatiently with the boats. It turned out that the evaders were somewhere between 450 and 850 yards off from where they should have been. Dobie gave them a few choice words before overseeing their embarkation across the river.

In total, 138 men successfully crossed the Rhine to safety. After crossing the river, the evaders followed a path of white tape that had been laid out for them. They were guided to a farmhouse that the Americans were using as a HQ where they met with an enthusiastic response. Donald Burgett was among those involved in the rescue:

> The British paratroopers were all smiling. They had suffered through an unspeakable hell in their battles against armour and multitudes of enemy foot soldiers, including *Waffen* SS troops. Then they had been forced to hide under the very noses of the enemy for a nerve-wracking month with the aid and care of the Dutch people. They must have dreaded each scraping footfall, each crunch of gravel outside, the thud of hob nailed boots on the floor overhead. The anxiety they felt while hidden in the cellars, dugouts and bunkers by Dutch civilians who faced certain death at the hands of the Germans if they were caught had been barely durable.[24]

None of the evaders had been killed in the evacuation and up until this point none had been wounded (although one or two had lost their way on the journey). But Tony Hibbert saw to it they did get off with a clean casualty sheet. Sitting on the front of a packed jeep on the way to the reception area, his leg was snapped when an oncoming vehicle collided with the jeep he was mounted on.

In the reception area, the British paratroopers were fed and watered, and for the first time in weeks, they were able to relax. Airey Neave was in attendance: 'I soon recognised the "Voice", the officer who had spoken to me on the power station line from Nijmegen to Ede. This was Major Digby Tatham Warter, to whose calm and ingenuity the success of 'Pegasus' owed much'.[25]

At 9 p.m. on 28 October, the Wildeboers and other resistance members switched on their radios to listen to the BBC Home Service broadcast, waiting for the prearranged message to be announced that would confirm the success of the mission. At 9 p.m. on the dot, the broadcast came through: 'Message for Bill. Everything is well. All our thanks'.[26]

A postcard showing the St Elisabeth Hospital. Together with his second-in-command, Capt. Frank, Digby escaped by climbing through the window of his room. He has marked where the hospital is located in pen. (*Photo from Digby's collection*)

Above left: Digby donning his beret.

Above right: Brigadier Lathbury, photo taken after Operation Pegasus.

15

Post-Arnhem

The Battalion had fought with the utmost gallantry, in inconceivably difficult conditions, and had denied the use of the vital Bridge to the enemy for 80 hours.

Major Tatham Warter, Officer Commanding 2nd Parachute Regiment

It was well-known that a large number of evaders still remained behind enemy lines and that a second evacuation would be needed. As soon as Operation Pegasus was done and dusted, Neave, Fraser, and their intelligence team began to plan 'Pegasus II'.

Meanwhile, from Eindhoven, the evaders and resistance members who had joined them in the evacuation were flown to Lincolnshire, England—the home of the 1st Airborne HQ prior to Market Garden. Among them was Jan Kooijman, who noted: 'The very next day Tatham Warter flies us in his private plane from Lincolnshire to London and put us off at 'the Dutch authorities'.[1]

For Digby and the evaders, returning to Lincolnshire presented scenes in stark contrast to those they had left behind. The losses sustained in the operation were clear for all to see. The place was eerily quiet; a skeleton of its former self. But a handful of men from the battalion were already there—men who had made it out in the main evacuation from Oosterbeek. These men had been the first to realise that almost every member of the battalion had been lost.

Having travelled by sea with 'B' Echelon, Colour-Sgt Jimmy Sharp had not taken part in the battle, but when the division had made its evacuation under Gen. Urquhart, he had set out to welcome the battalion back:

> We prepared the billets at Nijmegen for the Div coming back. They started to arrive at approx 2300 hours and I kept asking: 'Has anyone seen any 2nd Battalion?' But, no one had. The first, a medical corporal attached arrived at about 0600 hours the next morning and when they were all there the Battalion muster was 17 men and none of these had been with the battalion at the Bridge. I don't think I was the only one there with tears in my eyes.[2]

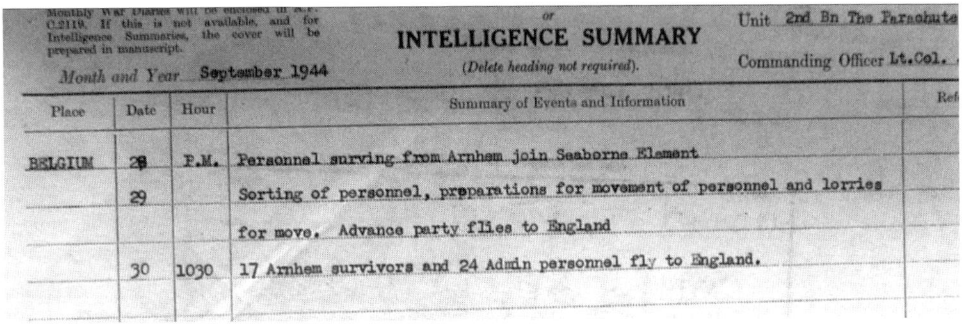
Monthly War Diaries will be enclosed in A.F. C.2119. If this is not available, and for Intelligence Summaries, the cover will be prepared in manuscript.

or

INTELLIGENCE SUMMARY

(*Delete heading not required*).

Unit 2nd Bn The Parachute

Commanding Officer Lt.Col.

Month and Year September 1944

Place	Date	Hour	Summary of Events and Information	Ref
BELGIUM	28	P.M.	Personnel surving from Arnhem join Seaborne Element	
	29		Sorting of personnel, preparations for movement of personnel and lorries	
			for move. Advance party flies to England	
	30	1030	17 Arnhem survivors and 24 Admin personnel fly to England.	

A sombre entry in the battalion war diary records that a mere seventeen men plus members of the admin team were all that was left of the battalion.

Den Portman, who had been wounded on his way to the bridge and taken to the Hartenstein Hotel, was one of the lucky seventeen. He described returning to meet Colour-Sgt Sharp as something he 'shall always remember':

> On this misty field by a small preach tree, he called out in his authoritative voice 'Fall in 2nd Battalion'. Seventeen men, exhausted from their exploits of the last ten days 'fell in'. He looked us over, 'Is this the lot?' he said, and his usually strong expression changed, his chin trembled and his eyes welled up in a veil of tears as he realised that the decimation of our Second battalion had been complete.[3]

Digby set about writing to the next of kin of his men, which he sent with an account of the battle he had written up, 'to give an idea of the importance of the task, and the gallant part played by members of the Battalion in this historic battle'.[4] This included those whose sons were 'missing'—the majority of whom were now POWs.

On 27 October, he wrote a heartfelt letter to the father of Maj. David Wallis:

> Dear Mr. Wallis,
>
> You will have had my telegram by now telling you about David. I'm afraid it must have been a most terrible blow to you. It had been quite impossible to let you know anything before as I am the first person to get back with any news of the Battalion.
>
> David was killed at about 8 p.m. on Monday 18th Sept. He had taken over command of the Battalion on Sunday night when the Colonel assumed command of the whole force at the Bridge. I saw a lot of him and can tell you that he was quite magnificent. He was quite fearless and spent most of his time where the battle was the hottest. He was just as cheerful as he always was and inspired everyone with his great confidence. It is a very great loss to us all, particularly to me as he was one of my greatest friends. He had many of the finest qualities that a man can have. I was quite close when he was killed and know that he died instantaneously without any pain.
>
> I'm afraid it is the end of the Battalion as I very much doubt if anyone else will get back now, until the war is over. I will send you a short description of the 2nd

Battalion's battle when I have had time to prepare it, or better still, if you are going to be in London during my leave I could come up and tell you the whole story. Perhaps you could let me know your plans—I can be found at Blethington 39.

Fountain tells me that he has sent off all of David's kit.

Please accept my deepest sympathy—I think I know what it will mean to you.

Yours sincerely,

Digby T.W.[5]

When it comes to gallantry awards, the 2nd Parachute Battalion has always felt it was hard done to in regards to those received for Operation Market Garden. In total, sixteen officers were recommended to division for awards. Of these, five were approved and submitted by division. Two received foreign awards, and one a lesser award. Of the 'other ranks', just one of twenty-nine recommendations would be accepted. One other would receive a foreign award while seven more would receive lesser awards than those recommended. One of these men, Bob Lygo, whose DCM recommendation was downgraded to a MM, deserves special mention. Throughout the battle, as No. 1 of a PIAT detachment attached to No. 3 Platoon, Pte. Lygo took it upon himself to take on any vehicles that crossed his path, particularly on the Tuesday when, in the face of concentrated fire, he scored a number of hits on enemy armoured cars and tanks, thus allowing the platoon to keep possession of their house. At the time, Lygo was isolated from the remainder of the platoon and working on his own initiative. When engaging the tanks, he had deliberately exposed himself to heavy fire to work forward to a position from which to fire. Truly a well-earned MM.

As with all battles, many acts of bravery went unrewarded. Even so, in the words of Bob Peatling, who fought at the bridge, 'When one considers the tributes paid and the sacrifices made, the awards do appear to be on the mean side.'[6]

For Arnhem, the battalion received two DSOs, one was in fact a bar (denoting a second DSO for the recipient) awarded to Lt-Col. Frost, and the other went to Digby.

Notification of Digby's award appeared in the *London Gazette* without a citation. Fortunately, the Tatham Warter family still have the original documentation:

Major Tatham-Warter commanded a Company of 2 Parachute Battalion which dropped west of ARNHEM in HOLLAND on 17th September. The task of the Battalion was the vital one of capturing, the main Rhine Bridge and this officer handled the leading Company with such dash and skill that the bridge was in our hands before dark after considerable casualties had been inflicted on the enemy and 30 prisoners captured. Later, when the C.O. took command of all forces on the bridge Major TATHAM-WARTER assumed command of the Battalion. He commanded during the next three days when the Battalion without any re-supply of food or ammunition, resisted incessant and determined attacks by vastly superior forces

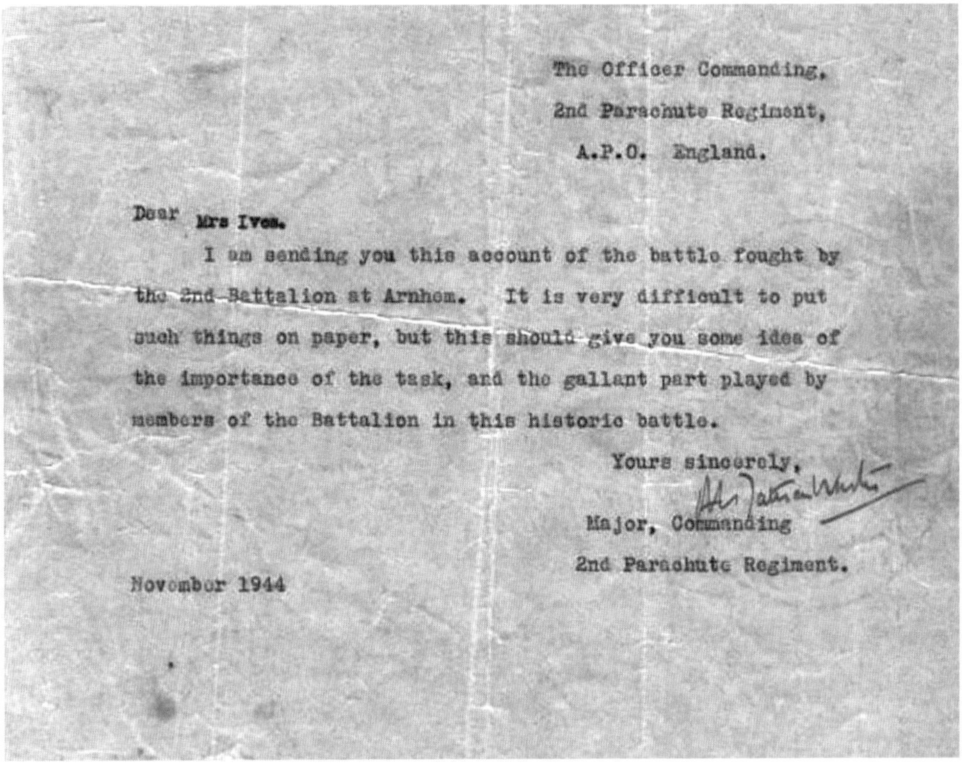

The Officer Commanding,
2nd Parachute Regiment,
A.P.O. England.

Dear Mrs Ives.

I am sending you this account of the battle fought by the 2nd Battalion at Arnhem. It is very difficult to put such things on paper, but this should give you some idea of the importance of the task, and the gallant part played by members of the Battalion in this historic battle.

Yours sincerely,

Major, Commanding
2nd Parachute Regiment.

November 1944

Above: An accompanying letter sent by Digby with his report on the battle to the next-of-kin of his men. (*Paradata*)

Right: Digby's DSO certificate of award that hung proudly in his home.

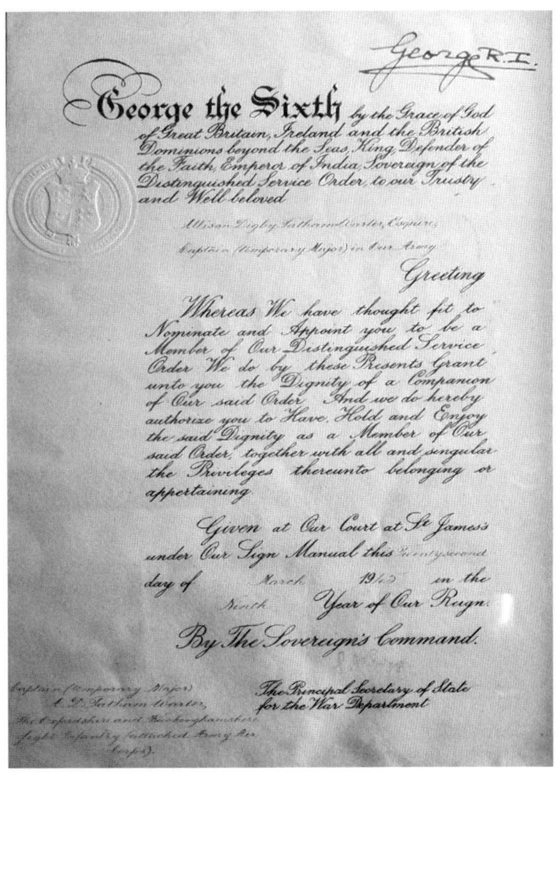

George R.I.

George the Sixth by the Grace of God of Great Britain, Ireland and the British Dominions beyond the Seas, King, Defender of the Faith, Emperor of India, Sovereign of the Distinguished Service Order, to our Trusty and Well-beloved

Greeting

Whereas We have thought fit to Nominate and Appoint you to be a Member of Our Distinguished Service Order We do by these Presents Grant unto you the Dignity of a Companion of Our said Order And we do hereby authorize you to Have, Hold and Enjoy the said Dignity as a Member of Our said Order, together with all and singular the Privileges thereunto belonging or appertaining.

Given at Our Court at St James's under Our Sign Manual this day of March 1945 in the Ninth Year of Our Reign.

By The Sovereign's Command.

The Principal Secretary of State for the War Department

> including tanks. Throughout this period, Major TATHAM-WARTER displayed magnificent qualities of courage, leadership and the utmost determination.
>
> He was to be found invariably at the most threatened point in the defence, where his personal example was an inspiration to all. On one occasion he was rendered unconscious by the blast from an 88 mm Tank Gun firing point blank at the house he was in, but he recovered and resumed command. Later, when captured by the enemy, he escaped and showed great initiative in making contact with the Dutch Resistance organisation. He organised and assembled a force of one hundred escaped airborne troops, so that they could play their part when the Germans should begin to withdraw.
>
> Finally, when orders were received to withdraw this party through the German lines, Major TATHAM-WARTER was largely responsible for the planning of a most brilliant and successful operation in which 130 armed men escaped through the German lines and crossed the Rhine. For a month, behind the German lines, this officer moved about regardless of his personal safety and was an inspiration to all those who saw him.[7]

At Grantham prior to Operation Market Garden, John Frost had pulled Maj. Tate to one side to speak with him about dragging the men out of bed on a Sunday morning to train. He had told Maj. Tate (killed in action at Arnhem) to give them the day off and that the battalion would earn their first VC in their next battle. Frost's prediction was correct. As a result of Digby's efforts, Lt Grayburn would be posthumously awarded the VC, far exceeding the MC he had told his men he was going to get prior to going into action.

After a failed recommendation for a bar to the MC, Tony Frank was awarded the American Silver Star and was mentioned in despatches. Robin Vlasto was unsuccessfully put forward for a mention in despatches and got nothing.

Digby could not get it out of his mind the fact that a number of unfortunate paratroopers remained hiding on the wrong side of the Rhine—men he had been unable to get out owing to them not having time to get to the rendezvous. Digby's time behind enemy lines had not dampened his enthusiasm and he felt he could be of some use in Pegasus II. A week after his return to England, he travelled to London to speak with the authorities to propose his next mission.

Digby's plan was to be parachuted back into Ede to organise and lead the remaining paratroopers out. He explained his plan to the authorities, but much to his dismay, they refused permission for him to go back.[2]

Operation Pegasus II went ahead on 18 November, several kilometres east of where Digby had evacuated. Not a single man made it across the river that night. The operation was a complete failure.

By the time of the Germany Army's unconditional surrender in May 1945, the battalion was back to full strength. Most of the new arrivals were either inexperienced recruits or members of the 4th Parachute Brigade that had been badly mauled at Arnhem and disbanded. On 4 May, the brigade was detached from the 1st Airborne Division and, other than the 1st Parachute Battalion, which was ordered to Denmark, remained in Britain in reserve. Seizing the opportunity, Digby acquired an army jeep and set out across the Channel and on to Holland to check up on the Wildeboers and his other Dutch friends whose safety he was concerned for having not heard anything of them since Operation Pegasus. They were thrilled to see him and he was equally pleased to find that they were safe and well.

POWs began to return from their places of incarceration, including John Frost, who found the battalion completely reformed in his absence. Frost admitted to a pang of jealousy that another man was in command of *his* battalion, but his wounds would take time to fully heal and he could not resume command just yet.

Upon his return, Frost noted:

> John Marshall, our second-in-command from Tunisian days, was now commanding and Digby Tatham-Warter was with them. He had escaped from the hospital in Arnhem, and was picked up by the Dutch Underground and, after an amazing series of escapades through which he sauntered with his customary sangfroid, helped to organise a mass evacuation of British prisoners from enemy-held Holland to our own lines. On his return he had written a report about the action at the bridge, in which he told the story which had gained, rightly, the award of the Victoria Cross to Jack Grayburn for his quite incredible guts and devotion to duty during our battle.[8]

Photo of Digby and the Wildeboers taken on 1 June 1945 during his visit following the German surrender. Digby had borrowed a jeep and hurried to Holland to check on the wellbeing of his friends. Much had happened since they had last met, but the Wildeboer family had weathered the storm and Digby found them in good health.

Left: A photograph from Digby's album taken during his return visit to the area in 1945. The reverse of the photograph describes it as the 'Sheep House'.

Below: A letter to Digby from Joop Haffmans to show his appreciation at what Digby and his fellow countrymen did for them.

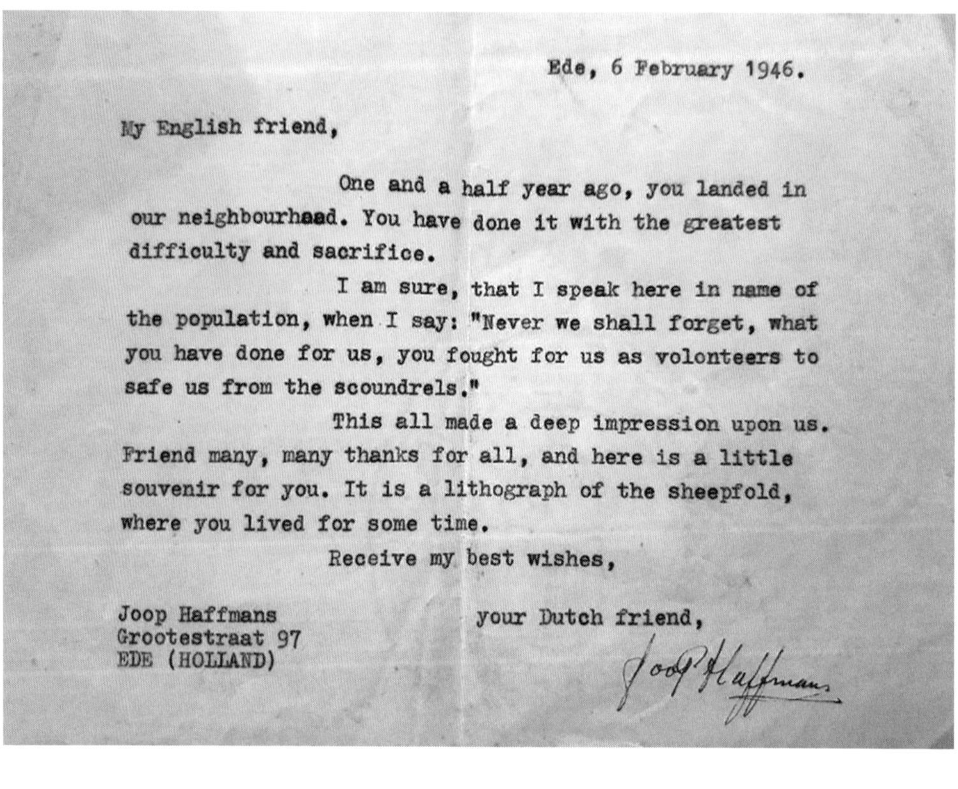

Ede, 6 February 1946.

My English friend,

One and a half year ago, you landed in our neighbourhaad. You have done it with the greatest difficulty and sacrifice.

I am sure, that I speak here in name of the population, when I say: "Never we shall forget, what you have done for us, you fought for us as volonteers to safe us from the scoundrels."

This all made a deep impression upon us. Friend many, many thanks for all, and here is a little souvenir for you. It is a lithograph of the sheepfold, where you lived for some time.

Receive my best wishes,

your Dutch friend,

Joop Haffmans

Joop Haffmans
Grootestraat 97
EDE (HOLLAND)

Digby had always enjoyed army life, but his views changed post-war when the brigade was transferred to the 6th Airborne Division and sent to Palestine after the disbandment of the 1st Airborne Division.

The news that they were to go to Palestine was initially greeted as a positive and it was thought the climate and good airfields gave excellent prospects for training. But expectations were soon dashed.

The situation in Palestine, where Britain was responsible for the government and security, was one of disorder and civil unrest. Based in Haifa by the coast, it was never intended for the 6th Airborne Division to be drawn into internal security duties. Nevertheless, that is exactly what happened and they soon found themselves involved in bitter conflict against Jewish groups fighting for an unlimited number of Jewish immigrants to be allowed into the country.

Frost, who had been commanding a divisional battle school in Norway, was recalled to resume command of the battalion.

In his memoir, he noted:

> By 1946 two Jewish terrorist organisations, the Stern Gang and the Irgun Zvai Leumi, had been raiding British installations and perpetrating atrocities on Arabs and British soldiers, with the aim of forcing a relaxation of restrictions on Jewish immigration, and of preventing an Arab/Jewish partition of the country. These activities, on the whole, were supported by the rest of the Jewish population, and a most unpleasant atmosphere prevailed.[9]

British soldiers were ardently detested, particularly the airborne, who were labelled as fascists.

Frost added:

> The rights of the indigenous Arab population were considered irrelevant by the terrorists and their supporters, and elsewhere in the world, we, the peacekeepers, were vilified. Anyway, as usual in such circumstances, British soldiers grinned and bore it. Their traditional good humour often succeeded in breaking through the wall of hatred surrounding them.[10]

Paratroopers, trained to use maximum force and to kill their enemy when opposed, now found themselves in an internal security peace-keeping role where minimal force and restraint was required in all situations no matter the provocation.

When time allowed, Digby taught the local Arabs to shoot sand grouse and spent time hunting—primarily desert fox. But by and large, the place held little appeal to him and it is fair to say that he detested his time in Palestine. Before the year was out, both Frost and Digby, and many other veterans of the war, had left the battalion.

While Frost took up a role with the Staff College, Digby decided to take up a secondment with the 5th King's Africa Rifles (KAR) that was actively looking for experienced British officers to join them. The opportunity appealed to Digby, and on the recommendation of his aunt and uncle in Kenya, he decided to make the move.

16

A New Beginning and the Mau Mau

As a British protectorate since the late nineteenth century, there were significant advantages for white settlers looking to make Kenya their home. Its railroad made it an important cog in the empire and highly strategic for transportation in the African continent. Following the Scramble for Africa, the continent had been carved up among those European countries that had an interest through trade and business. In 1890, the country had become a part of British East Africa, and in 1920, shortly after the First World War, the former East African Protectorate was annexed by Britain to become 'Kenya', named after the 17,000-foot Mount Kenya, its highest mountain located in the highlands.

With its 250-mile coast on the Indian Ocean, the 224,960 square miles of modern Kenya borders Sudan and Ethiopia to the north, Tanzania to the south, and Uganda to the west. Geographically, Kenya is split between the highlands to the south-west and the lowlands, which make up two-thirds of the country. By the 1930s, some 30,000 settlers lived in and around the central highlands. A volcanic fertile vault known as the Great Rift Valley stretches from the Jordan Valley south to Mozambique through Kenya. The many ethnic groups include the Kikuyu and Masai. As 1950 approached, the population in Kenya stood around 6 million. Today, it is fast approaching 50 million.

As a child, Digby had always enjoyed visiting Kenya with his family, usually in the school holidays or when his father was in India on business. By moving to the KAR, Digby was perhaps thinking beyond his military career, for Kenya with its cheap land and labour offered fantastic farming prospects and fit well with his love of the outdoors.

The KAR were based in Mogadishu in Somalia bordering Kenya at the time. Digby remained with them until 1948 before cashing in his pension to buy a farm.

Shortly after his arrival from Palestine, Digby became engaged to a young lady by the name of Susan Ridley. They planned to marry, but Digby jilted her before the big day after meeting Jane Boyd, the daughter of Capt. Roderick Boyd and granddaughter of Arthur George Egerton, 5th earl of Wilton. Digby was smitten and they were soon engaged.

The cancelation of Digby's marriage to Susan in order to become engaged to Jane 'raised eyebrows' throughout the community, but Digby cared little for what people thought.[1]

Digby and Jane had first met at a military social party in Kenya, and love at first sight it certainly was not. Jane was fifteen or sixteen at the time, and had used her best powers of persuasion to get her mother's permission to attend the event with a friend. When Jane was dared to go up to 'that tall fellow' and undo his braces, Jane took up the challenge. Shuffling over to Digby, Jane carried out the deed whereupon Digby turned and gave what Jane described as 'a most filthy look'.[2]

Jane had then left Kenya to attend finishing school in England where she remained for nine months. Jane was engaged to a man named Robin Long and they were planning to marry, but this was called off after Digby and Jane reconnected and struck up a mutual attraction after meeting again at the Nanyuki Races. Robin was universally considered to be a very nice man. Jane felt very sorry for her ex-fiancé, and Digby certainly had no issue with him.

I asked Jane how Digby came to propose, and her reply was perhaps what one might expect from a man of Digby's character. 'He didn't propose,' explained Jane, 'he simply considered himself much the better man and began planning the wedding!'[3] Faced with such competition, Robin could do nothing.

Breaking the unwritten rule in the officers' mess that politics, religion, and women were not to be discussed, Digby was previously overheard talking with his friend Sam Weller about which of the Boyd sisters each of them wanted to marry.

Given the situation, Jane's mother insisted their engagement should not yet be announced and they should wait a year before tying the knot. They agreed to wait and the engagement was not officially announced. Digby, however, had previously bought a stunning engagement ring for his ex-fiancé which had since been returned to him. Digby had given Jane the option of having Susan's ring or a new one, although he had stressed that he no longer had the budget to purchase such an impressive ring again. At any rate, Jane was more than happy to accept the old ring which she considered beautiful. 'I'm not fussy, it's a lovely ring. I'll keep this one,' she told Digby when he had suggested he could buy her another.[4]

Digby and Jane were engaged in 1948 and married on 6 August the following year. Ex-Ox & Bucks officer Bobby Hornsby-Wright, who had also settled in Kenya, was Digby's best man. Digby and Bobby had served together in India where they had both developed an interest in pig-sticking. Bobby had been severely wounded in the stomach during the war and his wound would cause him much discomfort throughout his life. Bobby was simply adored by the Tatham Warters and decades later, upon Digby's passing, would continue to care for the family.

As a wedding gift, Digby gave Jane a pony. It was not something she felt she particularly needed, but Digby made good use of it himself.

First there was the ring; then came the questionable wedding gift; next came the honeymoon. Digby had been saving hard for them to go to Kashmir, India, but when the time came, he discovered that Sam Weller, who looked after 'Sometimes Farm'—named as such because he was sometimes there and sometimes not—in which Digby was invested, had already spent the funds that Digby had earmarked for his honeymoon on the farm. Instead, the newlyweds set out by boat to travel the coast, visiting, among other places, Mombasa, Lamu, Malindi, and Zanzibar.

Left: On 6 August 1949, Digby married Jane Boyd, daughter of Capt. Roderick Bulteel Boyd, a farmer in Nanyuki. Digby worshipped Jane and was utterly devoted to her throughout his life.

Below: Newlyweds Digby and Jane.

Right: Jane Tatham Warter (*née* Boyd), the love of Digby's life. Jane passed away in 2021 having spent the best part of thirty years as Digby's widow.

Below: Newlyweds Digby and Jane.

Newlyweds Digby and Jane. Digby's best man, ex-Ox & Bucks officer Bobby Hornsby-Wright, stands by Digby's side.

Both Digby and Jane loved to fish, but when Digby arranged for them to spend a day at sea in an old clapped-out boat that looked like it was on the verge of sinking, Jane had her doubts. Digby, however, seemed oblivious to any risk. The boat owner and several others accompanied them, but as they set off, the line became entangled and one of the fishermen received a large hook through his hand. Firmly embedded, and with a fair amount of blood, they were forced to abort the trip, much to Jane's relief.

The honeymoon was not all bad, since part way through they got chatting with 'a very nice man' who, after hearing of their tattered plans of an Indian honeymoon, took pity on them and let them stay in one of his large and somewhat elegant houses.

By this time, Digby had left the regular army, taken his military pension, and purchased his small farm—'Eburru', near Gilgil in the Rift Valley. Set on volcanic land and spanning 5,000 acres, it would prove difficult to farm and would never be seriously productive, but Digby would strive to make it a success. Eburru in local Masai language means 'steam'. The area was very sloped and rugged with steam rising from the ground, which Digby captured to use as his water source. Despite his struggles, he would send food parcels containing tins of butter and other items notoriously difficult to obtain to his family in England who were under strict rationing and who were very appreciative of his efforts to provide for them.

'Eburru'—the Tatham Warter family home prior to Independence. Located on volcanic land in the Rift Valley, 'Eburru' in local Masai language means 'steam'. Digby used to capture this to use as his water source.

The area where the Tatham Warters lived was dubbed 'the white highlands', since only white Europeans were allowed to settle there during the colonial era. A number of ex-paratroopers moved out to Kenya after the war, including David Dobie who arrived in 1947 or 1948. His son, Charles Dobie, relates that his father had a contact 'who asked him to join him in a business involved with agricultural implements representing a Czech tractor manufacturer among other things'.[5]

In 1949, Dobie began importing Mercedes cars and set up a very successful business, D. T. Dobie, the Mercedes-Benz franchise for East Africa which stills thrives today. The story behind Dobie's Mercedes business is a fascinating one indeed.

Charles Dobie relates:

> My father subsequently met a German at a (motor) show (at either Hanover, London or Nairobi) who turned out to be somebody he had fought against in North Africa. A truce had been called to rescue personal valuables from the fallen soldiers on both sides. Over a cup of tea during the truce they got to know each other. So a few years later at this trade show, this German gentleman it turns out worked for Mercedes-Benz and that is how my father managed to secure the MB franchise for East Africa.[6]

Charles was also told by his mother that after the war, decorated British officers were funded by the newly established bank, S. G. Warburg, to start their own businesses and that his father took that seed capital to Kenya.

Digby and Jane with daughters. Caroline and Joanna (Jo). Caption in Digby's photo album reads: 'Joanna Mary Tatham Warter's Christening at Eburru on April 5th 1952, aged 7 months'.

The Tatham Warter family was soon growing. In June 1950, Jane gave birth to Caroline, the first of three daughters. Joanna (Jo) would be born in September the following year and Belinda (Binny) in November 1954.

Digby was very active in various social aspects of Kenyan life. During his service with the 5 KAR from 1946–48, he had formed a pack of hounds and made what was described as a 'spirited yet unsuccessful effort to introduce pig-sticking' to the area.[7]

Fortunately for Digby, polo was extremely popular in Kenya and he was soon playing at the highest level. Polo would be a major part of his life for many years and he was considered one of the best, playing for the Kenyan National Team and gaining a handicap of six.

Don Rooken-Smith, who would later play alongside Digby at international level, had known of him prior:

> My first association with Digby went back to 1949/50 as a schoolboy, when my Father also played polo at Bwana Begg's 'Kinyatta' ground, at Gilgil. Renamed 'Manyatta' after uhuru.
>
> The Kinyatta Polo Club at that time was perhaps the strongest playing Club of Kenya's 14 others ... and their senior team of Bwana Begg, Hugh Ferguson, Digby and Ray Scholes won most tournaments at that time.
>
> In early 1956 I was a member of a Kenya polo tour to Ethiopia, captained by Digby, and managed by the GOC EA Armed Forces—Gen. Loony Hinde....
>
> Our final polo match was against the Ethiopian Army, attended by HH Haile Salassie, whom we were presented to. The umpiring was unbelievably biased, in

order to ensure the Army won ... which was later explained as—'no one beats the Ethiopian Army in-front of the Lion of Judah', so we are making sure no heads roll ... which apparently included ours!![8]

Rooken-Smith continues:

> In mid 1956 a Rhodesian Polo Team toured Kenya. I was in the bush actively pursuing the mau/mau, so was not involved with polo. However Kenya had won the first Test and badly lost the second at Naivasha, and I had been selected to play under Digby, for the third test at Njoro. My CO was unimpressed with one of his subalterns taking off to play polo, and only the intervention of Gen. Hinde made it possible for me to play ... and we won! The Kenya team selected that day ... Jeremy Allen, DRS, Nick Allen and captained by Digby ... went on to successfully represent Kenya for a number of years.
>
> In 1957 the Kenya Polo Association sent a return team to tour Rhodesia. All the members motored to Rhodesia, and wives were included. Sir Charles Markham managed this side, with his usual no nonsense attitude, and a very good time was had by all. We won two of the tests, and Digby's record against Rhodesia was 4 won/2 lost.

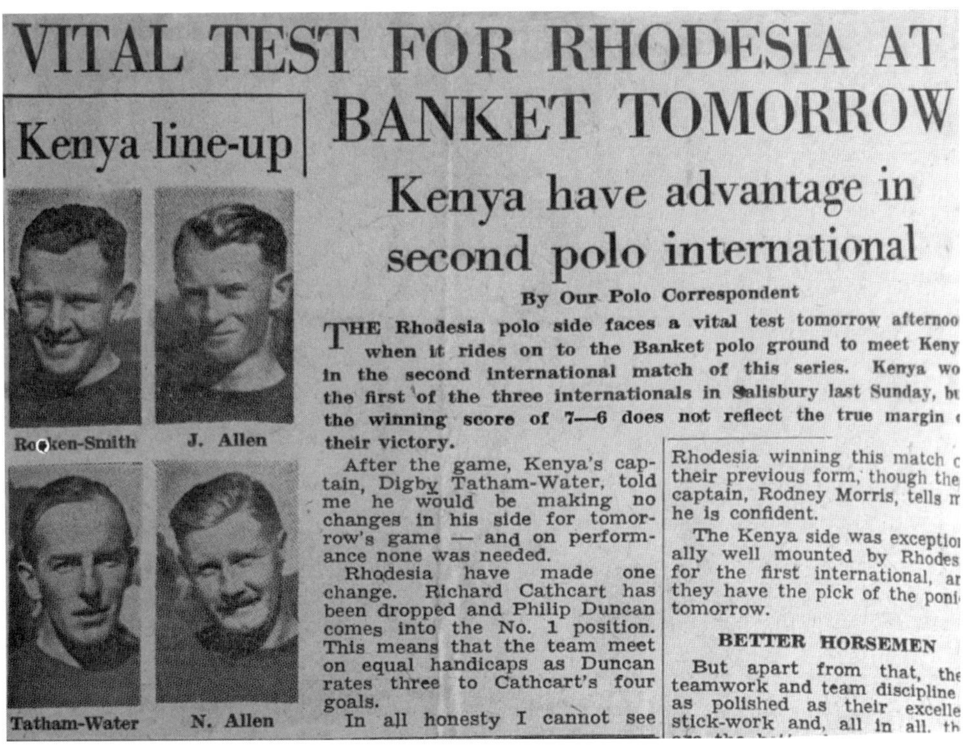

VITAL TEST FOR RHODESIA AT BANKET TOMORROW

Kenya line-up

Rooken-Smith J. Allen

Tatham-Water N. Allen

Kenya have advantage in second polo international

By Our Polo Correspondent

THE Rhodesia polo side faces a vital test tomorrow afternoo when it rides on to the Banket polo ground to meet Keny in the second international match of this series. Kenya wo the first of the three internationals in Salisbury last Sunday, bu the winning score of 7—6 does not reflect the true margin o their victory.

After the game, Kenya's captain, Digby Tatham-Water, told me he would be making no changes in his side for tomorrow's game — and on performance none was needed.

Rhodesia have made one change. Richard Cathcart has been dropped and Philip Duncan comes into the No. 1 position. This means that the team meet on equal handicaps as Duncan rates three to Cathcart's four goals.

In all honesty I cannot see Rhodesia winning this match o their previous form, though the captain, Rodney Morris, tells m he is confident.

The Kenya side was exceptio ally well mounted by Rhodes for the first international, ar they have the pick of the poni tomorrow.

BETTER HORSEMEN

But apart from that, the teamwork and team discipline as polished as their excelle stick-work and, all in all, th

Captain of the Kenyan Polo Team, Digby Tatham Warter, bottom left, with teammates in an article in the build-up to their game against Rhodesia.

Left: Captain of the Kenyan Polo Team, Digby Tatham Warter.

Below: Digby (right) with teammates Francis Foster (left) and Mickey Buswell (centre) at the Nairobi Polo Tournament

> In 1959 a strong South African side toured Kenya, and altho' we came close, they won every time they played. Digby had actually played against a SA side in 1951, under Will Broadfoot.
>
> In 1960 a British Army side toured Kenya, and I never understood why they did not play against Kenya. However their final game was against a side selected by Col. Hal Swinburne Ward, the President of the KPA. Digby captained the winning side at Njoro, which included John Chart in place of Nick Allen.
>
> Over the years I knew Digby best on the Polo field, both with and against (on his wonderful mare 'Vision'). He was always the consummate Gentleman … a very good polo player, a good sport and an excellent on-field captain … it was my great privilege to have played under him, and I shall always remember him with pride and appreciation, for my many times on the polo field with Digby. He enjoyed the polo parties as much as anyone, and I shall always remember the term he used often, when wanting nothing more to do with some one … 'just hook it, will you!'[9]

The 'polo parties' described by Rooken-Smith may well be referred to as 'drinking sessions', which Digby and his fellow polo enthusiasts considered part and parcel of the sport. Digby's daughters recall with some amusement the many times they would sit with their mother waiting for Digby to finish so they could go home. But there would always be 'just one more', followed by another and another. Post-match merriment was always rowdy and the women and children thought it best to leave the men to it.

Eddie Fernandes, who played polo both against Digby and with him on the same side, remembers him 'completely controlling the games from the back'. Eddie first learned of Digby when he was farming in Gilgil (Eburru) when his own father was playing polo. 'We used to come across to Gilgil and he came across this side,' Eddie related, 'and we'd always play against Digby. We never played with him unfortunately,

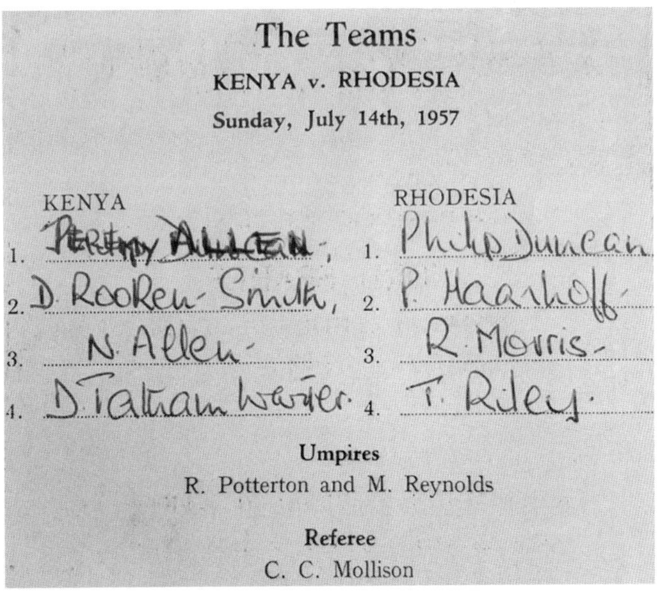

The Teams

KENYA v. RHODESIA

Sunday, July 14th, 1957

KENYA	RHODESIA
1. [illegible]	1. Philip Duncan
2. D. Rooken-Smith	2. P. Haarhoff
3. N. Allen	3. R. Morris
4. D. Tatham-Warter	4. T. Riley

Umpires
R. Potterton and M. Reynolds

Referee
C. C. Mollison

Kenya *v*. Rhodesia, 1957.

and of course we got to know his story—or a bit of it. A lot of people talked about him—it was only just after the war—and so we'd all heard a lot about Digby and Arnhem and so we had respect for him because we were all young chaps and just left school.'

After asserting how good a player Digby was, Eddie added:

> He trained his own horses and was a very good horseman and he taught all his daughters how to ride, and he did very well in the show-jumping world and he ended up here as the best player in the country.
>
> I didn't really know much about his farming world except we did go over there on occasion and see them and had a meal with Digby and Jane with my parents usually when there was a polo tournament going on over there. Then he left there and came to Nanyuki, this side, and bought a farm and started playing at the Nanyuki Polo Club and I thought now this is my chance to play with him. I got to play with him once and there is actually quite a story with it because we were playing at Gilgil in a tournament. There were four teams in it over three days and each team had to play the other three teams—an American tournament. We won our Friday match, won our Saturday match, and Sunday was going to be the big final between our team at Nanyuki and Digby's old team from over there at Gilgil. Our friends from West Kenya, they had other ideas and Saturday night someone gave Digby a Mickey Finn or something and God!—he was in no state to play good polo on Sunday![10]

'Well, we've lost this already,' Eddie had sighed as he turned to see Digby in full party mode necking another drink mere hours before the big game.[11]

> Anyway, it was great fun playing with him and he was a very good captain—very good, because we played with him quite a lot on the weekends and we knew him very well and he was great to play with. He was very commanding. Polo is like any of these games—there are four players on each side and he had a great way of handling those men. He usually played at Number 3 so he was at the back controlling the game and he was very clever at doing that and placing his men up front. He was very very good at that. He was a very good team leader that's for sure.[12]

Despite his popularity and large social acquaintances, Digby showed no interest in joining his old college's association formed by former students residing in Kenya.

One of them, Desmond Fitzgerald, related:

> Normally, at Wellington, you did not make friends outside your dormitory or house. So, although I was at Stocken's with Digby Tatham-Warter for a bit and actually sat next to him at the new boy's table in hall, we were never friends. However, this hardly explains why, from the day when we were first in Kenya together and for the next 40 years, he steadfastly ignored me, refused to acknowledge our close association at Wellington in 1930 and would never have anything to do with the Old Wellingtonian Society of East Africa, which Peter Vernon-Evans and I ran for about 20 years.[13]

Kenya line-up

Rooken-Smith J. Allen

Tatham-Water N. Allen

Above left: The Kenyan national Polo team, Kenya tour, Rhodesia 1957: Don Rooken-Smith, Jeremy Allen, Nick Allen, and Digby Tatham Warter.

Above right: The final match of the 1959 tour where both teams lined up together. *From left to right*: Don Rooken-Smith, Nick Allen, Digby, and Keith Frazer of South Africa.

Below: A polo team thought to consist of members of Digby's Mau Mounties during the rebellion, including John Chart (left). Digby stands second left.

Mau Mau Rebellion

The 1950s saw the culmination of growing tensions in Kenya. The Mau Mau Rebellion, also known as the Mau Mau Uprising, or Emergency, was the culminating response to native distain towards colonial rule. What had began as a movement by intellectual students had spawned into a militant group intent on forcing change through acts of violence towards colonials and their supporters.

A main grievance was the perceived 'theft' of land by white settlers who first began to arrive when the native population was estimated to have been in the region of 2,000,000. Much of the country at that time was unpopulated or rarely utilised, meaning the claim of 'theft' was deemed very questionable. The rapid increase of the native population did little to stem the issue. Today the population sits in the tens of millions.

Mau Mau activities increased through 1952. A number of murders were committed, including the brutal assassination of a key colonial officer—a chief—who supported British rule. The violence increased, and soon, small-scale attacks and sabotage against European properties were commonplace. Farms belonging to white residents were raided and burnt, their cattle slaughtered and the occupants maimed and murdered. Tensions reached boiling point after these brutal killings of white settlers. As the Mau Mau movement gathered momentum, so too did the determination of those in opposition. Many Kikuyu sided with the Kenyan Colonial government, but as the troubles increased, any Kikuyu not willing to take the oath of allegiance to the Mau Mau ran the risk of being killed or assaulted.

On 20 October 1952, the Kenyan government declared a state of emergency. The army were brought in and the Mau Mau fled into the bush. Troops, both British and African, were supplemented by the Kenyan Police, strengthened by the addition of men and women into the Kenyan Police Reserve. A number of ex-colonials eager to do their bit formed groups of irregular units. David Dobie, operating from Nairobi, would form 'Dobie Force', or 'D-Force', a special unit described as a 'vigilante group' that carried out covert operations and commando-style attacks against key Mau Mau targets. Officially, the Security Forces refused to acknowledge the existence of such groups, although they undoubtedly knew they existed and worked with them when carrying out these 'special operations'.

In November, Digby, at his own expense, formed and raised a mounted infantry unit whose main purpose would initially be to patrol the large ranches on the Laikipia Plateau north of the Aberdares, although this would later expand as the unit grew. In setting up his contingent, Digby handpicked serving members of the Kenya Regiment for his unit—men who could ride, shoot, and ideally provide their own horses. Digby would be known as 'The Galloping Major' and his unit, the 'Mau Mounties'. His unit was considered elite.

Initially, Digby selected eight men, and he put them through a rigorous yet somewhat condensed training regime. One of these men was Robert Foster, who noted:

> The original members of the 'Mounted Section' forgathered in the grounds of the Naivasha [Polo] Club in November 1952 and had extensive training under Digby.

> Initially there were eight of us. Digby Tatham-Warter, Tony Nuttall, Mike Pelly, Jossleyn Morean, Cyrus Morral, Micky Buswell, Francis Foster and Robert Foster. We arrived mostly with polo ponies, as these were by far the better trained, and an assortment of guns. Shot guns were favoured by the Fosters and Buswell, and most of us had side arms. We started off with our own saddles and tackle, but these were sent home later when we were kitted out properly, mainly with ex-World War II saddlery, equipment, tents etc. Also, friendly farmers loaned us young horses which we broke and trained, so, eventually, all our own horses were sent home.[14]

On 23 December, Digby considered them adequately trained and ready for the job-at-hand. The following morning, Christmas Eve, they set out on a 40-mile ride to a farm on the edge of the Aberdare Mountains. In the early hours of Christmas morning, they departed for the Nyeri Polo Club at Mweiga, which they reached at 8 p.m. after travelling down an old donkey track and negotiating 'miles and miles of bamboo'.[15]

Polo was very popular in Kenya and there were various clubs around the country. Digby did not let the emergency impact his love of the game and seized the chance to play whenever the opportunity presented itself. Throughout the fighting, he would often lead his party towards polo clubs to get his fill.

As time wore on, it became clear the troubles would be prolonged and the government stepped in to provide horses and equipment for units like Digby's Mau Mounties. What had started as an 'all-white force' evolved to include African NCOs and troopers. The influx of 'whites' into Digby's unit also continued and according to one member Digby took on 'some very colourful characters!'[16]

David Charters joined Digby's unit in 1954 after entering the local police station in Nakuru to offer his services to the Security Force. National service had at this point been enforced, and conscripts had no choice where they ended up. But the system allowed those who volunteered to pick their own unit, so according to Charters, 'anyone with half a brain would volunteer'.[17] When asked, Charters, having rode horses all his life, told the policeman he wished to join the mounted section. The policeman replied that the commanding officer of the mounted section in the Rift Valley was 'a difficult chap' and wasn't sure if he'd be willing to take him on. 'Well, let's give it a try, shall we?' Charters replied.[18]

The policeman picked up the phone and rang Digby to tell him that Charters desired to join his unit. 'All right, send Charters up on Friday night and I'll have a look at him,' was Digby's reply.[19]

That Friday, Charters met Digby at what he described as a 'beautiful farm in the middle of a forest on Eburru, overlooking a lake, Elmenteita'.

Charters noted:

> The night I arrived I was offered a drink… I as a young man was not a drinker at all but Digby gave me sherry and I drank sherry after sherry after sherry. When I went to bed I was feeling absolutely dreadful.[20]

Left: Digby, seen here during the Mau Mau Rebellion carrying his equipment. Tony Nuttall, an original member of the Mau Mounties and friend of the Tatham Warters, is smiling behind him.

Below: Downing tents and moving camp, from Digby's Mau Mau album.

During the troubles.

Charters was plastered and woke in the morning feeling extremely rough—a fact that could not have escaped Digby, who that morning informed Charters that they would be going to the camp to have a look at the horses at the other side of the lake to see if he was suitable. Charters—who was far too ill to eat—went out on an empty stomach feeling as sick as a dog. After showcasing his skills as a horseman, he was glad of an early night. At 4 a.m., however, he was abruptly woken by Digby who told him to get dressed. A 'gang' had been spotted in the forest and they were going on foot to have it out with them.

Charters accompanied Digby's party in their search. They travelled for seven hours straight, up and down heavily forested tracks to a height of 6,000–7,000 feet. 'It was a terrible initiation for me,' Charters related. 'I did not think I was going to survive!'[21]

The patrol, unable to locate the Mau Mau gang, returned to base whereupon Digby turned to Charters and told him, 'Okay, I'll take you on.'[22] With hindsight, Charters wondered if there was ever a gang in the first place.

When I informed David Charters of Digby's alleged methods of leadership during the Second World War, chiefly that some sources described him as being a strict disciplinarian, Charters did not recognise these traits at all:

> I am surprised that Digby was said to be a strict disciplinarian. I am aware of no such attitude. He was simply one of us trying to combat a movement we all detested and which we felt was a threat to the community. His personality was such that we would have been devastated to disappoint him—perhaps one can characterise this as a subtle form of discipline? [23]

The fear of disappointing Digby or letting him down was common among all who had dealings with him. Ironically, Charters's thoughts about not wanting to let down his commander are reminiscent of Digby's own feelings during the Arnhem operation where he was conscious that if there was any flaw in his performance he would be letting down his commander, John Frost.

Charters remembers that Digby 'directed us to areas he thought we could be useful but did not interfere with the way we went about our work.'[24] In not breathing down the neck of those under him, Digby's method of leadership in the rebellion bore distinct similarities to Frost's own technique.

Charters was acutely aware that he and the other member of Digby's contingent were 'thoroughly unskilled' in the art of war and 'a dreadful comparison to his paratroopers', yet not a word of criticism was directed towards any of them from Digby for the duration of the conflict. Those who served under him considered him an inspiring leader. Charters for one had cherishes memories 'of being privileged to be a part of Digby's Mounted section'.[25]

The section's accommodation was often tented and their patrols often consisted of just three or four troopers, often two 'whites' with a couple of 'Askaris'. Digby directed operations and nudged his men to places where he felt they were most needed or where he surmised Mau Mau fighters would potentially be located.

Right: Askaris move through the bush during the Mau Mau Rebellion. A number of African troops served in Digby's unit. (*Photo from Digby's personal photo album*)

Below: A patrol from Digby's Mau Mounties returns to base. (*Photo from Digby's personal album*)

Above: Digby's Mau Mounties Bill Hindley (left), David Charters (third left) and two askaris in the bush. (*Photo from Digby's personal album*)

Left: The Mau Mounties take a break from patrolling to refresh and water their horses. (*Photo from Digby's personal album*)

An Askari veteran of the Second World War poses with his rifle. His medals sit proudly on his chest. (*Photo from Digby's personal album*)

Notwithstanding the fighting, Digby always found the time for sport. 'We found time in the evenings in our tents when we had a "four" to play bridge,' remembered Charters, 'but Digby's game of choice was polo (he held a handicap of six) and insisted we learn and play when near a polo field.'[26]

Don Rooken-Smith recalls Digby and his 'Mau Mounties' played in a number of polo tournaments during the rebellion.[27]

'He was a superb horseman and one of the best polo players in Kenya,' related one of his men by the name of Ryan, 'He could, however, be a right-royal pain in the nether regions':

> When he had par-taken in well, if not wisely, of the juice of the barley from Scotland he could become quite belligerent and would offer to fight anyone to whom he felt antagonistic, usually with very little reason—on one occasion a whole section of the Kenya Regiment! However, he was a thoroughly decent man, and a good caring commander universally respected and admired, so he was seldom taken up on this.[28]

Ryan went on to narrate a story when Digby's unit was stationed at their HQ—a 43,000-acre cattle ranch at N'dabibi belonging to Gilbert Colville—where Jane was also staying. When not in the bush, Digby lived in one of the houses with Jane and the men in tents adjacent to the house.

It was in fact Ryan's first day with them, having transferred from another unit and he had been detailed to take rations with him to the HQ. These rations included whiskey, which Digby was soon into. Under the influence of his favourite tipple, Digby became 'a bit aggressive' so was carted off to bed by Jane.[29] The men then retired to their tents. 'That was not, unfortunately, the last we were to see or hear of him that evening', related Ryan:

> At about 2.00a.m he appeared outside our tent line and demanded that we all rise, get dressed and parade, preparatory to going out on patrol. This we duly did but, having inspected us, he dismissed us all and we returned to our still-warm sleeping bags.[30]

The men returned to their tents to sleep, but Digby had other ideas. An hour or so later, he was back, ordering them out for a second time to parade and prepare for a patrol. His men obliged and were dismissed once again, but at 4:30 a.m. when he came back for a third time they began to protest. Eventually, Jane came, berated him, and took him back inside.

In April 1954, British and African troops, with police and Kikuyu guards, launched a sweeping operation in the forests to flush out the Mau Mau. The State of Emergency would remain in place until 1960, but by all intents and purposes, the rebellion was over. Families that had been forced to leave their homes could now return.

Digby never spoke of his experiences to his wife or daughters, but his unit was said to have been involved in some serious fighting. A number of years after the event, Digby's son-in-law would overhear Digby reminiscing with a friend, speaking about the time he had 'got thirteen of them'.[31] It was a brutal conflict.

The uprising cost the lives of countless Mau Mau fighters. Government figures claim that 11,503 were killed, include more than 1,000 Mau Mau who were executed at the cessation of hostilities, but there is little doubt that the number was significantly higher. Colonial deaths amounted to thirty-two, though considerably more were wounded.

The Mau Mau had been defeated, but in the years that followed, the cause they had fought for would not simply vanish. Many still yearned for independence.

Digby's mounted patrol returns to camp.

The Mau Mounties 'In Masai Country'.

Left: This photo, from Digby's personal photo album, was taken during the Mau Mau Rebellion.

Below: A Mau Mau hut is put to the torch. (*Photo from Digby's personal album*)

17

Life in Kenya

Having perhaps implied how fierce Digby came across, I shall always remember when something amused or pleased him, how his face lit up and his smile became the warmest expression of joy and approval, which won one over immediately.[1]

Digby was in many ways a 'larger than life' character, outspoken and sometimes irascible, yet the most loyal of friends with the warmest of natures.[2]

In 1955, Lt-Gen. Sir Gerald Lathbury arrived in Kenya as the commander-in-chief (C-in-C) of East Africa Command to direct operations. Unlike Digby, and Frost and Dobie, and many others, Lathbury had remained in the army and his career had gone from strength to strength. After commanding the 3rd Para Brigade in Palestine and attending the Imperial Defence College in 1948, he had been appointed GOC of the 16th Airborne Division and the commandant of the Staff College in Camberley before his posting to Kenya.

Lathbury was not convinced that the troubles had ceased with the amnesty, and in December 1955, he wrote that there should be 'no illusions about the future. Mau Mau has not been cured; it has been suppressed. The thousands who have spent a long time in detention must have been embittered by it. Nationalism is still very potent.'[3]

Upon his arrival, Lathbury wasted no time in making contact with his old friends Digby and David Dobie. Lathbury's wife, Jean, and their young daughters, Virginia (Ginny) and Annabel, who had accompanied Lathbury to the country, were introduced to the Tatham Warter family. They became firm friends and the two families remain in close contact to this day.

Lathbury's daughter, Ginny, remembers their time spent with the Tatham Warters with great fondness:

> My first memories of Digby and his family were sometime in 1956 when we arrived in Nairobi. My father had been appointed C in C of the British troops out in Kenya and was in charge of ridding the country of the Mau Mau insurgents.

Soon after our arrival he took us all up to Eburru where Digby farmed pyrethrum and lived with Jane, Caroline and Jo who were very small at the time. I was just 11 and my sister Annabel 7. We all became tremendous friends. Mum immediately got on with Jane and she already knew Digby a little. I have the impression now that dad was very pleased to see Digby again and valued his vastly superior knowledge of Kenya and the tribes. Sadly he had a very demanding job so was unable to see as much of them as we all did.

I loved riding and was allowed to ride around the farm with Digby. He also asked me to ride a beautiful Welsh pony called The Blessing which he had schooled and wanted to show at the Royal Agricultural Show in Nairobi. I was lucky enough to win the championship show pony Class so felt very proud although I was only a passenger on a superbly schooled pony. Belinda, their youngest daughter yet to be born was a great horsewomen very much after Digby's heart.

This period was long before the safari days but we would all go camping to lovely places. One holiday I remember very well was to Lake Baringo where a family called Roberts lived and we camped near the house. It was completely wild in those days and full of birds and a good many crocodiles. Digby was leant a boat by David Roberts and taught us to water ski. I think Caroline must have been old enough too. Anyway there is no quicker way to learn than on a crocodile infested lake. I think Jane and mum were slightly horrified.[4]

'Virginia Lathbury on "Blessing" with Digby', Mitchell Park, 1956. Ginny would ride 'Blessing' to victory at the Royal Agricultural Show in Nairobi winning the championship show pony Class yet Ginny insisted she 'was only a passenger on a superbly schooled pony'.

Gerald Lathbury as the C-in-C in East Africa, 1955. Lathbury had a remarkable army career. As brigadier, he commanded the 1st Parachute Brigade at Arnhem

Gerald Lathbury and his family would remain in Kenya until 1957, at which point, they returned to England where he took the position of director-general of military training at the War Office.

European Holiday Trip

In April 1955, Digby and Jane set off by boat at Mombasa to embark on a lengthy five-month trip of a lifetime across Europe, visiting England, France, Belgium, Holland, and Germany where Digby collected his new car—a brand-new black Mercedes—the purchase having been arranged through David Dobie. In buying the vehicle, Digby was forced to swallow his pride—the car, of course, being of German manufacture.

Their trip was made all the better because Digby had arranged to meet with his old friend, Bill Wildeboer. The two men were very excited to see one and other again and for their respective wives to meet for the first time.

Of course, Jane had an amusing incident to relate to the Wildeboers that involved Digby who, while driving through the mountains in Switzerland, had completely ignored a set of traffic lights through a one-way zone, surmising nothing would be coming the other way. When a lorry came driving towards him, he was forced, after a few choice words towards the driver who refused to back up, not only to stop but to reverse the whole way back along the narrow road, swearing and cursing all the way. 'He thought he was the king of the world,' laughed Dicky when relating the story, 'but in Switzerland he found out he wasn't.'[5] It was one of the very rare occasions Digby had to cede defeat.

Digby and Jane stayed with the Wildeboers at their family home and were shown around 'some beautiful parts of Holland by Hilly', Bill's older daughter, which included a trip to Amsterdam where a most enjoyable time was had by all.[6] Nobody

Above: Digby stands with the Wildeboers outside their home at 32 Lunterseweg. Digby's Mercedes, picked up on the holiday, can be seen parked to the left. The secret dugout that Digby hid in when taken in by the Wildeboers was situated behind the small building on the right.

Below: 1955, Digby and Jane's European holiday. Digby (right) stands with the Wildeboers.

had any way of knowing at the time, but this would be the last time Digby would see Bill who passed away shortly afterwards.

Digby and Jane were able to visit many places of historical interest during their holiday and also spent time fishing. In Salza, France, Digby almost drowned after his waders filled with water and tipped him upside down. From the bank, Jane was horrified and could do nothing but watch him struggle but, thankfully, 'he somehow got himself out'.[7]

In England, they attended Ascot races and visited family and friends. Somewhat sheepishly, he showed them his brand-new German Mercedes and drove members of the family to a circus in Gloucester. His niece, Jane, found it 'lovely to travel in'.[8] She was, however, disappointed when Digby was presented with a copy of a highly detailed and meticulously researched family history going back many generations, that had been lovingly compiled by his father, Henry, some decades earlier. But Digby had no interest in such things and was not concerned about his family's ancestry. Upon opening the first page and taking a quick glance, he threw it down, calling it 'a waste of time'.[9] Digby's young niece felt differently and picked it up. To this day, this family history is still cherished by Jane who will ensure it is passed down to future generations.

Digby probably visited Ian Fleming, the family friend and James Bond author who he tended to visit each time he was in England. On another later visit to England, Digby would meet with Peter Scott—the son of the famous Antarctic explorer Robert Falcon Scott—who he met in the village of Slimbridge in Gloucestershire that is perhaps best known as the home of the Wildfowl and Wetland's Trust's Slimbridge Reserve that Peter Scott had established. Digby was visiting with his family at the time and Scott, upon hearing about Digby, would ask to meet him. They shared a mutual passion for wildlife and nature and would strike up a close friendship. Scott and his family would later visit the Tatham Warters in Kenya and would be thrilled when Digby arranged for some flamingos to be flown to England for him.

Digby also has a connection with Hollywood stars including Nigel Green whose many roles include the unforgettable Colour-Sergeant Bourne in the 1964 film *Zulu*.

Green was on the set of *Cowboys in Africa*—a TV series broadcast from 1967–68. The production team had rented land from Digby on which to camp, and Jane together with a friend and the girls were watching them lasso some animals. One man began to show off in front of Jane and her friend—both of whom were looking very glamorous—when an eland skewered him with its horns. With his stomach ripped open and his guts on the floor, the unfortunate man was whisked away in a helicopter to receive urgent medical care. It was a traumatic experience for the girls, but perhaps more so for the skewered individual who, much to the surprise of Jane and other witnesses, survived his horrific injuries.

Old comrades visited Digby too, including John Frost who fell in love with Kenya and wanted to move there to open a hotel. But it was not to be. Their families got on very well together, but as much as Frost's wife, Jean, loved Digby and Jane, she did not want to leave England to live there. In fact, she point-blank refused to entertain the idea, telling Frost that if he moved to Kenya he would be doing so by himself. Perhaps not surprisingly, Frost promptly dropped the idea.

Above: Digby with his new Mercedes, during his lengthy European holiday.

Digby and Jane at the Mercedes Museum in Germany during their 1955 European holiday. Digby collected his Mercedes during the trip, the purchase having been arranged by David Dobie.

Digby and Jane attend Ascot Races.

European holiday, 1955. Digby in Grossglockner—the highest mountain in Austria and the highest mountain in the Alps east of the Brenner Pass.

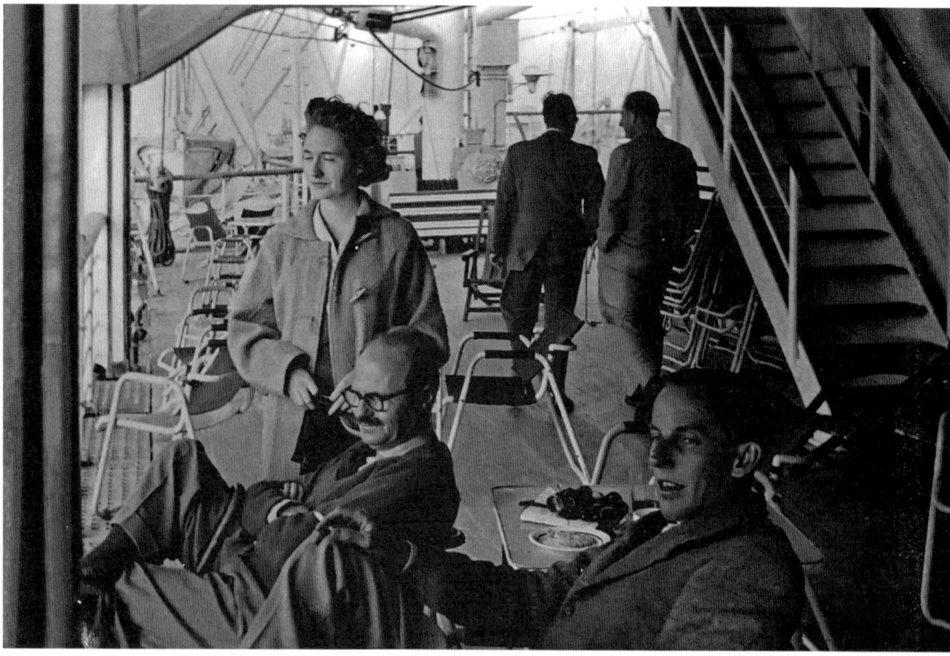

At sea, 1955.

Digby and Jane at sea during their 1955 European tour.

A page from one of Digby's albums of photographs taken during the filming of Cowboys in Africa.

Back in Kenya, Digby concentrated on his farming. He was very dynamic and pioneering crossing native cattle with Channel-island breeds, which resulted in fantastic livestock and dairy produce. The farming at Eburru was very difficult, but Digby worked extremely hard to make it work. 'It was rugged and harsh,' remembers his nephew, Anthony Barkas, 'but everything was immaculate. The cattle were top class…'[10]

Among Digby's successful endeavours was his ability to produce pyrethrum—an insecticide made from drying and crushing certain plants and mixing them with water. Today, it is one of the world's most common insecticides and thousands of tonnes are exported from Kenya each year.

Digby regularly trapped and disposed of the game that preyed on his calves and sheep. But there were other threats too. 'One Sunday out,' recalls Anthony Barkas, 'the house staff shrieking that a very large snake was trying to kill one of the dogs. We rushed out to find the most enormous cobra I have ever seen (about 10 feet long), stretched out in the flower border along the bottom of the wall with all the dogs barking like mad. Digby casually took out his revolver and shot it in the head.'[11]

Digby would have loved a son, but it was not to be. But Anthony visited regularly and spent a lot of time with him. In the evenings, they would go shooting to cull Impala—'Boy's Own time together' as Anthony recalled it. Both nephew and uncle enjoyed it immensely and Digby never missed an opportunity to remind Anthony that they shared almost identical initials—ADTW and ADTB.

Anthony remembers that Digby 'encouraged daring behaviour, but without taking silly risks':

> Not a very good example, but when I was at Pembroke House and staying with them at Eburru, they had a wonderful old Victorian pram, with big wheels and superbly sprung. This, I with my friends would ride from the top of the garden, over the terraces and at great speed towards the treacherously thorny hedge at the bottom of the garden. The object was to get to the hedge and pile out in time not to do oneself serious damage. Or, if the run was perfect, approach the wicket gate in the hedge and leap over it into the adjacent field. However this was usually occupied by a couple of very angry Jersey bulls, who wouldn't hesitate to run one through if they had the chance. We succeeded to get the bulls-eye once or twice, leapt the gate and avoided a serious goring.
>
> Inevitably there were some dreadful spills on the way down and a little damage done to the pram and the garden (and of course ourselves), but Digby never admonished us for such activity though of course Jane was concerned about the pram, her lovely garden and possibly any injuries to us.[12]

But the family's time at Eburru was not destined to last.

Kenya Gains Independence

The Mau Mau had been defeated, but Gerald Lathbury had grasped the fact that a fragile situation remained and he had predicted that the unrest would not simply vanish overnight. His suspicions had proven to be correct. Political wrangling had continued long after the emergency had ended, and in December 1963, Kenya gained its independence.

Independence brought huge change to the settler communities, most of whom sold their farms under a settlement scheme where owners were paid to relocate.

Of the five farms in the Eburru area, all but one sold up and moved. The Tatham Warters relocated to the Nanyuki area to buy Olechugu, a farm that was more profitable than Eburru and a place where Jane particularly would be much happier.

Digby had always been very regimental and well organised in all that he did. The farm was no different and was impeccably run with nothing but the highest standards being acceptable. The Olechugu house staff were issued with uniforms and were expected to perform duties to the best of their abilities at all times. He set rules which were not to be broken and he did not tolerate slackers.

For the children, life on the farm was great fun. Digby had taught them to ride from a very early age and they were very proficient. Each morning, the girls would lie in bed with Digby and Jane and have morning tea. Digby had always refused to sleep in the same bed as Jane, claiming she 'hogged the sheets'. Instead, two smaller beds were pushed together, yet on Digby's insistence, they still had to have their own separate sheets. In the mornings when they woke, the girls would make their way into their parents' bedroom. This often resulted in a scramble since only two of them could squeeze into Jane's bed, meaning whoever got there last had to climb in with Digby who invariably complained that they were wriggling about and moving too much.

Digby had a strict daily routine. After a cold bath, the essential cup of tea, and a full breakfast to start the day, he would carry out a tour of his land and put the staff to work, checking that everything was as it should be. Jane and the girls would accompany him on their horses and ponies. It was great family time.

Lunch was always at 1 p.m. sharp, with no exceptions. After lunch came his nap which lasted precisely one hour. For this, he usually napped on a mattress outside. After another brew, he would head back out to tend to the farm.

Following the Settlement Scheme and the moves that came with it, Digby and many of the other 'older fellows' practically ceased playing polo, 'and ponies became scarce'.[13] Digby began schooling his own ponies and thrust himself into show-jumping. He would also judge competitions and design the courses.

When inspecting the jumps prior to a tournament, Digby sometimes took Ducky with him. 'No one can have any idea how precious Ducky was,' related Digby's daughter, Caroline.[14] Indeed, no biography of Digby would be complete without mention of their beloved pet duck.

Having nudged its way into the Tatham Warter household, Ducky the little black river duck had become a big part of the family. Its gradual integration began when Ducky—who lived by the nearby river—began following the house staff into the Tatham Warter home when they were serving morning tea. Over time, Digby taught it to jump onto his bed to kiss him and Jane good morning with a peck on the lips.

Life in Kenya. Digby holds Binny on a baby elephant while Jo looks on.

Digby and Jane with some of the many dogs the family would own over the years. Photo taken at Eburru in 1962. Later that year, they would sell Eburru under the Settlement Scheme and relocate to Olechugu in Nanyuki.

There was the added incentive, for once Ducky had completed this courtesy, it was given its morning feed.

Soon, Ducky was accompanying the Tatham Warters everywhere they went, including trips out in the car, where it would sit on the back shelf behind the girls or any other passenger who happened to be in the vehicle. On longer journeys, the family would stop to give Ducky a water break.

Ducky went with Digby to his show-jumping events. On one occasion, Digby—who was kitted out in full attire with trademark bowler hat—was walking the course prior to the event. As Digby inspected the jumps, Ducky waddled along beside him, much to the amusement of the crowd. But when Ducky reached the water jump, all thought of following Digby around the course had suddenly vanished. Ducky jumped into the water and refused to budge. The crowd erupted with laughter while reporters snapped away with their cameras. The next day, the newspaper's front page featured Ducky in the water.

During another not-so-amusing tournament, the newspaper headline—A Major Disaster'—was published with a photo of Digby—who was commonly referred to as 'the major'—falling from his mount. It was a clever pun on words, but not a headline Digby was too fond of.

It was not just polo and show-jumping; Digby had very many interests in which he excelled. Anthony Barkas relates:

He was also a very keen fisherman and enjoyed sailing. He started deep sea fishing from his tiny sailing dinghy (Goldfish), which terrified the life out of me when we seemed to be miles off shore and the wind began to get up. And even more scary when he jumped overboard and swam about in the deep blue. The rest of us were quite happy to sit out the heat on the boat and hope that a large dark form (a shark) didn't suddenly appear! He then graduated to a lovely small fishing boat called Sea Hawk. It was only about 20 feet long, with a pair of outboard motors, a cockpit with a big fighting chair and a retractable awning, a cabin that slept two, a front deck and a roof where half the team sunbathed and kept lookout for the approaching bill fish. Every year he and Jane would cruise up and down the Kenya coast, primarily after a monster Marlin or Sailfish, as well as the myriad of other species in the sea. They would go with friends and stay with other friends or in pubs along the way—and indulge in wonderful seafood every night.

Also every year my family and the Tatham Warters would rent a house along the coast during the Christmas holiday and fish from Sea Hawk for hours and hours. We used to leave at dawn and flog the waters all day and return almost at dusk, completely exhausted, but ready to repeat the performance the next day. And this often went on for almost the whole three weeks' holiday. Our success rate was not high. Then one day in 1964, we hooked and landed a monster Sailfish—which still stands today as the All Africa Record, at over 164lbs. Much to both Jane and Digby's chagrin, my father was in the fighting chair at the time and so the record fell to him. But their pride was in the little boat that Digby had lovingly captained to achieve that record. Sea Hawk gave them both huge pleasure for many years. Digby also had a bit of success fishing on Lake Rudolf (now Lake Turkana) and he managed to haul a golden Nile Perch weighing in at 144lbs! Again the biggest of its kind ever caught. A truly spectacular fish.[15]

Digby and his friend, John Dugmore, display the results of their fishing endeavours. Digby holds his 30-lb Nile perch and John his smaller yet still impressive 18-lb catch.

Above: Posing with a catch.

Left: 'Digby with his 155lb Marlin'. Digby was very fond of the sea. He loved sailing and fishing.

Digby enjoying Kenyan wildlife

Digby, Jane, and Binny with a selection of animals on their farm.

Goldfish—the Tatham Warter family boat. Digby never had a son, but he spent a lot of time with his nephews and sons of his friends, teaching them to ride and hunt among other things.

Ginny (Lathbury) also has fond memories of her time with Digby:

> When we left Kenya after dad had successfully dealt with the Mau Mau there was a gap of a few years before I went back by myself and stayed with all our friends and got myself a job in Nairobi. By this time the land around Eburru was to be taken over by the Africans as Independence had just taken place whilst I was there in 1963. The TW family moved up to Nanyuki to the farm.
>
> Digby started his Safari business with Hilary Hook around this time but we had many wonderful private safaris with Digby's little igloo tents and some fairly primitive shower arrangements. Superb food around the camp fire and animals everywhere. This was long before all the smart lodges and endless bus loads of people.
>
> I was always in awe of Digby but loved him and all his family more than I can say. It is a well known fact that he could be difficult but I was lucky and rarely saw anything other than his charming side. Our mother Jean used to make him very cross with her unpunctuality and always wanting him to stop the vehicle for her to take another photograph! Really they were the greatest friends.[16]

They were indeed great friends. The Tatham Warters and the Lathburys would remain in close contact throughout their lives, and the daughters of Digby and Gerald remain in touch today. Together with the daughters of John Frost, Tony Hibbert, and Bill Wildeboer, they have spent time together at Arnhem and Oosterbeek during anniversary events.

Digby set up the Young Riders Pony Club where parents would leave their children with him for five to seven days, during which time he would teach them to ride, jump, and perform certain skills. Digby was very patient with the children and always succeeded in getting the best out of them. They were terrified of him and found him intimidating, but, like with his girls and indeed his soldiers, their biggest fear was that they would let him down or disappoint him. One pupil remembers how Digby used to stand with his riding crop and bowler hat starring intently at the rider. It was a very intimidating sight.

Binny was a daredevil, a very talented and fearless rider, and the daughter whose character closely resembled that of her father. At the Young Riders Pony Club when a student was having some difficulty on a feisty pony that refused to jump, Digby instructed Binny to mount it, bring it under control, and make the jump. If she could not do it, nobody could. But it was no use. The pony still would not jump. Digby then took his whip to the pony but on going to give it a hard whack, he missed and hit Binny instead. Binny winced in pain and the young club members looked on in horror, but the silence was quickly broken when Digby erupted into laughter. At this point, everyone else who moments before had been horrified, burst out laughing too, all except Binny.

On the final 'graduation', the children would put on a horseshow for the parents where trophies and awards were presented to them. The entire thing was meticulously planned and very popular. Many people in Kenya owe much to Digby for their ability to ride.

Belinda, Digby, and Caroline.

Digby and Ferro. 'K.B.H.S One Day Event at Molo, September 1962'.

The intimidating Digby Tatham Warter speaks to his pupils. Many testify to his domineering presence, which they found utterly terrifying. Notwithstanding, he was a fantastic teacher and always got the best out of the children.

Digby, Caroline, and Belinda.

Left: 'Kitale Show—1962'. Digby and Ferrow.

Below: Digby and Ferro, one day event, Molo. 1962.

Binny and Bess at the Pony Club Inter-Branch competition where she won The Murray Cup.

When his team of girls, 'The Warter Babies', won a first-class prize, Digby sent them to collect their cup dressed in loin cloth nappies with dummies in their mouths. Digby found it hilarious, but the officials and others in attendance were not very impressed. 'Digby egged us on like he always did,' Gilly, one of the girls, remarked.[17]

On another occasion, he had them collect their prize dressed as school children. 'What are they playing at?' was one comment that was heard from the shocked audience. 'This is not dignified' was another.[18]

It was, of course, all Digby's idea.

Digby judged horse shows and built the cross-country courses at Mount Kenya, which were always formidable with difficult obstacles. Digby sometimes had Eddie Fernandes and Rose Caldwell constructing and checking the courses. Digby would then walk round himself and, if need be, have them tweaked. Digby always said he did not want to scare the horses but he wanted to 'scare the shit out of the riders'.[19] With that in mind, the courses were constructed to be physically achievable for a horse yet difficult for the rider—and scary.

Digby and two of his 'Warter Babies', Heather (left) and Rose (right), accept an award in Nairobi.

Digby looks on as his daughter, Binny, receives The Murray Cup at the 'Pony Club Inter-Branch at Kenyatta', 1967.

Above left and above right: Digby grins for the camera.

Digby during a race event.

Safari

For all his seemingly ferocious manner and imperial background, Tatham-Warter was forty years ahead of his time in introducing the concept of safaris in which the game was shot by camera rather than gun.[20]

An ardent naturalist, he organised and accompanied high-level safaris and was an originator of the photographic safari.[21]

Digby set up his safari business after moving to Olechugu in conjunction with Hilary Hook. 'This turned out to be a most successful venture,' Anthony Barkas recalls. 'Olechugu Safaris very quickly acquired an excellent reputation. Rich and smart clients from England and America especially, became attracted to his luxurious safari outfit. As one might expect, everything was immaculate and catered for all the needs of such clients.'[22]

Hook was a retired colonel and veteran of the Second World War who had also played his part in stemming the Mau Mau rebellion. His army career, like Digby's, had begun on the unattached list destined for the Indian Army. He would later gain prominence in the BBC documentary *Home from the Hill*, broadcast in the 1980s, where he discussed his thoughts on colonialism and the end of the British Empire together with polo, pig-sticking, and elephant hunting.

Hook had lived on the slopes of Mount Kenya about forty-five minutes from Digby at Eburru where they used to socialise and shoot snipe together. To promote their new venture, the ex-army officers had flyers printed and circulated in England. The punters were soon arriving.

Digby and Hook spent days out on reconnaissance, travelling hundreds of miles into Uganda, among other places, at a time when crossing borders was non-problematic. Over time, clients would fly from all over the world to go on their safaris and many would return again and again. The fact that Digby and Hook were both real characters was part of the attraction. 'Many of their wealthy clients were to remark on their culture shock on first meeting these two eccentric English gentlemen and the subsequent experiences through which they were led—which was, of course, precisely what they were paying for,' wrote one newspaper.[23]

Anthony Barkas remembers 'the campsite routine on safari was run by Jane in an orderly, military fashion, with all the appropriate touches':

> Everything had to be perfect. And with Digby's experience in the bush, the game finding and viewing was to be conducted with professionalism, comfort, a good narrative and to achieve huge satisfaction and pleasure of the guests. Between them, Digby and Jane ran wonderful safaris and they were regularly invited to stay with their clients (most of whom became friends) back in the UK or USA, so they made every effort to accept when they were in country.[24]

Digby would run his safaris for twenty years, in which time he forged a worldwide reputation for his organisation and professionalism. In the early days, safari was seen

On safari.

A day in the life...

Digby with Jean Lathbury 'in camp'. Digby and his family spent much time with the Lathbury's and often took Jean and her daughters on safari. Gerald Lathbury, Digby's former brigadier, was usually too busy in his job to accompany them.

Vaso Nyiro River, Samburu, April 1971. Digby with Hilary Hook. Together the two men ran very successful safaris.

Above: The Tatham Warters dine together on safari.

Right: Digby and Jane Tatham Warter with camera in hand. Jane was an exceptional photographer. This was something that used to grate Digby because she was better than him. Note Digby's signature without hyphen.

Digby and Jane on safari. Jane and another photographer take simultaneous shots.

very much as 'a macho thing', but Digby and Hilary Hook broke the mould by taking their wives on safari with them. Jane did the cooking and photographed the wildlife. Digby also fancied himself as a photographer but, much to his chagrin, Jane's photos were always better.

Anthony Barkas related that Digby 'had foresight and planned everything carefully', while Sue Brown, who as a young lady helped Digby on safari during the school holidays when Jane stayed home with the girls, related that everything was meticulously planned and Digby's clients were full of praise for his organisational skills.[25] Ginny (Lathbury) called his methods of organisation 'regimental'.[26]

Digby often led family safaris where, according to his nephew, he 'was clearly the man in charge and everyone would look to him to provide the leadership and excitement':

> As children we would occasionally be terrified by the night noises outside our tents and the following morning we would be scolded by Digby and told 'not to be so stupid, there is nothing to be afraid of…' In those days whenever we saw elephant, they were either threatening to charge and we had to be ready to drive off in a great rush and hope not to stall the car, or if the elephants and other game were too far away, Digby would bang the sides of the car to see how they would react—hoping that we would be in for a little exciting charge and chase! (Nowadays, things are very different and we sit motionless in the car with elephants all around us.)[27]

Sue Brown described a similar story of Digby 'rounding up' elephants in his jeep with them going absolutely berserk.

On one safari as they set up camp for the night, Digby and companions discovered a fresh buffalo carcass and a pride of lions nearby. So during the night, when needing to visit the latrine, Jane was understandably worried about walking out to it in the pitch darkness. For reassurance, she asked Digby to accompany her, but he flatly refused, telling her there was nothing to worry about.

Another time, Digby climbed down from high ground to stand face to face with a hippo to see how it would react. Perhaps unsurprisingly, Jane refused the offer to join him.

Whether facing bullets in war, facing down wild animals, swimming in shark-infested waters, jet-skiing among crocodiles, or any number of other questionable acts, Digby, throughout his life, did not show any sign of fear or lack of nerves. Yet there was one thing that put the absolute fear of God into him. That thing was bees. Digby was petrified of bees. In fact, it is fair to say that he had a phobia of them and he would go crazy if he saw one. On one occasion, when a bee got into his car, he immediately slammed on the brakes and jumped out cursing.

The Tatham Warters kept many animals over the years, some more ferocious than others. The most savage of them all was undoubtedly their banded mongoose, Bandy, who seemed to have a constant thirst for blood. Bandy 'bit at the drop of a hat' and did not think twice about attacking anyone she came into contact with, particularly the children who had a habit of teasing her, although she needed no provocation.[28] One particularly vicious attack came as the family were about to depart on a car journey. Bandy had wanted to accompany them and trotted over to the car with the intention of jumping in. As Caroline went to pick her up, Bandy sunk her teeth into her hand and refused to let go. Caroline still carries the scars. 'She was a tyrant,' she recalls.[29]

Jane was the only person Bandy never attacked. When Jane was ill in bed, Bandy would climb in alongside to protect her and let no one near.

The family used to get their own back on Bandy by playing tricks on her, usually with precautions firmly in place. Bandy adored eggs and used to devour them as a special treat. A favourite trick was to put Bandy in a room and put a ping pong ball in there. In an excited state, and thinking she had been issued a treat, Bandy would attempt to eat it and go mad with rage when realising she had been duped.

Manx, a second mongoose with a small section of tail, would often accompany the family on their safaris. Manx, described as 'sweet as anything', was starkly different to the psychotic Bandy.

The family had many horses and ponies, and Digby always kept dogs, including in later life two Australian Blue Healers as company and as guard dogs. They would bite anyone entering Digby's workshop as he carried out his carpentry. Another dog, an Australian Cattle Dog by the name of Buckaroo, would terrorise everyone, much to the amusement of Digby who found this hilarious and thought Buckaroo had a great sense of humour. 'Despite this he was a lovely dog and seriously not a problem,' explained Caroline, 'unless he was sitting by Daddy's feet.'[30]

To Digby and Hook, reconnaissance was always an ongoing process as they strove to find as yet unexplored territory. They enjoyed nothing more than locating un-walked areas, planning their routes, and finding new locations where they could camp with their clients.

Bandy, the blood-thirsty and ferocious mongoose, emerges from her doll house. Bandy liked nothing more than to sink her teeth into the Tatham Warters. Only Jane was immune to its aggressive tendencies. Photo dated between August 1960 and October 1961.

Digby explored inaccessible and previously uninhabited places where none had gone before, but this brought frustrations. Digby was expert at finding the perfect locations for setting up his camps. He made his own river crossings, too, but the problem was that by doing so he made a previously inaccessible place accessible, and wherever he went, others followed. Essentially he was putting in the time and effort, only for others to use his trails, camp in his established areas, and make use of his crossing points. He was understandably very protective of his camps.

Once Digby had located a spot for a camp and set his campsite, he considered it his, and nobody else could use it. More than once he had to force out other parties using his spots as he returned to them. Ulf Aschan, an associate of Digby, explained that he would yell 'Find your own fucking camp!' to those he found using his locations.[31] At Digby's Camp on the Masai Mara Game Reserve, one unfortunate young member of a safari team, an Englishman, put up a camp. 'This man had a reputation,' Ulf explained, 'and was not one to play around with, but Digby chased him out faster than you can say "Get the fuck out of my camp", or words to that effect.'[32]

Ulf almost camped there himself but was warned off by a local Masai (or Maasai) who told him in no uncertain terms that it was 'Digby's Camp'.[33]

The Masai Mara is now a huge national game reserve in Narok and Trans Mara Counties, contiguous with the Serengeti National Parks in Tanzania, bordering Kenya. In those days, there was no problem crossing borders and no permission was required, but the Mesai Mara did not then have the influx of tourists it has today. Today, Digby's camp site, as described by Ulf, is an extremely popular tourist camp called

Rekero Camp, situated on the Mesai Mara Game Reserve and is considered a 'perfect location' and 'prime position'.[34]

Despite its modern name, older generations still refer to it as 'Digby's camp'. Digby's river crossing is still there today.

The family went on a safari in the Masai Mara, which was totally uninhabited at the time. Live chickens were taken with them in baskets which the girls befriended and gave names to. One by one they began to disappear. When the girls asked where they had gone, Jane told them that hyenas had taken them. This was considered kinder than telling them they had just eaten the chicken for lunch.

But conditions were not always so harsh. Digby's safaris were hugely impressive affairs. Provisions included portable showers and, of course, plenty of alcohol. Sue Brown remembers that being on safari with Digby was like a week-long house party. The booze flowed.

Locations required travel by aeroplane and when Digby's daughter, Binny, became a pilot, she suggested to her father that he should book the company she worked for and she should fly for him. Digby asked why he would do this since he already had arrangements in place with a different company. Binny responded 'Because I am your daughter!' which Digby accepted as a good enough reason to give it a try.[35] But things did not go according to plan. On her first outing—to collect Digby and his group from a Masai Mara safari and return them to Nairobi—she could not get the nose of the aeroplane open to store the luggage. Binny struggled while the party and a very angry Digby looked on, but it was no use. 'That's it, I'm never using you again!' he yelled.[36]

Binny's blushes were spared when a guest managed to get the nose open. Digby had soon calmed down and, of course, he did use her again.

Digby had a number of sayings for which he was well-known. 'Just hook it will you!' was but one of them, usually shouted when he wanted nothing more to do with someone. 'Assumption is the mother of all fuck ups' was another (perhaps he had the Arnhem operation in mind!) and was usually said after somebody had used the words 'I assume' in their sentence. When a friend or family member had been hard done to or was upset over something or other, he would tell them to 'put it by', meaning for them to forget it and move on.

In a similar vein to 'just hook it will you!', 'Never darken my doorstep again!' was invariably yelled at some unfortunate guest who had stepped out of line, although on one occasion at least, he came up with a more creative way to be rid of someone.

After a party at his home, Digby rose in the morning to find his garden strewn with debris from the previous night's antics. As the house staff tidied the rubbish, Digby had caught a glimpse of Paddy Gratten, the chairman of the Mount Kenya Horse Show Society—of which Digby was president and Jo the secretary—stirring in the corner having slept there all night. 'And you can fuck off with the rest of the garbage!' was Digby's only comment.[37]

Such quips were a regular occurrence, but Digby loved nothing more than when someone gave it back. Certainly he formed a better opinion of those who did so.

Food was a 'means to an end' for Digby. He ate because he had to, not because he particularly enjoyed it. An exception was what he referred to as 'Officers' Mess Potatoes'. Essentially, they were very burnt potatoes that held little appeal to anyone but him.

Copter pilot tells f crash

By JOHN PLATTER

TECHNICAL fault which resulted in a helicopter crashing on Mt. Kenya last Wednesday has still not been traced, the pilot of the craft, Ian Adam (pictured right) said in Nairobi yesterday.

ith a passenger, Ian Sutherland, he suddenly found he had lost all power when on a reconaissance flight over the mountain looking for suitable landing spots. He was about 200 ft. above the ground and rapidly descended to 100 ft. "the dead man's curve."

knew we were going in. I remained tied in my seat. Ian Sutherland was flung clear, and just as well because he'd have hit a rock otherwise. Our tail snapped and one of our rotor blades ended up 200 yards from the crash," he said.

New craft

either of them was seriously injured and shortly afterwards some picnickers, Mr. and Mrs. Digby Tatham Warter, picked them up and took them to Nanyuki Hospital.

ast night a new Hughes 300 was due to be offloaded at Embakasi. It will be assembled today, ready to continue demonstrations Trans World Helicopters are doing for the Kenya Police, who are interested in using more helicopters especially for rescue work.

This was Ian Adam's first crash. As chief pilot for Trans World Helicopters, he has 8,500 flying hours "under his belt." He has just completed a tour in Tanzania, where similar demonstrations have been conducted on behalf of the Government and other agencies.

After stopping for a coffee at the Mt. Kenya Safari Club they flew up the mountain on Wednesday morning to try to find a suitable landing base for future mountain rescue operations.

On Thursday and Friday they were going to take the police up. He had not found one — he wanted at least a 50 ft. clearing. It was at about 12,000 ft. that he saw the road and spotted the Tatham Warters picnicking and came down to see if the road would be suitable.

"I don't know what happened. We just lost power and we're trying to find the cause now," he said.

How does he feel about using the same craft on the same flight next week?.

Potential

"Oh, fine. I'm not bothered at all. There would be no progress if people just turned away after every crash and gave up. That's why it's so important for us to get a new helicopter here fast.

"We came down on Wednesday, we've got a new machine here by Sunday, which is not bad going."

He said there was a tremendous potential for the use of helicopters in East Africa.

Trans World are working in conjunction with Wilken Air Services in the craft's distribution here.

Left: Newspaper article describes that a technical problem resulted in the helicopter losing its power. Digby and Jane had been having a picnic when they saw it coming down and later took the occupants to hospital.

Below: 'Helicopter crash. Mt. Kenya. 1966'. In 1966, Digby and Jane observed a helicopter coming down. Racing to the scene, they rescued the occupants and took them to hospital. The incident featured in local newspapers. Digby's vehicle can be seen in the background.

Digby and Jane with daughter Binny. When Binny became a pilot, she flew Digby and his guests to their safaris and collected them although her first effort did not go entirely according to plan.

Digby in camp.

Above: Digby sits at the head of his table with guests on safari.

Left: Digby relaxes with his pipe wearing what appears to be a Life Guards cap that presumably belonged to a friend.

At a large family gathering at Binny's home, the lady doing the cooking was given instructions from Digby for 'Officers' Mess potatoes' which he swore were the best. Everyone eagerly awaited the results. 'Now this is how you should produce your roast potatoes,' Digby proudly said as they were brought out. Everyone hated them but Digby refused to accept their opinion and insisted they were delicious.

Digby's daughters shared many stories of their childhood, many of which had amusing undertones, although they could not have been amusing at the time. Caroline, for example, related a time when they were sitting in a Nairobi restaurant during a family meal where bread rolls were served with the starters. On taking a bite, Digby called over a member of the establishment's staff to complain about the hardness of his roll. In response, the staff member politely pointed out that that they were meant to be hard, but this did not satisfy Digby who then proceeded to illustrate just how hard the roll was by hitting the man on the head with it to prove his point. 'Feel that!' he told the waiter as he struck him. As fellow diners looked on, Caroline wished the world would swallow her up.

Above left: Digby and Jane.

Above right: Digby sits on a camel in a photograph dated 1976.

Above left: Digby and Jane.

Above right: Digby (left) with Jane (third left) with friends.

Above,opposite and next page: Digby, an avid reader (and huge fan of *Fawlty Towers*).

FAWLTY TOWERS

Fanny Hill

18

A Bridge Too Far

Digby Tatham-Warter was famously depicted in A Bridge Too Far, *Richard Attenborough's 1977 film of the Allied defeat at Arnhem in 1944, as a crazed toff leading a bayonet charge sporting an old bowler hat and a tattered umbrella. But his character, personality and achievements were substantially greater than suggested by the film's rather trite cameo.*[1]

In 1974, Cornelius Ryan's classic book *A Bridge Too Far* was released to critical acclaim. It brought Operation Market Garden to the attention of a wider public. Film rights were soon sold, and production began on the spectacularly large movie. It was released in 1977 and boasted a huge ensemble cast of established international actors. Many key individuals were portrayed in the film, but there were a number of notable omissions, including Maj. Allison Digby Tatham Warter.

John Frost, who was an on-set advisor, was portrayed on screen by actor Anthony Hopkins. Later, when he released his book *A Drop Too Many*, Frost voiced his disappointment and regret that Digby had been omitted from the movie, not least because he considered Digby's role in the battle of 'crucial importance'.[2] Despite his disappointment, Frost understood the production was on such a scale that it was impossible to include everyone, and that 'with the time and space available, one had to accept that there would have to be a certain amount of cannibalization of characters to overcome the problem...'[3]

By 'cannibalism', Frost was referring to the fictional character of Maj. Harry Carlyle (played by Christopher Good) who shared distinct similarities to Digby, including the carrying of an umbrella. Frost, however, felt strongly that the character did not do Digby justice and that the part was 'slurred so as to be of little account'.[4]

Frost gave much credit to Digby for his actions during the battle, and he was disappointed that Digby did not get a more prominent part, particularly since it was he who had commanded the battalion in the latter stages of the battle when all hope had gone:

Frost noted:

> When there were no buildings left to go to, our men dug weapons pits in the back gardens of the ruined houses, but it was difficult to site these with effective fields of fire. Digby Tatham-Warter and other officers were tireless in directing men to new positions as and when they could. They kept control right to the end so that, when the wounded were evacuated and despite the resultant improvement in the enemy's position, our men could go on fighting til they were physically overwhelmed.[5]

The character of Maj. Carlyle also bears similarities to Lt Grayburn whose actions were amalgamated with Digby's through Carlyle on screen. Perhaps this is why the character was given a fictional name.

One scene in the movie sees Maj. Carlyle casually stroll on to the bridge, umbrella in hand, with the intention of crossing it with his men. In reality, it was Lt Grayburn who attempted this. He was hit in the shoulder by gunfire during the attempt, just like Carlyle in the film, who is seen staggering away holding his upper arm after coming under fire from the pillbox. Like Grayburn, Maj. Carlyle dies of wounds in the film.

That the character largely based on him was seen to die on screen was the cause of some frustration for Digby. 'His' onscreen death would often be brought up by people he spoke to. Graham Toze describing the recollection of his NCO father, Graham Toze, who at the time was based in Kenya, explained that, 'After "refreshments" and a sly mention of the film the Major was known to stand up, vigorously pat himself down and bark "Do I look bloody dead to you!"'[6]

A stand-out scene that has gone down in movie history encapsulates a typical form of humour for which Brits are known. It begins with Frost and Carlyle on the roof of a house overlooking the bridge. A German officer with a white flag cautiously approaches from the other side. As he reaches within shouting distance, Carlyle calls out that he is far enough, and asks him what he wants. The German then shouts up that his general says there is no point to continue fighting and that they are willing to discuss surrender. Frost then instructs Carlyle to 'tell him to go to hell' which in turn prompts Carlyle to shout down to the German: 'We haven't the proper facilities to take you all prisoner. Sorry'.[7, 8]

At this point, the bemused German lowers his white flag, turns about, and walks away, thoroughly confused. The scene was extremely well received by the British public, but did not sit well with those who had actually been there. John Frost thought it was absurd and hated it. On set, Frost had rejected the original version of the scene which he thought was even worse. Although not happy with the final cut, Frost felt it was an improvement on what it was going to be prior to his intervention that had forced a rewrite.

In the original script, the scene played out differently, although still strikingly similar in spirit. Frost and the German general were to meet under the bridge to discuss terms for surrender. Frost was then to tell the general that he could not accept their surrender due to a lack of facilities. Frost called it 'laughable' and had protested, successfully, for it to be changed. The scene that featured in the movie was the compromise, but Frost could not hide his disappointment. 'In the end,' he related, 'a very unsatisfactory and most unrealistic compromise was reached in that one of "my" officers sarcastically informed the Germans that "we" could not accept their surrender.'[9]

Ironically, this scene, referred to by Frost as 'very unsatisfactory', has arguably become the most iconic and memorable scene of the entire movie and is now considered a classic piece of cinema history. Many viewers incorrectly assume the scene in the film is based on what actually happened in the battle. During the real battle, the Germans did in fact offer Frost the chance to surrender. This occurred on Tuesday 19 September, and he did—albeit indirectly—tell Germans to 'go to hell'.

The German commander, Maj.-Gen. Heinz Harmel, the GOC of the 10th SS Panzer Division, was very frustrated and in his own words 'beginning to feel damn foolish' at failing to crush British paratroopers at the bridge.[10] He was acutely aware they were low on both ammunition and supplies and that their numbers had been reduced heavily in the fighting. With tanks and artillery at his disposal, Harmel was determined to blow every building held by the paratroopers to bits, but before he did so, he felt compelled 'in view of the fight they were putting up' to offer them the chance to surrender before the destruction began.[11]

L/Sgt Stan Halliwell was an engineer with the 1st Parachute Squadron who had been captured earlier in the day while attempting to reach an isolated section of the defence with some extra ammunition. As a POW, he was instructed by Harmel's staff

Heinz Harmel, *c.* 1944, who commanded the SS Division Frundsberg during Operation Market Garden.

to return to the British lines under an escort and flag of truce to offer the British the opportunity to surrender, to assert to his comrades that they had no hope of being reinforced, and that further resistance was futile. Halliwell was to speak with Frost and arrange for him to meet Harmel under the bridge to discuss the terms. His captors told him in no uncertain terms that he was expected to act like a gentleman and return to them with Frost's answer.

It soon became evident that the paratroopers were in no mood to accept a truce. As Halliwell made his way towards them with his German escorts, fire erupted from the British positions. Halliwell charged forward ahead of his captors to identify himself, shouting to his comrades that he was British and for them to stop firing, which they did. With battle raging on all sides, Halliwell then spent the next ten minutes frantically running round the British perimeter looking for John Frost to relay the message. Eventually, after what seemed like an eternity, Halliwell found him and put the German proposal of surrender forward. At this point Frost instructed Halliwell to 'tell them to go to hell'. When Halliwell asked if he really had to go back just to tell them that, Frost said it was up to him. There was no question of the outcome. With a grin, Halliwell dashed off to take up a position alongside his mates.[12]

It was not just Frost who was unhappy with the movie's surrender scene. Several years after the film's release, John Frost met with Maj.-Gen. Harmel, his opposite number who had made the offer of surrender. Harmel was quick to tell Frost that he found the scene 'quite ridiculous'.[13]

But the scene was not quite as far-fetched as one may think. On the 19th in the Van Limburg School after a fierce firefight, Capt. Eric Mackay of the Royal Engineers received an offer of surrender when a German, waving a 'not very white hanky tied to a rifle' emerged from a building further up the road. 'He shouted surrender,' Mackay recalled. 'I promptly assumed that they wanted to surrender, but perhaps they meant us.'[14] Regardless, Mackay yelled back for the German to 'get the hell out of here'. His men joined in: 'Bugger off! Go back and fight it out, you bastards,' shouted one. [15]

The German got the idea, turned about, and walked away having failed to achieve whatever it was he had set out to do. Perhaps Mackay's experience was the inspiration behind the scene that made the final cut of the film, either that or it was simply a coincidence that something very similar had in fact taken place.

In reference to the huge cast of established actors, Brigadier Hackett would call the film 'A Star too Many'. It was not popular with all veterans, and Digby utterly detested it.

The Kenyan premiere of *A Bridge Too Far* was held at a Nairobi cinema with Digby in attendance as a VIP. By the time it had finished, he had had a few drinks and made an emotional speech on the stage that left those in attendance under no illusion as to how he felt about it.

Digby felt the film could never compare to the real thing, and what he perceived as American bias did not sit well with him at all. As a rule, he hated stateside movies, referring to them as 'American crap'.

The movie caused a number of myths to develop regarding Digby and his brolly. In the film, just before his death, Maj. Carlyle responds to John Frost who asks, 'why on earth do you always carry that bloody umbrella?'[16]

'Bad memory,' replied Carlyle. 'Always forgot the password. I knew no Jerry would ever carry one. I had to prove I was an Englishman.'[17]

This is another great scene, but in reality Digby carried the umbrella as a form of identification, nothing more nothing less. He also did not take it with him into the battle, as the film depicts. It was found in one of the houses by the bridge.[18] He did not have trouble remembering passwords. A creative script-writer is the source of this untruth.

Prior to the release of the book and later the film, Digby's immediate family, friends, and acquaintances were already aware that he had carried an umbrella in the battle. They cannot recall quite how they came to hear about it—it was just one of those things that everyone knew—but are certain they did not hear of it from Digby himself.

When the movie was released, Digby's niece asked why he carried it and Digby replied that it was for identification purposes but did not elaborate. The obvious advantage of carrying it is that he became instantly recognisable to his men who, in the chaos of battle may be attempting to seek out their leader among other paratroopers who looked distinctly similar at a glance. Additionally, the chances of him being mistaken for a German were significantly reduced. After all, 'only a bloody fool of any Englishman would carry an umbrella into battle.'[19]

19

Later Life

Digby was the figure—at home and wherever he was, around whom everything seemed to revolve. He was big. He had a presence. He had a deep, authoritative voice and commanding manner. Things usually were done his way. He could be gruff, demanding and expected everything to be of the highest standard. He didn't take fools kindly and was not afraid to tell people what he thought of them or their performance. He set the standards himself and was meticulous in achieving and maintaining them.[1]

Digby was admired by all ranks of the Parachute Regiment and received frequent visits from those stationed in Kenya. He was also a regular VIP attendee at their various events. It was through the paras that Digby came to be diagnosed with emphysema. During the late 1970s/early 1980s, one of their doctors had heard his awful cough; when he enquired, Digby told him he had had it for a long time. The doctor insisted he had it looked at. Digby took the advice and visited his doctor who confirmed the ailment.

The main cause of emphysema—a lung disease causing shortness of breath—is smoking. Digby had been a heavy smoker for decades, since his early army days at the very least. When Digby was advised that his life would be prolonged if he stopped smoking, he quit cigarettes immediately. But he continued to smoke his pipe and cigars, which he considered to be less harmful. The condition worsened, and after a severe coughing fit at Heathrow Airport—where he smashed his pipe on the floor in frustration, covering one or two onlookers with ash in the process—he vowed to never smoke again. Digby was true to his word, but the damage was already done, although it would be another decade before he would succumb to the illness.

As a result of his health, Digby sold his farm and purchased a lovely home on Simba Lane in Nanyuki, popularly known as Lunatic Lane because of an old legend alleging that every full moon, a naked man would gallop up and down the road on his horse. It was around this time that Digby stopped his safaris. In 1983, his daughter, Jo, and her husband, Danny, took over the business.

Among the officers of the Parachute Regiment to visit Digby was Col. Herbert 'H' Jones, the commanding officer of 2 Para, who became a great friend of Digby and Jane.

On their first meeting, H paid an impromptu visit to Digby's home on Simba Lane by helicopter. Digby and Jane were entertaining guests and playing backgammon on the veranda when the buzz of the helicopter caught their ears. It came into view and landed on their lawn. Emerging in full uniform from the helicopter was H who approached Digby and saluted him. He then turned to Jane and saluted her, too, before introducing himself. He won a lot of respect for that. Digby's son-in-law, Danny McCallum, who was present at the time, admired the way H conducted himself and 'was impressed with H as an officer and as a gentleman'.

The Tatham Warters took to H immediately, and Jane became very fond of him, despite the fact that the back draft from the helicopter had blown her beloved creepers from their roof as it landed.

H often visited the Tatham Warters and lunched with them regularly, and Digby was invited to all the regimental cocktail parties and other events at Nanyuki Sports Club—their military camp. They had dinner parties in the mess, and on one occasion, during the 'Beating of Retreat', H presented him with a bronze sculpture of a paratrooper in full regalia. On another occasion, in the 2 Para officers' mess at the Nanyuki Show Ground, a local ranch manager (who will remain nameless) who had allowed them to use his land for live field firing was invited to the dinner, but failed to arrive at the allotted time. The man was telephoned to ensure he was aware of the occasion. He said he was and informed them he would be arriving imminently. H

Statuette presented to Digby by Col. H. Jones of the 2nd Battalion Parachute Regiment shortly before the Falklands War. The inscription reads:

TO MAJOR A D TATHAM-WARTER D.S.O.
O.C. A COY 2 PARA
1944
FROM ALL RANKS 2 PARA
1981

told the mess sergeant to delay the dinner until the man arrived, but an hour passed without him showing, so H gave permission for dinner to be served. Just as everyone settled at the table, the guest arrived in a drunken state.

In describing the event, H's biographer, John Wilsey, wrote:

> The Mess was about to have a problem on its hands more serious than a delayed dinner and an inebriated guest. The ranch manager, sitting one away from H and now drinking copiously, began loudly and roundly to condemn the Parachute Regiment in general, and 2 Para in particular, citing the Regiment's youth, lack of tradition, and alleged poor record of behaviour and bad field discipline when camped on his ranch. This was fighting talk, touching, as it did, on sensitive areas. It was no comfort to the officers present that he had abused the hospitality of other regiments in similar terms over the years.[2]

H and the paratroopers showed remarkable restraint in not reacting to the man's provocations. The trouble continued into the next morning, at which time Digby—who was absolutely furious at the man's behaviour—got involved and sorted the issue immediately. The man responsible, who had a deep respect for Digby, apologised to him profusely before apologising to the regiment.

H felt the incident was worthy enough to be recorded in his official post-exercise report dated 20 January 1982:

> His behaviour that night became worse and worse; the other guests left at approx 0200, but Mr X did not leave until 0400, at which time he was escorted from the Mess by me. His behaviour ... can only be described as intolerable. Unfortunately he continued to drink elsewhere in Nanyuki, and telephoned me at about 10-00 hours to continue his threats and abuse. At this point Major (Retd) Tatham-Warter (an ex member of 2 Para) intervened, and as a result Mr X calmed down, and apologised verbally, and later in writing.[3]

The incident soon became hot topic throughout the ex-pat community and also in the Muthaiga Club where 'more enticing flesh' had been added 'to the bones of the story'.[4]

The 2nd Parachute Battalion left Kenya shortly after.

That the troublesome individual respected Digby in such a way is no surprise when one considers just how much of an impact he had with those who knew him. Anthony Barkas remembers that 'Digby was very much the hero of so many people. In particular all those in the Parachute Regiment, who held him in such high esteem—from his exploits in the war':

> Those battalions which used to train in Kenya around the Nanyuki area would flock to his house and attend with awe. He was always loud, held very strong views and latterly was not afraid to share them, normally emphasised with an ample distribution of the F-word! They all loved him for it. I am reminded that in February 1982, whilst his battalion of Parachutists was training in Kenya, Lt. Col. H Jones and

> his RHQ team came to dinner with Jane and Digby. I was there too. They departed shortly afterwards to the Falklands Islands.[5]

Digby's language and demeanour went down a treat with the paratroopers, just as it had all those years back during his years of service.

An episode in the 1960s following Kenyan Independence was one such incident typical of the man. Incidents such as this would horrify officials but delight the men. With independence came huge change, and at the time, it was said that 'a series of British Defence Advisers would be told by the High Commissioner to "Look after Tatham-Warter"'.[6]

The story goes:

> One such officer, late of Digby's regiment, was not entirely clear what this meant but soon found out when, after an introductory 'I suppose you're another bloody mealy-mouthed Diplomat', his charge took him off to a Beating of Retreat by a British Infantry Battalion. As Tatham-Warter, a VIP guest, stood for 'Sunset' his trousers slowly, and in time with the lowering Standards, dropped to his ankles. He later claimed 'loss of weight' although the cognoscenti had their doubts.[7]

Digby was a product of his time, and those I spoke with made no secret of the fact that he could be rather bolshie and eccentric. Indeed, this heightened his popularity within the Parachute Regiment.

He was never afraid to speak his mind. He was also stern, chauvinistic, undiplomatic, and politically incorrect. Never was this more evident than when he entered the Muthaiga Club and made for his friend Ulf Aschan who was dining with a man described as 'a great snob', who was half English, half Persian, and 'filthy rich'. 'Mixing with the natives now are we Ulf?' Digby uttered as he walked past their table.[8]

Those who knew Digby sometimes wondered whether he acted as he did for his own amusement or whether it was simply a part of his character and came naturally. Perhaps it was both.

Ulf Aschan told me: 'Digby was incredibly outspoken, and more often than not was extremely rude to people' and thought 'his lovely wife was very tolerant'.[9]

'Digby absolutely adored mum,' related Caroline, 'and rightly so. She was very good to him.'[10]

Jane, over the years would tell Digby when he was out of line. This often came in the morning after a night of drinking, but he had no problem in apologising if he felt it was warranted.

Not everyone appreciated Digby's language or manner, and there were certainly times when his behaviour got him in trouble. A court case in 1986 caused ructions throughout Kenyan colonial society after Digby, during a birthday party, insulted another attendee to such a degree that the person—a Danish man—felt the need to take the matter further. 'Don't be mean, you fucking Dane!' Digby had yelled to the guest, not once but twice, 'illustrating the fact that it was meant.'[11]

Digby sits with his family. Jane looks down on her husband (top right). Daughter Caroline sits bottom left below Jo, with Binny sitting bottom right.

'Naturally,' the solicitor's letter explained, 'our client was horrified to hear this, it vexed him that he should be abused in this fashion.'[12] Taking legal advice, Digby settled the matter with a financial pay-off to avoid a court case.

'Of course the austere exterior belied a self-mocking humour and a fundamentally anti-establishment attitude (it never, after all, had been *his* establishment),' noted an article published upon his death:

> Those picked, after rigorous selection, to join Digby's very tight circle of friends were allowed a clear view of a complex character shaped by a background which today would simply not be understood. Within this exclusive circle, mostly though not entirely from his own world, he was a warm, loveable man who would do anything for his friends and a wonderful even notorious host.[13]

Rose Caldwell told me: 'He wasn't afraid of telling people what he thought—usually after he'd had a drink. But we got used to it'. While Michael Kingscote during the first few seconds of our first conversation admitted: 'He was exceedingly arrogant and upset a lot of people'.[14, 15]

'He was a tough bugger. He didn't tolerate incompetence,' related son-in-law Danny McCallum.[16]

He enjoyed a drink but there was never a danger of it becoming an addiction. Digby was far too strong for that to ever happen. He implemented a rule upon himself whereby he could not touch alcohol before 7 p.m. Granted, he often watched the clock for the hand to strike seven, but he stuck to it rigidly.

When he was out of line, Digby would always apologise. That is why the incident with 'The Dane' was silly. By all accounts, 'The Dane' was a very serious man with no sense of humour, whereas Digby had an enormous sense of humour and the language he used was perfectly normal to him.

The ten-week Falklands conflict began on 2 April 1982 after Argentinian soldiers invaded and occupied the Falkland Islands in the South Atlantic. 2 Para, having recently completed their training in Kenya, were among those mobilised to deal with the threat.

With his old battalion, with H at the helm, destined to play a major part in the battles that would inevitably come, Digby keenly followed the BBC news to keep up to date with the war's progress.

Towards the end of May, Digby's daughter, Jo, was in the North Kenyan Polo Club when Digby and Jane entered the premises. Jo could tell immediately that something was wrong. Indeed, it was. Jane, by now in floods of tears, broke the news to Jo that H had been killed. Jane would later say that she had had a terrible feeling that H would not survive the war. Digby, close to tears himself, was devastated at the loss of H who was awarded a posthumous VC for his actions.

His VC citation reads:

> On 28th May 1982 Lieutenant Colonel Jones was commanding 2nd Battalion The Parachute Regiment on operations on the Falkland Islands. The Battalion was ordered to attack enemy positions in and around the settlements of Darwin and Goose Green. During the attack against an enemy who was well dug in with mutually supporting positions sited in depth, the Battalion was held up just South of Darwin by a particularly well-prepared and resilient enemy position of at least eleven trenches on an important ridge. A number of casualties were received. In order to read the battle fully and to ensure that the momentum of his attack was not lost, Colonel Jones took forward his reconnaissance party to the foot of a re-entrant which a section of his Battalion had just secured. Despite persistent, heavy and accurate fire the reconnaissance party gained the top of the re-entrant, at approximately the same height as the enemy positions. From here Colonel Jones encouraged the direction of his Battalion mortar fire, in an effort to neutralise the enemy positions.
>
> However, these had been well prepared and continued to pour effective fire onto the Battalion advance, which, by now held up for over an hour and under increasingly heavy artillery fire, was in danger of faltering. In his effort to gain a good viewpoint, Colonel Jones was now at the very front of his Battalion. It was clear to him that desperate measures were needed in order to overcome the enemy position and rekindle the attack, and that unless these measures were taken promptly the Battalion would sustain increasing casualties and the attack perhaps even fail. It was time for personal leadership and action. Colonel Jones immediately seized a sub-machine gun, and, calling on those around him and with total disregard for his own safety, charged the

> nearest enemy position. This action exposed him to fire from a number of trenches. As he charged up a short slope at the enemy position he was seen to fall and roll backward downhill. He immediately picked himself up, and again charged the enemy trench, firing his sub-machine gun and seemingly oblivious to the intense fire directed at him. He was hit by fire from another trench which he outflanked, and fell dying only a few feet from the enemy he had assaulted. A short time later a company of the Battalion attacked the enemy, who quickly surrendered. The display of courage by Colonel Jones had completely undermined their will to fight further.
>
> Thereafter the momentum of the attack was rapidly regained, Darwin and Goose Green were liberated, and the Battalion released the local inhabitants unharmed and forced the surrender of some 1,200 of the enemy.
>
> The achievements of 2nd Battalion The Parachute Regiment at Darwin and Goose Green set the tone for the subsequent land victory on the Falklands. The British achieved such a moral superiority over the enemy in this first battle that, despite the advantages of numbers and selection of battle-ground, the Argentinian troops never thereafter doubted either the superior fighting qualities of the British troops, nor their own inevitable defeat.
>
> This was an action of the utmost gallantry by a Commanding Officer whose dashing leadership and courage throughout the battle were an inspiration to all about him.[17]

One, who was very familiar with the bond between Digby and H, who knew of H's awe of Digby's actions at Arnhem, told me: 'I wouldn't be at all surprised if Col. H was thinking of Digby as he charged with his men to his death and subsequent award of the VC'.[18]

Following her husband's death, H's wife, Sarah, often stayed with Jane and Digby at their home in Nanyuki.

In addition to emphysema, Digby also contracted Dupuytren's Contracture, which caused his little fingers and those next to them to curl up on both hands, yet this did not prevent him from becoming an excellent self-taught carpenter, a hobby he took up in later life. Digby made many fantastic objects and imported mahogany and walnut to make, among other things, jewellery boxes and sewing boxes of all sizes. His pieces were intricately detailed and immaculately finished with the most beautiful veneer patterns.

Ginny (Lathbury) saw Digby for the last time in 1984:

> The last time I saw Digby and Jane was when my husband and I went out for a holiday in 1984. Digby was beginning to suffer from his emphysema but they took us on a wonderful safari. I felt then that I would like to remember Kenya as it was then although I dearly wish I could go back once more. The last time I saw Jane was here [England] about 7 or 8 years ago.
>
> Neither Dad, Digby, or their great friend David Dobie who also ended up in Kenya ever talked of their exploits and bravery at Arnhem which I think was the only time they were together during the Second World War. So many brave soldiers were the same and we have, even as families, had to read about their bravery in the history books or news clippings. Of course there is the famous film A Bridge too Far which I remember going to the Premiere with my father who spoke little even then![19]

Above: On safari: the Tatham Warters, Lathburys, and friends.

Right: 'England April–June 1972 at Bures Manor and Saville Gardens with the Lathburys'. In the bottom photo, Digby stands with Jean Lathbury, Gerald Lathbury's wife.

1984 Pegasus Reunion

In 1984, Tony Hibbert in conjunction with some Dutch friends began to plan an Operation Pegasus reunion to coincide with the forty-year anniversary of Operation Market Garden. Great efforts were made to invite all those involved in the operation, including members of the Dutch Underground and those civilians who had assisted in their hour of need. Hibbert wrote to Digby and invited him to attend. Digby accepted.

In preparation, Bill Wildeboer's daughter, Hilly, did sterling work in tracking down the lady who had originally taken pity on Digby and Tony Frank and hid them in her barn. Despite being extremely old and frail, she was very excited to attend the reunion and be reunited with Digby. When they met, Digby kissed her and they embraced with tears in their eyes.

When word got round that the reunion was to take place, many of the Dutch Underground immediately thought of Digby, including 'Flip', who wrote to Digby to see if he was going. In response, Digby in a letter dated 17 July 1984, wrote:

Dear Flip,

Thank you very much for your letter. Yes, of course I remember you very well and have happy memories of our bicycle rides together. I know that I would not have survived very long without your able guiding and help. I also remember well the incident of the German car in the ditch. They were quite grateful to us, I think. At any rate they were not particularly unpleasant to us!

It is very good to hear from you after all these years. Probably the last time we met was in 1955 or '56 when my wife and I stayed with the Wildeboers for the last time.

It is very good of you to ask me to the reunion party at Renkum. I had heard from Tony Hibbert about it and have written to him to say that if we come to England as planned we will definitely be at Arnhem for that weekend. I am sure that Dicky Wildeboer must have put you in touch with Wilhelm Dollerman from whom you got my address. However I have now heard from them both and have written to ask if Jane and I can stay with one or both of them over that weekend.

The reunion party at Renkum will be far the most important part of the celebrations for me. In fact the main reason for coming to Arnhem that weekend is for the opportunity to see some of my old friends again. But, it will be sad to be in Ede without Bill, especially, and Tony and Barend.

Although I expect there will have been much change in the countryside it would be fun, if there is time, to see the woods where we assembled for the escape and the route we took down to the river. Perhaps Marten could show me the way again.

It is very good news that old Mrs. Wildeboer is still alive and well. I don't know why but I thought she had died a few years ago. It will be very good to see her again.

I need not tell you how much I am looking forward to being with you all again after all these years.

Yours ever
'Peter'[20]

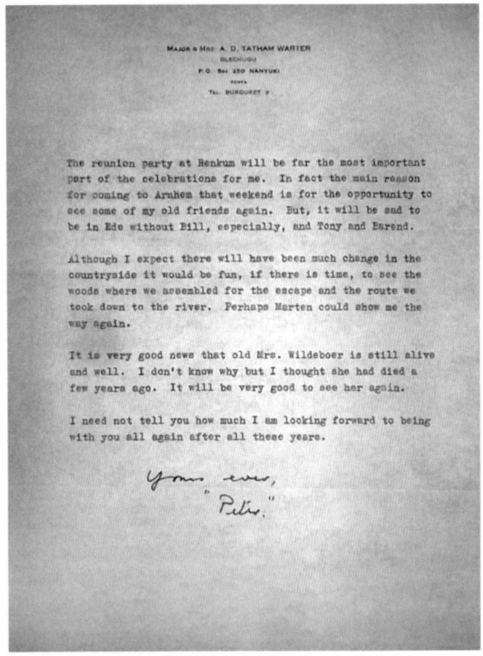

MAJOR & MRS A. D. TATHAM WARTER
OLECHUGU
P.O. Box 250 NANYUKI
KENYA
TEL. BURGURET 9

The reunion party at Renkum will be far the most important part of the celebrations for me. In fact the main reason for coming to Arnhem that weekend is for the opportunity to see some of my old friends again. But, it will be sad to be in Ede without Bill, especially, and Tony and Barend.

Although I expect there will have been much change in the countryside it would be fun, if there is time, to see the woods where we assembled for the escape and the route we took down to the river. Perhaps Marten could show me the way again.

It is very good news that old Mrs. Wildeboer is still alive and well. I don't know why but I thought she had died a few years ago. It will be very good to see her again.

I need not tell you how much I am looking forward to being with you all again after all these years.

Yours ever,
"Peter."

In reply to a letter from 'Flip' regarding the 1984 Pegasus Reunion, Digby signed off his letter as 'Peter'—the alias used during his time with the resistance after the failure of Operation Market Garden. (*Rene Kemna*)

Digby and Jane travelled to Holland with their youngest daughter, Binny, and her German husband, Friedrich. They took Digby and Jane in their own car—a Mercedes, complete with German number plate. Digby directed them straight to 32 Lunterseweg—the home of the Wildeboers, only to find they no longer lived there. He tracked down Dicky at her workplace who explained she now lived in her own home as did Hilly, while their mother resided in a retirement home. Digby arranged to stay with Dicky for the duration of his stay.

At Dicky's home, the night before the commemorations, a large number of the Dutch Resistance turned up to see Digby again. Digby had brought with him some Famous Grouse whisky which was soon cracked open together with vast amounts of strong spirits that his old friends had brought with them. 'Well, they never stopped talking and drinking,' remembers Dicky who had to turf them out in the early hours of the morning, telling them to sober up quickly for the event.[21] Despite his night's heavy drinking, Digby was up and ready the following morning. After questioning Dicky as to why the house staff had been up in the early hours vacuuming the house, he was informed by Dicky that they did not have house staff and that Dicky herself had been cleaning the house ready for the morning's guests.

Dicky drove Digby and Jane to a ceremony after he had refused to travel in Binny's Mercedes. He did not think it was the day to travel in such a car.

Later that day, Digby and his family attended the Operation Pegasus reunion-party—the event he had most been looking forward to. He was intensely nervous. Many of the evaders were in attendance, as were numerous members of the Dutch Underground. The absence of Bill left a large hole, but his wife, Hil, was there. It was the first time they had met since Bill had died, and almost thirty years had past since then. Neither could speak the other's language, but that did not matter. They sat together with tears in their eyes, staring intently at each other while holding hands and hugging. At that moment, nobody else mattered and it was as if they were the only two people in the room. Jane and Dicky stood watching them. 'It was as if we didn't exist,' Dicky explained.[22]

Dicky relates that her mother was not an affectionate lady and throughout her life did not show any affection towards her. Such was the strong bond forged between her and Digby, she was full of affection for him. This is something that Dicky has often thought about and it was a strange feeling to see her mother act in such a way. Dicky admits to a pang of jealousy because she herself was never on the receiving end of such warmth.

Tonny de Nooy had also died, but his wife attended the reunion on his behalf and presented Digby with a large bunch of flowers which completely stunned him. He could not grasp why a women would give a man flowers and enquired to Dicky who told him it was because she had heard all about him from Tonny and wanted to show her respect and admiration.

After some persuasion from Hibbert, Digby gave a talk on Operation Pegasus and reminisced fondly with those in attendance on what they had pulled off. Digby called the reunion a 'great occasion'.[23]

Today, the bond between the Tatham Warters and the Wildeboers remains strong and both families continue to meet whenever they can. In September 2019, when Digby's daughter, Caroline, and her husband, Tim, travelled to Holland to attend the seventy-fifth anniversary commemorations, they stayed with Dicky. Dicky also used to visit Digby's mother, Kathleen, in England where she was introduced to many friends of the Tatham Warter family, with Kathleen telling them proudly of the link between the two families and how they had taken care of her son during the war. She was particularly pleased when Digby's mother introduced her to the world-renowned champion jockey Lester Piggott, who was a good friend of the family. Dicky also went to Kenya and went on safari with the family, later turning down an offer by the Tatham Warters to move there (owing to it being a completely different lifestyle to all that she knew).

Digby's Memoirs

Digby's memoirs came about through the determination of his family, particularly his daughter, Jo, who urged him to put his experiences in the war down on paper. 'I can't do it,' he had told his family, but with pressure from Jo, who offered to assist by writing it as he used a Dictaphone to speak into, the book was duly published.[24] The title *Dutch Courage & 'Pegasus'* details Digby's time with the resistance and leaves the reader in no doubt as to his admiration of the Dutch residents who took the fight to the Germans when under occupation. Digby had decided he did not want to speak too much about the battle itself as 'much had been said of that already'.[25]

It is unfortunate that Digby did not go into any detail of the battle. He had already written official reports and did not see the point in adding more. Nevertheless, Digby's memoir holds much historical importance and Jo deserves a lot of credit for her efforts to see it printed, particularly since Digby's health by this time was rapidly declining.

As his health deteriorated, Digby's morning ritual of a cold bath stopped and he began to live life differently. His family knew something was seriously wrong when he went off his whisky. Eventually he was confined to his bed and hooked up to oxygen to help him breath. At the point of his death on 21 March 1993, Digby had been bedridden for over a year, during which time he had lost all interest in life. It was a sad end for a man whose life had been so full of energy and excitement.

Shortly before Digby's death, there was potential for a family rift to be healed, yet sadly the matter would remain unresolved.

As a child, Ann Meredith had been integrated into the Tatham Warter household when Digby himself was just a boy. This had occurred shortly after the death of Digby's father. Ann had faced a number of difficulties when joining the family, but Digby had looked out for her and had been very kind when others were not. Digby and his siblings were told that Ann was the daughter of the sister of one of their staff, and it was under this guise that she had entered the household. But Digby's parents were holding a great secret, a secret that had been accidently and unexpectedly revealed during the Second World War.

Back in 1921 during a trip to Kenya to visit her family, Digby's mother, Kathleen, had met Jim Elkington, a charming ladies man who had been instantly taken in by Kathleen's beauty and lively nature. Jim was married, but this had not stopped his roving eye. Kathleen had spent some time with Jim on his farm in Elementeita where they hunted and got to know each other intimately, free from the presence of his wife who was staying elsewhere.

In early 1922, Kathleen became aware that she was pregnant with Jim's baby. To hide this from her husband, she had remained in Kenya for the majority of her pregnancy before returning to England a week or two before giving birth. But she had not returned home. Instead, she had given birth in secret at a nursing home in Reigate so nobody would know. Her plan, however, had been foiled by the matron who knew her husband's aunt who recognised Kathleen and informed Henry.

Henry was a kind good-hearted man, adored by everybody who knew him. Kathleen certainly adored him, but he was much older, and whether or not she loved him in that way is something the family is not too sure about. Nevertheless, despite her infidelity, she was devoted to her husband and spurned Jim's efforts for her to leave Henry.

Quite how Henry reacted when informed of Ann's birth is not known, but life had continued as normal and they remained together as a married couple. Ann was brought up not too far from the Tatham Warter household by the sister of one of their nannies in what Ann described as 'one of the most loving households one could ever have wanted'.[26]

Under this guise, Ann would occasionally visit the Tatham Warter's and play with the children. Henry was happy to spend time with her, too.

Ann was very much 'one of the family', explained a niece, who added that 'Henry was very sweet to her'.[27] She was brought up to call her biological mother 'Aunty Kay'.

An article written by Tom Lawrence, based on his conversations with Ann, relates:

> Ann can just remember going to the Tatham-Warter house and being put on a pony and led by Kathleen's husband Henry, whom she remembers as a very kind man. One can surmise he was very accepting of her, but was bound by the social conformities

> of the time. At some point Henry and Jim met at a race meeting to discuss the matter of Ann, however what was discussed and concluded nobody knows.[28]

During a further visit to Kenya in 1924, Kathleen once again spent time with Jim, and at this point, he begged her to leave Henry and marry him, but Kathleen steadfastly refused. Following Henry's passing in 1928, she would remain his widow until her own death in 1978, aged ninety-seven. By this time, Jim was already dead, having passed away before Henry.

In January 1925, while Kathleen was in Kenya resisting Jim's attempts to persuade her to leave her husband, Jim had shot himself in the head while 'cleaning his gun'. He died five days later from his injuries, aged forty-nine. A court of enquiry was held in which Kathleen was cleared of any misdemeanour, and she returned to England.

Tom Lawrence, who has researched Jim's story extensively, wrote:

> Needless to say tongues have wagged as to the nature of his death, and whether it was suicide or not. As sure as night follows day various theories have been put forward, each to its own end, and now, some eighty [*sic*] years later it is difficult to ascertain which is true and which is not.
>
> It was said that Jim had give up drinking at this stage, as he had, in the past, drunk rather heavily, and that 'Mrs Jim' had sent him down a case of whiskey, which he took to in the disappointment of Kathleen's refusal to leave her husband, and this lead to him shooting himself in a state of alcoholically aggravated depression. Equally, it could have been an accident, drink induced or otherwise—he was a man familiar with guns, but even then it is remarkable how many people who do know what they are doing with guns have accidentally shot themselves.[29]

Ann's true identity was finally revealed during the Second World War after she had applied to join MI5, the headquarters for which was located near to where she lived.

When summoned from the waiting room for her initial interview, the director addressed Ann as Miss Warter to which Ann replied that she was in fact Miss Meredith. In response, the director handed Ann a copy of her birth records that they had pulled as a part of their checks. They stated her name was Ann Meredith-Warter. From this, the cat was out of the bag.

Ann went on to serve with MI5 but her exploits are largely unknown. She was bound by the Official Secrets Act that all MI5 employees had to sign, and Ann took this very seriously. The only clue came many years later when the members of a group she was with were asked whether any of them had ever been under fire and Ann—then an old lady—reply that she had.

The news that they were in fact brother and sister did nothing to dampen Digby and Ann's close relationship. Ann used to visit Digby in Kenya, and *vice versa*, and Ann enjoyed a lovely relationship with Digby's wife, Jane, and the girls.

Sadly things took a turn for the worse when Ann began to show an interest in finding out about her biological father. Digby was not happy, and when she made it known that she wanted to write a book about him, Digby washed his hands of her completely.

Shortly before Digby's death when bedridden and gravely ill, Ann travelled to Kenya to see him in the hope of putting the past behind them. But when Ann arrived at the house, Digby told Jane and his daughters he did not wish to see her and asserted that they were not to let her into his room. Digby died soon after, without reconciliation with his sister.

In the past, Digby had expressed an interest in being buried at sea, but he also loved the Africa landscape. When the time came, he was cremated and his ashes buried. Digby's final resting place sits on the top of a hill, known now as 'Digby's Hill', on what is now the Lewa Wildlife Conservancy. The views from his grave are stunning. 'Digby's Camp', which he used when on safari, is located on the conservancy nearby.

In January 2020, I visited Lewa Downs with Dave and Sue Brown and Digby's daughters, Caroline and Jo. As we stood by Digby's graveside, Sue, who had been a great friend of Digby, wondered what he would have thought of the charred remnants of a recent campfire that was almost touching his solitary grave on the hill. These remains—evidently from a recent safari group having a few drinks around the campfire—were the only sign of life in the area. The spot was peaceful and secluded. 'I can't work out whether Digby would have welcomed them or told them to "Fuck off,"' Sue retorted.[30]

Digby was a unique character whose life was full of enjoyment and he lived it to the full. Following his death, *The Times* published an obituary which included the following words:

> Gerald Lathbury, Tatham-Warter's brigade commander, once remarked (probably in Digby's defence): 'But every battalion needs a Digby!' Officers, and many of the men, serving to-day would almost certainly agree.
>
> He left an indelible stamp on everything he did and had only one standard in all things—his own.[31]

EIIR

The British High Commissioner
is commanded by Her Majesty to invite

Major & Mrs A.D. Tatham Warter

to a Reception to be given by
The Queen and The Duke of Edinburgh
at the Hotel Intercontinental, Nairobi
on Sunday, 13th November, 1983 at 6 p.m.

A reply is requested to:
British High Commission
Telephone: Nairobi 335944 Ext. 219

Dress: Lounge Suit

Invitation from the British high commissioner.

APPENDIX I

Digby Tatham Warter's Report

The following report was written by Digby while hiding in Van den Ven's orchard with his adjutant Capt. Tony Frank:

The GOC Airborne Division,

Sir,

This is an accurate account, as far as I can give it, of the battle at the bridge. I have written it in case no one else is able to give you the story.

I have the honour to be Sir,

Your obedient servant

AD Tatham Warter, Major

D-DAY. The Bn was dropped accurately in first class conditions. There was no opposition on dropping zone. 'A Coy captured six vehicles and 12 POW's at rendezvous. Moved off at approximately 1530 hrs with 'A' leading. After approximately two miles 'A' Coy held up by machine gun and mortar fire. A left flanking movement by one platoon drove enemy back and we were able to continue keeping slightly to South. It seemed we had struck the flank of the enemy positions as we could hear sounds of battle on 3Bn route. No further opposition until we reached railway, when a few snipers in station caused slight delay. Just East of railway an armoured car appeared and caused some delay and casualties. It pulled out before we could bring PIAT or 6 pdr to bear. This armoured car appeared two or three times, but 'A' Coy were able to get round through the back gardens. The railway bridge (Charing Cross) was blown as 'C' Coy were crossing.

'B' Coy were ordered onto Den Brink where they met considerable opposition and suffered casualties. At this stage wireless communications with 'B' and 'C' Coys broke down. Nothing more was ever heard of 'C' Coy. Meanwhile 'A' Coy pushed on south of Den Brink and entered town keeping close to the river. They encountered several small parties of enemy with light automatics, but these soon packed in when outflanked. Altogether some 30–40 POW's were taken by 'A' Coy during this advance. 'A' Coy reached bridge at approximately 2000 hrs and occupied buildings 8 and 10 and area A. Enemy traffic was crossing bridges at this time. At 2045 hrs, 'A' Coy put in an assault with one platoon South end of bridge. They were met by a light flak gun from South end of bridge and an armoured car on the bridge. The platoon suffered 8 casualties in the first 50 yards and the attempt was abandoned. The CO had now arrived and decided that the South end must be taken from the south. He sent a patrol under Major Murray (1st Para Sqn RE) to recce for barges and to contact 'B' Coy at Putney (pontoon bridge) with order to cross and take South end of the bridge. This patrol never made contact with 'B' Coy. Meanwhile Bn HQ and HQ Coy arrived and occupied houses 2, 3 and 5. Shortly afterwards Bde HQ and attached troops less Brigade and IO arrived.

Lieut Col Frost took command of the force which now consisted of 1 Para Bde Gp less 1 and 3 Bns, 'B' and 'C' Coys 2 Bn. Brigade HQ tps were disposed as follows: Approximately 45 men (RASC and Sgts) under Capt Briggs in houses 14, 15, 16, 17. Bde Def pl despatched to cross river and take South end. (Still no news of 'B' Coy). They failed to cross and later occupied 12 and 13. Remainder in 1, 2 and 4. All tps East of the bridge were placed under command OC 'A' Coy.

D+1. Major Lewis, 3 Bn with the remnants of his Coy, (one pl and 12 men) arrived. Major Lewis and 12 men occupied house 17 and the pl was ordered to occupy 12. This pl was never seen again. At approximately 0500 hrs, 'B' Coy less 1 pl arrived and occupied 7. They had met strong resistance at Putney and suffered some casualties. At first light 'A' Coy evacuated area A. During the night some enemy ammunition and petrol trucks were set on fire in this area and a strong counter attack from South of bridge was driven back with casualties. 'A' Coy now held 8, 9 and 10.

Later a party of sappers under Capt O' Callaghan RE, A/L Coy were placed under command 'A' Coy. The bridge was kept under careful observation and the sappers reported that it was not prepared for demolition.

During the morning armoured cars attempted to cross bridge from South to North—6pdrs accounted for six and PIAT for four—a total of 10 armoured cars and half tracks being destroyed. The Bn area was heavily mortared throughout the day and House 9 received a good deal of light flak from South of river. During the late afternoon and evening a strong attack supported by mortar fire and two MK III tanks developed from the East along river bank. Bde Def pl suffered heavy casualties from tanks in 12 and 13, and withdrew to join Capt Briggs in 14 and 15.

House 10 then bore the brunt of the attack and one pl of 'B' Coy was moved into 11. The attack was finally driven off. One tank was accounted for by PIAT and one by 6pdr. Just before dark, Houses 17, 11, 9, and 1 were set on fire by enemy and subsequently burnt down. Bde HQ in 2 narrowly escaped fire. Throughout the day there had been rumour and great hopes of 1 and 3 Bns arriving, but by night it was accepted that they would not get there. Later, hopes were revived when we were told 2 S Staffs followed by 11 Bn were on their way to join us.

Soon after dark Major Wallis who had been commanding 2 Bn was killed and Major Tatham Warter took over command, handing over 'A' Coy to Captain Franks. Area A was occupied during the night by 'B' Coy and another attempt from the South was driven back. The small Bn reserve of ammunition was distributed mostly to troops East of the bridge. During the night it was decided to strengthen our positions East of the bridge. Orders were issued for 'A' Coy to move East of bridge and occupy ruins of 11 and area under bridge at B. 'B' Coy were to take over 8 and ruins of 9. This plan was put into effect early D+2.

D+2. The East attack of the bridge was resumed with heavy mortaring and attempted infiltrations throughout the morning. At midday three tanks got into position near the river and started to shell 10 at point blank range. The pl holding the house suffered casualties and had to evacuate into Area 'B'. Two PIAT were despatched and closed with the tanks and scored three hits. Two more tanks were observed, after obtaining three more bombs from 'B' Coy, the party returned to see the tanks pulling out. Meanwhile some enemy had occupied 10. The pl counter attacked and reoccupied the house. The pl commander was severely wounded and the pl suffered several casualties. An attempt was then made to rescue House 13. This resulted in heavy casualties and the attempt was abandoned. Shortly after this a heavy gun South of the river started to shell block 8. The top two stories of all these houses were demolished and 'B' Coy suffered some casualties.

Two armoured cars penetrated along river bank to 9, where one was accounted for by PIAT. The other withdrew. At about this time Capt Franks was wounded, but remained in command until dark: pressure continued throughout the evening. Block 8 and House 10 were now set on fire, forcing the remnants of 'A' Coy into area 'B' and the ruins of 11 and 'B' Coy into block 7. Just before dark a Tiger tank drove down the lines of houses 1, 2, 3, 5, and 6 firing two or three shells into each house. The two remaining six pdrs could not engage it, but its withdrawal was hastened by bombs. During this episode the CO was injured and severely affected by blast. Major Gough was placed in command of 2 Bn. He later handed over to Major Tate. Meanwhile Houses 16, 14 were set on fire, and Capt Briggs' position began to look sticky. The position as a whole was now greatly weakened. We had suffered heavy casualties—particularly in 'A' Coy. Ammunition was getting very short. We had lost a key position East of the bridge, House 10. The enemy were occupying all houses to the North and West of our positions. Although they did not attempt infiltrations from this direction, they were able to keep us under continuous automatic fire, to which we could not afford to reply. The number of wounded were reaching serious proportions—they were all kept in the extensive cellars of Bde HQ (2).

D+3. During the morning pressure from the East continued. Capt Briggs' party were finally burnt out and fell back on 'A' Coy. Between them they held area B and the ruins of 8 and 9 throughout the morning. They put in a series of small counter attacks at different times on enemy setting charges under the small arch. Finally tanks were brought up to area B and blasted them from every position they held. There were no PIAT bombs left. Previous to this most of block 7 had been destroyed and 'B' Coy had been withdrawn to 5 and 3. At about midday the remnants of 'A' Coy (approx 15) and Capt Briggs party (25) were withdrawn to the main position.

Earlier in the morning Col Frost and Major Crawley had been wounded. Major Gough took over active command of the force referring important matters to Col Frost. Capt Hoyer-Miller took over 'B' Coy. Major Tatham Warter now resumed command of 2 Bn. Houses 1–6 were now strongly held and alternative positions were prepared in the gardens. All the remaining houses in the sector had been burnt down. It was anticipated that the remaining houses would be fired and we intended holding the gardens until they had burnt out and were cool enough for us to return. We appreciated that the enemy would not be able to use the houses either and furthermore they would not be able to serious damage us with tanks from any directions. During the afternoon four or five tanks crossed the bridge from North to South. The 6pdrs were unable to fire as they were now under direct small arms fire. Later in the afternoon the enemy brought an 88mm gun into position West of block 7 and started shelling 3, 5, 6.

We now received the news that 30 Corps were to attack the South side of river at 1700 hrs definitely. We were full of confidence that, even if this should not develop, we would be able to hold on throughout the following day. The mortars engaged the 88mm gun with good effect, silencing it for quite long periods. Throughout the battle the mortars had done most valuable work engaging targets South and East of the Bridge. Just before dark the enemy started to set fire to 3, 5 and 6, and houses to the West, by firing phosphorous bombs into already demolished roofs. They were soon burning fiercely. Just after dark Bde HQ in 2 caught fire. The wounded had to be moved into 4, but before this was completed this house was also on fire. There was nowhere else to move the wounded as all houses at the back of our position that were not burnt down were held by enemy. Col Frost then ordered all opposition from Bde HQ to cease and the wounded to be surrendered. This meant the Bde HQ party approx 120 men, under Major Hibbert moving North to new positions. Strict orders were given to 2 Bn NOT to open fire on enemy.

The enemy took advantage of the situation to bring large numbers into the area of 2 and 4. A German officer entered our garden and demanded assistance to remove all the wounded. Later he demanded our surrender. Several of his men followed him in and the situation became tricky as we were powerless to open fire on the enemy or counter attack until we had been certain that the wounded had been evacuated. To add to this confusion we were surrounded on three sides by burning houses and the enemy were throwing grenades into the gardens from the area behind 4. It was clear that this position was no longer tenable, so after consulting Major Gough who had now joined 2 Bn, the CO ordered a move to our adjoining warehouse which was known not to be strongly held, 'A' Coy took the house with little opposition and the Bn, Sappers and Anti-tank gunners followed. The enemy soon had this building partially surrounded and it was clear that it was quite undefendable. The CO then decided to split the Bn into two more manageable parties, one under himself and the other under Major Tate. The two parties were to find separate areas for the night, and to reassemble at the original positions at 0515 hrs.

The CO's party set off, but before long came under MG fire at very close range. The party became divided, half eventually occupying a building some 200 yards from the original position. Soon after, a party of RASC from Bde HQ under Capt Gill joined us with the information that Bde HQ had been unable to find a defence position and had to split up into parties of 10 to make their way out of the town.

It was now clear that we were no longer a fighting force, and that as the area was very thoroughly surrounded, a similar fate must have befallen Major Tate's party—this proved to be the case. It was then decided to hide in the area in the hope that 30 Corps would arrive before we were discovered. A thorough search was made of the whole area the following morning and most of the Bn and Bde HQ were rounded up.

When the 2Bn left the garden position it consisted approximately of: CO: Major Tatham Warter, Adjt: Capt McLean, 'A' Coy: Capt Frank and 15 men, 'B' Coy: Capt Hoyer Miller, Lieut Flavell and 35 men. HQ Coy: Major Tate, Capt Panter, Lieut Monsell, Lieut Tannenbaum and 60–70 men.

After the evacuation of wounded from Bde HQ there were no means of dealing with further casualties. 60–70 more wounded were brought in the following morning. It is not possible to give accurately the total casualties, but the MO's estimation of 2 Bns wounded was 210.

There has been no news of 'C' Coy.

End of report.

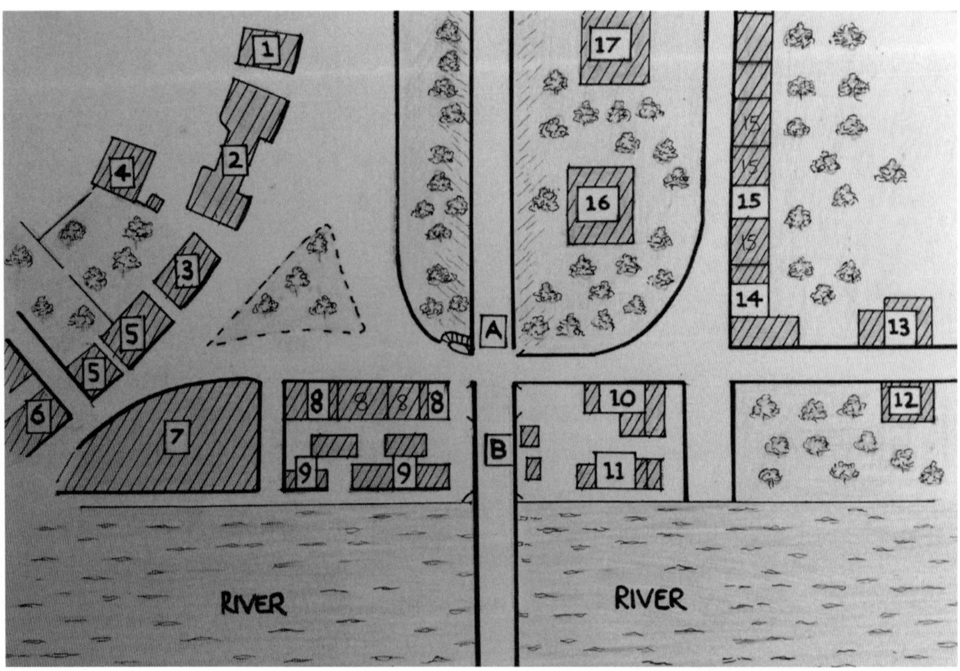

An exact representation of Digby's map that accompanied his report on the battle. (*Artist: Eric Thornton*)

A discrepancy exists surrounding the location of Battalion HQ. Various sources state the small building positioned at an angle on the corner was used as the HQ (see for example F. Steer's *Arnhem: The Bridge*). This white building is widely considered to have been the HQ, but other sources (see for example J. Frost's *A Drop Too Many*) show the next building in line to be the HQ.

It is distinctly possible that Digby himself is responsible for or at least played a part in this confusion. Following the battle when Digby wrote his report, he sketched a drawing of the perimeter, numbering each of the buildings and giving detail on what they were used for. Digby records the building next to Brigade HQ as the Battalion HQ, but when his sketch is compared to the aerial photographs of the area, it is evident that he omitted to include the corner building in his illustration. This omission is deceiving as without the inclusion of this building, it gives the impression of the two HQ buildings being next to each other when in fact they were not. Authors have undoubtedly assumed the location to be next door after viewing Digby's sketch, not realising he had not included the corner building—possibly because it was not manned (it was after all very exposed) or because it was not relevant to the battle.

APPENDIX II

Digby Tatham Warter Evasion Report

Evasion Report: 21st September - 23rd October 1944
by Major A. D. Tatham-Warter
2nd Parachute Bn.

First Contacts

Captain Frank and I escaped from a hospital in ARNHEM in the night 21/22 Sept and hid about two miles west of the town. After a week we heard that Brigadier Lathbury had done much the same thing and was lying up quite close. We soon made contact with him and later heard of 10 men also in the area. On the 3rd October the HQ of the underground movement of EDE got in touch with us and asked us to move to EDE to help them in:

(a) Sending information to 2nd Army
(b) Taking care of the men of 1 Airborne Div hiding in their area.

The following day I was moved by bicycle to EDE and the same day visited about 45 men, mostly of 133 Para Fd Amb and 10 Bn who were hiding in farms about 3 miles from EDE. Later that day I was taken to meet KING, a Belgian S.A.S. officer operating in the district. The latter was most helpful and contracted to arrange a supply drop of weapons, food and cigarettes on a D.Z. in operation further North. He also put me in touch with an escape route which will be called W.

On 4th October it was decided to move the Brigadier and Capt Frank to EDE which was considered a safer area and offered some opportunity for escape. Pete [Piet], the ex-leader of the ARNHEM underground, volunteered to move both these officers, who were wounded, by Red Cross Car. He accomplished this safely on the morning 6th October and both were established in houses in EDE.

Intelligence

It was obvious that there was little I could do in this line. Their method of collecting information was very efficient. These included thorough patrolling of the whole district to locate artillery, dumps, etc. a night and day round count on all roads, all troop movements and concentrations. This information was passed to 2nd Army via KING and also by a method to be known as 'Q'. Plans and sketches were photographed and sent over the river either by courier or by picked men of ours by Route 'W'. It seemed a most efficient organisation and produced definite but not always good results from the R.A.F. and R.A.

The only limitation was that the area two km North of the River was 'out of bounds' to civilians and so no accurate information as to enemy dispositions on the River could be obtained.

Escape Methods

(a) Route 'W'. This was the existing method and it was never really satisfactory. The Rhine crossing was about 30 km West of EDE and was comparatively easy, the main difficulty being the WAAL. We sent 11 men at different times by this route and 3 were captured. Later we sent an officer, Lieut Adams, to establish a post North of the WAAL with a view to speeding up the process. He was replaced by an 'I' officer from 2nd Army who was caught and the route was finally blown.

(b) Route 'R'. This was a much shorter route, being one due South of EDE, and only involved one River crossing. When all arrangements were made we sent off an American Pilot to try it out. Luckily for him the route was blown while he was still three miles from the River.

(c) The Air. Before the Brigadier arrived we evolved a plan for getting him flown out. Unfortunately in the only suitable areas, the fields were so small that nothing bigger than an Arty O.P. A/C could land with safety. We suggested to 2nd Army that this could be done at dusk. They turned this down but offered to bring a Lysander in at night if we would flood-light the field diagonally. We turned this down.

We were left with the rather insecure route 'W', which it was quite impossible to use for large numbers, and was at the best of times precarious.

Further Contacts

The next person of note to arrive in EDE was Lt-Col Dobie, who turned up one day after some very harrowing experiences. Shortly after this Pete [Piet] repeated his former exploit by delivering Brigadier Hackett intact, but very weak from his stomach wound. He was put to bed in the town under the care of a Dutch doctor.

We kept getting reports of men in hiding within a radius of 30 miles and agents were always sent to investigate. Sometimes these reports were true and at the end of the ten days we had collected about 80 men, including six officers and several pilots, RAF and American, in the neighbourhood of EDE. We then decided that EDE was getting congested and Pete [Piet] of ARNHEM opened a new base at REEMST, about six miles North East. Pete [Piet] then discovered Tony Hibbert, Capt Robinson, Lieut Hindley and several men who were hiding some distance North East of Arnhem. It was intended to move this party to REEMST at a later date. At the end of a month the numbers were approx 80 in and around EDE and 40 at REEMST.

Supply Drop

The supply drop we had asked for was successfully carried out about 7th October on a D.Z. some way to the North. The weapons and food reached us, but four years of war and home grown tobacco got the better of our Dutch friends sense of honesty and very few cigarettes survived transit. We couldn't grumble as they kept us very well supplied out of their meagre stock of home grown tobacco. The weapons were hidden in a farm near EDE and proved very useful later. Later we asked for, and received, a further drop, which included clothes for escape which had always been a great problem to the Dutch. We should have liked a more regular supply system but the Boche made this difficult by discovering the D.Z. and new ones hard to find.

These supply drops were arranged through KING the Belgian S.A.S. officer, who I used to meet at a farm near EDE about twice a week.

Sabotage

Bill, the leader of EDE resistance, very wisely refrained from all sabotage except for cutting the railway when required. It is of interest that he received orders from his 'Brigade' Commander to carry out wholesale sabotage and slaughter of Boche officers. It he had done this EDE would have ceased to exist and both the Intelligence System and our safety would have been compromised. His prompt action on the railway was on one occasion directly responsible for the destruction of quite a number of light tanks. These were parked in sidings North of EDE. Bill cut the lines North and South and then asked the RAF to complete the job. The result was quite good. The line was cut on three other occasions and only four trains passed through during my stay in EDE.

I was once asked to provide a party to blow a train on an important line 20 miles to the North. We should have liked the job, but there were many difficulties and we felt it was the job of the Resistance men in that area, who had better facilities and were experienced in the work.

We were expecting the 2nd Army any day, and so, when we had collected about 80 men whom we could arm, we made plans for sabotage on all roads when the right moment should come. This would not be until a bridgehead was formed and the Boche had started to pull out.

The plan, roughly, was to work in small parties, five of our men with five Dutch, on all roads leading from EDE and ARNHEM and as far North as APELDOORN. Tony Hibbert was to take charge of the ARNHEM district while I worked at EDE and coordinated the whole operation. We hoped to make road movement, by night at any rate, impossible without a strong escort. The country was ideal as most of it was thickly wooded. Just when our plans were completed and the necessary dispositions were being made, we got word that our efforts would not be required for a long time and we started to think seriously of escape.

Relations with the Enemy

Once we had reached EDE we were not seriously inconvenienced by the Boche in and around the town. We were lucky in that there were very few S.S. in the district, though there were a great many *Wehrmacht* and later a few *Grune Polizei.* The situation got worse towards the end of our stay when it was realised that the district was in no immediate danger of attack, and the 'back room' boys, who had cleared out during the Arnhem battle began to creep back.

The two things that worried us most were -

(a) A call up of all bicycles which lasted about ten days, and entailed the blocking of most roads and a search of houses and farms for hidden bicycles. During this period we had to be very careful how we moved and there was always the danger of discovery in the search.

(b) Billetting—They made two or three attempts to take over the Brigadier's house and entered several others that we were using. For the last three days there were four men of a panzer unit in my house, which was most inconvenient as it was a busy time for us.

We were very lucky in only having three men caught and they were some way from EDE, so the Boche never had any reason to suspect that there were large numbers hiding in the district, and our disguises, though sometimes a bit eccentric, seemed to be effective.

It is of interest that the Boche chose the day after we left and crossed the river for a mass call up of all men from 15 to 60 years old, to dig defences. They had done it in all the towns in the neighbourhood and it is very doubtful if we should all have survived this very thorough process.

Col. Dobie's Escape

I have already mentioned Route 'W' and the fact that the officer we sent to establish it was replaced by an 'I' officer from 2nd Army. He sent word that the route was good and could take six men per day. Col Dobie was anxious to try his luck, so we sent him off on 14th October, carrying very important photos and plans of defences. Shortly after he left I received the information which changed our plans and got word to him before he crossed the River asking him to go into the question of a mass escape which we had already discussed in outline.

He had a most exciting journey, but got through at the same time as Route 'W' was finally blown. The full story of this and the arrangements he made South of the River have been written by him (See Annexure 1 attached [see below]). It is sufficient to say that without his detailed knowledge of our situation and the excellent arrangements he made, it is very doubtful whether the escape would have worked.

Planned Escape

Immediately after Col Dobie's departure we got news that Route 'W' was blown so we were doubtful if he would get through. As it was essential that some one knowing our situation and plans should be South of the River to make arrangements there, the Brigadier volunteered to try a crossing alone South of EDE—a night patrol by Capt Wainwright (156 Bn) showed that the area we had selected was much too strongly held so we had to think again. Tony Hibbert had been brought over to EDE and now took command of the party at REEMST. A daily conference was held at the Brigadier's house, which the Brigadier, Tony and I attended, and a plan was drawn up.

On 16th October we got the good news that Col Dobie was across and that night I talked to him by 'Q'. We found that his ideas fitted in very well with our plans and after fixing preliminaries we agreed to discuss full details the following night. He gave me another area for the crossing which was to be known as 'DIGBY'. The plan finally decided was very simple. We were to make our own arrangements for reaching the River; at midnight and every hour after that a Bofors would fire a burst due North over 'DIGBY'. When we were ready we would flash a red Vic and ten boats, with flank protection, would come across. Col Dobie guaranteed the fullest support from the South bank if we should get into trouble.

The Brigadier was sceptical as to the merits of a Bofors as direction signal, but we agreed to use it. Afterwards his doubts were more than justified.

Concentration

Having decided on the plan, the main problem confronting us was how 130 odd Englishmen were to be concentrated at the River. It entailed moving them a distance varying from 8 to 15 miles through country thickly populated by Boche, and finally through the defence lines to the River. We originally planned to do this by moving to a concentration point in the wood just North of DIGBY the night before, in two separate parties, one from EDE, the other from REEMST. It was a difficult undertaking as the area we should move through contained a great number of Batteries and all that goes with them. However we were spared this by a great piece of luck. At 1700 hours on Friday, 20 October, we got the news that the Boche had ordered the evacuation of BENNEKOM, which was a village only two miles from our concentration area, by midday Sunday. This meant that on the following day the road would be congested with refugees, so we at once decided to make use of this opportunity. Bill mobilised his whole organisation and starting at 0730 hrs on Saturday, the 90 men from EDE district were moved down in parties of two's and three's to the concentration area, three miles North of Digby, in a thick part of the woods. There were one or two ugly moments but by 1730 hrs the concentration was complete and the whole party had been equipped with their uniforms, weapons and food which had all been transported to the area by horse and cart.

There still remained the problem of the other 40 men from REEMST. We had decided to move them down in two lorries provided by the Dutch Red Cross starting at dusk on the evening of the crossing. According to plan, soon after dusk on the Sunday 22nd October the lorries picked up their load with Tony Hibbert in command, drove down, passing many Germans without incident, and drew up at the selected point on time. They had chosen a bad moment for as they debussed a German bicycle patrol came down the road and had to slow up, ringing their bells, to get past the congestion on the road. They didn't appear to notice anything wrong, not even the Dutch guides shouting instructions in English.

The whole party was now concentrated and organised into platoons and Sections. Our numbers were swollen by fifteen Dutchmen and two Russian Pilots who wished to accompany us.

The Approach

The area selected for crossing had been reconnoitred by myself in daylight on Saturday morning and by a very thorough Recce patrol led by Capt Wainwright on Saturday night. We had a Dutch farmer to lead us through the woods and the last 1000 yards to the river was across open meadows, through a gap 250 yards wide between two strong enemy posts, sited 300 yards back from the river. We then had to move West along the River bank for 800 yards to DIGBY. The River front was covered by a series of posts all sited 300 yards back on the winter dyke and the bank itself was known to be regularly patrolled. It would have been a hazardous move with a highly trained company, but with a mixed bag of 120 parachutists, largely R.A.M.C. orderlies, 10 British and U.S. pilots, two Russians and 15 Dutchmen, all of whom were unfit and many of whom had never seen their leaders in daylight, it soon became obvious that our chances of slipping through unobserved were remote. Before we reached the River the party most closely resembled a herd of Buffalo, and I think it was this fact, which probably mislead the Boche as to our numbers, added to the fact that the US parachutists on the South bank had been patrolling very vigorously on previous nights, that got us through. Although they were aware of our presence they were obviously windy to take us on. We moved off at 2100 hrs and reached the River at 2350 hrs. Captain Wainwright had led the party with great skill over the route he had reconnoitred and so far not a shot had been fired. Soon after we started moving West we bumped into a small patrol which opened fire and caused some consternation. Several enemy posts then sent up Red verey lights but fortunately the expected S.O.S. fire did not materialise.

The Crossing

At midnight we still reckoned we had about 500 yards to cover to DIGBY but were surprised to see the Bofors tracer passing what appeared a very short distance ahead. We moved on another 150 yards and then signalled for the boats; after 20 minutes waiting and still no boats we were beginning to wonder, when an American officer appeared and pointed out that if we moved another 400 yards West we should find all the boats waiting. We were very relieved, but decided then never to trust a Bofors again. We found Col Dobie waiting with the boats and rather annoyed that we had been so long. Still not a shot had been fired from the German positions, although we were clearly in view of them all the time; and we crossed without incident, to find a magnificent reception laid on for us.

APPENDIX III

David Dobie Report

Annexure 1 to Appx 'F'
Report on Operation to Liberate Personnel from Northern Holland
by Lt-Col. D. T. Dobie. D.S.O.

EDE

Monday 16 Oct 44

Had been asked to proceed to 2nd Army HQ with plans of defences of ROTTERDAM and certain photographs of defences etc in North HOLLAND. Went to underground HQ and saw Major Tatham-Warter, and went through plan of ambushing roads when 2nd Army cross the Rijn. All arrangements and communications fixed before I left.

1600 hrs.—I proceeded to Capt Haig and sent wireless message to London reference operation. Remained night at Capt Haig's.

Tuesday 17 Oct 44

Was guided by underground to region Amerongen—4077—where I crossed Neder Rijn to Maurik—4176. Underground at Maurik stated it was impossible to cross river Waal as there had been a fight the same day at TIEL, and two German soldiers had been killed. They agreed to give me guides the following day.

Wednesday 18 Oct 44

Arrived Tiel 1730 hrs but was told quite impossible to cross river owing to dusk curfew. Frans de Veldor, a boy of 19, volunteered to get me to river bank through town. This he did, and we reached another underground house on outskirts of town. There I was told I could not cross owing to numerous German posts and patrols on the northern bank. However, Frans de V. once more volunteered to take me across. This was accomplished by 2200 hrs by infiltrating between two German posts and crossing the river in a rowing boat. Contact was made with British armoured car patrol at Wamel—4367—at 2350 hrs.

Thursday 19 Oct 44

Contacted I.S.9 and went to 2nd Army HQ. Plans were delivered to G.1 Section. I then went to General Dempsey's Tac HQ and informed him of the presence of approximately 200 airborne north of the river Rijn, armed, organised, and ready for his advance over the Rijn. Ambush plan explained.

G.O.C. said I would have to evacuate them, if it was possible, and sent me to HQ 30 Corps, to make plan with General Horrocks.

Friday 20 Oct 44

Two crossings were decided on

1. For personnel North of Arnhem at area OOSTERBEEK 6975.
2. S.E. of WAGENINGEN–604759.

the date to be night 23/24 October/

1. to be carried out by 50th Div.
2. To be carried out by 101 U.S. Airborne Div.

Rough outline plan completed, and I passed plan by telephone to Major Tatham-Warter at EDE. Was informed by him that they had to get out night 21/22 October and could only go by the western crossing.

Saturday 21 Oct 44

Detailed plan completed with General Taylor, 101 U.S. Airborne Div. The 2nd Bn 506 Regt would carry out the task. 30 Corps RE to provide assault boats.

Plan

Information

1. Enemy.
Is holding North bank of river Neder Rijn with main positions on high ground some distance from the river bank. The bank itself is covered only with patrols and posts.

2. Own Troops.
Approx 130 officers and men of 1st Airborne Div are in area North of Neder Rijn. This party is organised, armed, and in a fit state to make its way by night to the North bank of the river.

Intention

3. 30 Corps will evacuate the party of 1st Airborne (Br) Div from the area North of the river Neder Rijn.

Method

4. 2nd Bn 506 Regt of 101 U.S. Airborne Div will supply an assault party in three groups—

Left; One patrol of one officer, 7 men and F.O.O.
Right; same party
Centre; Company Commander beach party under Lieut Heaps
(attd 1 Parachute Bn).
OC 30 Corps Engineers.

23 assault boats will be manned by 30 Corps R.E.

5. Covering party.
Local to the bridgehead by the remainder of the company during crossing. Remainder of regimental machine guns and mortars to line bank to support crossing and evacuation which will be carried out in one lift.

Indication of Crossing Place

6. Patrol from 1st (Br) Airborne will indicate crossing place by flashing 'V' with red light from North bank. Crossing will be effected immediately. A Bofors gun will indicate to airborne personnel crossing place by firing bursts of 10 due North over crossing places every clock hour, from 2400 hrs onwards.

Arty.

7. The operation will be supported by 30 Corps Artillery by -
(a) Box barrage at local bridgehead.
(b) Concentrations on known German positions.
(c) C.B. in whole area.

8. The crossing to be silent, and no firing by anyone unless ordered by O.C. crossing.

Command

9. Lt-Col. Dobie will command crossing and be responsible for evacuation.

10. All personnel will be in position ready to effect the crossing by 2300 hrs.

ADM.

11. D.A. & Q.M.G. will make arrangements for transport and reception. I.S.9 will make arrangements for planes back to England.

Inter-Comn.

12. (a) Walkie-talkie between flank parties and OC Coy.
(b) W.T. to command post duplicated by line.
(c) Command post Randwick—5975.

The co-ordinating conference was held at HQ 101 U.S. Airborne Div by General Horrocks.

Contact again was made by me with Major Digby Tatham-Warter, and final instructions passed. Was informed by him that concentration North of Rijn was already proceeding smoothly and had all artillery stopped in area 3 kms North of crossing place as some troops were already there.

Sunday 22 Oct 44.

Proceeded to HQ 2nd Bn 506 Regt and went over the plan in detail with Lt-Col Strayer, the CO of the Bn.

At 1900 hrs we proceeded to Command post at Randwick.

All preparations were completed without mishap at 2300 hrs. At 2400 hrs the Bofors gun indicated crossing place. About the same time we heard small arms fire from North of the river about 1,000 yards east of our crossing place. This later proved to be a German patrol which had run into the airborne personnel on the river bank.

At 0005 hrs the red light flashed 'V', but it was approximately 800 yards east of our crossing place. I immediately gave the order to cross, and we established a small bridgehead on the North bank of the Rijn. Germans were heard and seen 150 yards away in the woods. Lieut Heilecker proceeded at top speed eastwards to contact parachutists. I remained area bridgehead and organised defence.

At 0030 hrs two red verey lights were fired by Germans in the wood. Mortars opened up and landed near my left-hand patrol. A machine gun opened up from about 1,000 yards West. Shooting was inaccurate.

At approx 0100 hrs Lieut H. returned with the first party of parachutists, who were embarked and sent across. A red and a white were sent up by the Germans and some artillery fire came over in the Randwick area. Mortar fire continued, but no casualties were caused.

By 0130 hrs the remainder of the airborne personnel had come in.

By 0200 hrs all had been embarked, and I withdrew the covering party and reported back to the Command post.

The operation was completed without casualty, and 100 per cent success.

This information was sent to Airborne Forces HQ by wireless, and to 30 Corps HQ.

All personnel were transported to Nijmegen C.C.S., the total number being 138. The next day the party was flown to England.

Endnotes

Preface

1 *Oxford Dictionary of National Biography.*
2 De Wiart, Sir A. C., *Happy Odyssey* (London: Jonathan Cape, 1950).
3 Frost CB, DSO, MC. Maj.-Gen., J. *A Drop Too Many* (London: Cassell & Co., 1980).
4 Nichol J., & Rennell T., *Arnhem: The Batttle for Survival* (London: Penguin Books, 2012).
5 *Ibid.*
6 *Daily Telegraph*, 30 March 1993.
7 Frost CB, DSO, MC. Maj.-Gen., J. *A Drop Too Many* (London: Cassell & Co., 1980).
8 *Ibid.*
9 Dover MC, Maj. V. *The Silken Canopy* (London: Cassell Ltd, 1979).
10 *Ibid.*
11 Heaps, L. *The Grey Goose of Arnhem* (London: Weidenfeld & Nicholson, 1976).
12 Urquhart, Maj.-Gen. R. E. CB, DSO, *Arnhem* (London, Cassell, 1958).
13 *Ibid.*

Chapter 1

1 Called Eliza Mary in baptism and marriage registers but Mary Eliza everywhere else.
2 At least three members of the Warter family gave their lives in the First World War. In May 1917, Lt William Henry Warter who had gained his commission with the Wiltshire Regiment was killed in France while attached to the Machine Gun Corps, aged nineteen. 2Lt Joseph Gordon Warter, a Wiltshire Regiment officer attached to the 66th Squadron of the Royal Flying Corps, was shot down and killed in September 1917, and just two months later, Capt. Henry de Grey Warter (Digby's uncle), a career soldier in the Dragoon Guards, was also killed in action. He had been born in India in 1885. His father, who, rather confusingly was also called Henry de Grey Warter, had died on active service in India in March 1889 as a colonel in the Royal Horse Artillery.
3 *WalesOnline*, 22 January 2008.
4 *Daily Telegraph*, 10 March 1993.
5 Jane Randle (Digby's niece) to author, 2019.

Chapter 2

1 Beddington CBE, Maj.-Gen. W. R., *A History of the Queen's Bays (The 2nd Dragoon Guards) 1929–1945* (Winchester: Warren & Son Ltd, 1954).
2 Lt-Col. Henry de Grey Warter, RA (1837–1889).
3 Howard, J., & Bates, P., *The Pegasus Diaries* (Barnsley: Pen & Sword, 2008).
4 Ox & Bucks Chronicle 1938.
5 *Ibid.*
6 *Ibid.*
7 Ox & Bucks Chronicle 1939.
8 *Ibid.*
9 *Ibid.*
10 Howard, J., & Bates, P, *op. cit.*
11 *Ibid.*
12 *Ibid.*
13 *Ibid.*
14 *Ibid.*
15 *Ibid*
16 Ox & Bucks Chronicle 1939.
17 *Ibid.*
18 *Ibid.*
19 *Ibid.*

Chapter 3

1 Borden, M., *Journey Down a Blind Alley* (London: Hutchinson & Co. Ltd, 1946) (Note: MTC is often erroneously referred to as the Motor *Transport* Corps).
2 *Ibid.*
3 *Ibid.*
4 *Ibid.*
5 Unnamed British newspaper, *c.* June 1940, a still of which featured in the TV documentary, *Tin Hats & Silk Stockings* (1989).
6 Borden, M., *op. cit.*
7 *Ibid.*

Chapter 4

1 Borden, M., *Journey Down a Blind Alley* (London: Hutchinson & Co. Ltd, 1946).
2 *Ibid.*
3 *Ibid.*
4 *Ibid.*
5 *Ibid.*
6 Tin Hats & Silk Stockings Hadfield Spears documentary, 1989.
7 Sgt Jack Tebbutt diary.
8 Willett, P., *Armoured Horseman* (Barnsley: Pen & Sword, 2015).
9 *Ibid.*
10 *Ibid.*
11 *Ibid.*
12 *National Archives, WO 373/20/39*, recommendation for MC.
13 *Ibid.*
14 *Ibid.*
15 *Ibid.*
16 Willett, P., *op. cit.*
17 *Ibid.*

18 *Ibid.*
19 Borden, M., *op. cit.*
20 *Ibid.*
21 *Ibid.*
22 Sgt Jack Tebbutt stated that John was stood on his tank pointing directions to his men when an anti-amour shell hit him in the chest (not the head). Of course, a shell such as this could quite easily have struck the chest and caused decapitation.
23 *The Times*, 20 May 1943.
24 Recollections of Jane Randle (Digby and Kit's niece) as related to the author in 2019. It was Jane and her husband, Michael, who confiscated the firearm and handed it into the police.

Chapter 5

1 Howard, J., & Bates, P., *The Pegasus Diaries* (Barnsley: Pen & Sword, 2008).
2 *Ibid.*
3 *Ibid.*
4 Pegasus Journal, Volume xxv11 No. 1, January 1972.
5 For which there are various spellings.
6 Frost CB, DSO, MC. Maj.-Gen., J., *A Drop Too Many* (London: Cassell & Co., 1980).
7 *Ibid.*
8 *Ibid.*
9 *Ibid.*

Chapter 6

1 Lathbury DSO, Brig. G. audio recording by L. Heaps, IWM,
2 Heaps, L. *The Grey Goose of Arnhem* (London: Weidenfeld & Nicholson, 1976).
3 Steve Morgan, as related to the author in a 2018 interview.
4 Dover MC, Maj. V. *The Silken Canopy* (London: Cassell Ltd, 1979).
5 Frost CB, DSO, MC. Maj.-Gen., J., *A Drop Too Many* (London: Cassell & Co., 1980).
6 Dover MC, Maj. V. *op. cit.*
7 *Ibid.*
8 *The Times*, Digby Tatham Warter obituary, 13 April 1993.
9 *Ibid.*
10 *London Gazette*, 23 December 1943.
11 Ages correct at the time of Operation Market Garden in September 1944.
12 Sims, J., *Arnhem Spearhead* (London: Imperial War Museum, 1978).
13 *Ibid.*
14 Morgan, S., personal account recounted to author *c.* 2018 and written up by D. Betts (Steve's niece) as dictated by Steve and sent to author via email *c.* 2019.
15 *Airborne Forces: The Second World War 1939–1945 Royal Air Force*, Issued by the Air Ministry (A.H.B), [Restricted publication].
16 Archive video footage from 1969, the twenty-fifth anniversary of the battle.
17 Arthur, M., *Men of the Red Beret* (London: Hutchinson, 1990).
18 Hibbert, Maj. T., account, Pegasus Archive.
19 Middlebrook, M., *Arnhem 1944: The Airborne Battle*, (London: Viking, 1994) [edited version].

Chapter 7

1 Vlasto, Lt R., Cornelius Ryan Ohio University Archive.
2 *Ibid.*
3 *Ibid.*
4 *Ibid.*
5 Holt, Pte, account.

6 Cook, R., *A Tribute to the Life of Jack Grayburn*, *c*. 2013.
7 Holt, *op. cit.*
8 Frost CB, DSO, MC, Maj.-Gen., J., *op. cit.*
9 Sims, J., *Arnhem Spearhead* (London: Imperial War Museum, 1978).
10 Vlasto, R. *op, cit.*
11 Frost CB, DSO, MC, Maj.-Gen., J., *op. cit.*
12 *Ibid.*
13 Vlasto, *op. cit.*
14 Middlebrook, M., *Arnhem 1944: The Airborne Battle*, (London: Viking, 1994).
15 *Ibid.*
16 Frank, Capt. T., account, courtesy of *Paradata*.
17 Frost CB, DSO, MC, Maj.-Gen., J., *op. cit.*
18 Middlebrook, M., *op. cit.*
19 Frost CB, DSO, MC, Maj.-Gen., J., *op. cit.*
20 Tatham Warter Audio File, Leo Heaps Production Company, courtesy of Adrian Heaps (note: recording held by Imperial War Museum).
21 *Ibid.*
22 Middlebrook, M., *op. cit.*
23 *Ibid.*
24 *Ibid.*
25 Sliz, J., *Engineers at the Bridge* (Printed by Amazon, 2010).

Chapter 8

1 Frost CB, DSO, MC, Maj.-Gen., J., *A Drop Too Many* (London: Cassell & Co., 1980).
2 Tatham Warter, Maj. A. D., after-action report written in Holland, addressed to *The GOC 1 Airborne Division*.
3 Smith, D., Account, as published in *Without Tradition, 2 Para 1941–1945*, Peatling, R., 1994.
4 Middlebrook, M., *Arnhem 1944: The Airborne Battle* (London: Viking, 1994).
5 Morgan, S., *With a Machine Gun to Arnhem* (Lancashire: Brendon Publishing, 2020).
6 Heaps, L. *The Grey Goose of Arnhem* (London: Weidenfeld & Nicholson, 1976).
7 *Daily Mail*, 31 March 1993.
8 Heaps, L., *op. cit.*
9 *Ibid.*

Chapter 9

1 Ryan, C., Ohio University Archive.
2 Ryan, C., Ohio University Archive, Egan account.
3 Middlebrook, M., *Arnhem 1944: The Airborne Battle* (London: Viking, 1994).
4 Tatham Warter, Maj. A. D., after-action report written in Holland, addressed to *The GOC 1 Airborne Division*.
5 Frank, Capt. T., Silver Star citation, courtesy of *Paradata*.
6 Frank, Capt. T., account, courtesy of *Paradata*.
7 Morgan, Pte S. as related to the author, *c*. 2018.
8 Ryan, C., Ohio University Archive, Gough account.
9 *Ibid.*
10 *Ibid.*
11 Frost CB, DSO, MC, Maj.-Gen., J., *A Drop Too Many* (London: Cassell & Co., 1980).
12 Tatham Warter Audio File, Leo Heaps Production Company, courtesy of Adrian Heaps (note: recording held by Imperial War Museum) Note: Digby was not entirely sure how long he was out of action following his wounding. A subsequent source (*Daily Mail*, 31 March 1993) recorded it as eight hours.
13 *Daily Telegraph*, 30 March 1993, Digby Tatham Warter obituary.

14 Heaps, L., *The Grey Goose of Arnhem* (London: Weidenfeld & Nicholson, 1976).
15 Typed contemporary account by a Para POW (whose identity I was unable to confirm).
16 *Ibid.*
17 *Ibid.*
18 Heaps, L., *op. cit.*
19 Middlebrook, M., *op. cit.*
20 Heaps, L., *op. cit.*
21 Mordecai, T., account, courtesy of *Airborne Assault Museum.*
22 *Ibid.*
23 Ashley, Sgt N., account, courtesy of Steve Nichols
24 As related to his son, Sebastian.
25 Pte S. Morgan, *op. cit.*
26 Llewellyn-Jones, Capt. A. D., Return to Arnhem 40 Years on—September 1984, Pegasus Journal, December 199.
27 *Ibid.*
28 *Ibid.*
29 *Ibid.*
30 Heaps, L., *op. cit.*
31 Pte S. Morgan, *op. cit.*
32 Heaps, L., *op. cit.*
33 *Ibid.*

Chapter 10

1 Vlasto, Lt R., Cornelius Ryan Ohio University Archive.
2 Morgan, S., personal recollection recorded at Arnhem Bridge, Everist, R., & Everist, W., 2014.
3 *Ibid.*
4 *Ibid.*
5 *Ibid.*
6 Tatham Warter, Maj. A. D., after-action report written in Holland, addressed to *The GOC 1 Airborne Division.*
7 Frost CB, DSO, MC, Maj.-Gen., J., *A Drop Too Many* (London: Cassell & Co., 1980).
8 Hibbert, Maj. T., account, Pegasus Archive.
9 *Ibid.*
10 Sims, J., *Arnhem Spearhead: A Private Soldier's Story* (London: Imperial War Museum, 1978).
11 Frost CB, DSO, MC, Maj.-Gen., *op. cit.*
12 *Ibid.*
13 Middlebrook, M., *Arnhem 1944: The Airborne Battle* (London: Viking, 1994).
14 *Ibid.*
15 Morgan, S., *op. cit.*
16 *Ibid.*
17 Wallace, Sgt J., 'A' Coy, 2 Para, account.
18 Tatham Warter, Maj. A. D., after-action report written in Holland, addressed to *The GOC 1 Airborne Division.*
19 Ainslie, Lt T., account.
20 *Ibid.*
21 Back, L/Cpl H., Cornelius Ryan Ohio University Archive.
22 Tatham Warter Audio File, Leo Heaps Production Company, courtesy of Adrian Heaps (note: recording held by Imperial War Museum).

Chapter 11

1 Tatham Warter, D., *Dutch Courage & Pegasus*, privately published *c.* 1991.
2 Cornelius Ryan Ohio University Archive, Gough, Maj. F., documents.

3 Hall, Sgt E., Dutch Operation Pegasus I documentary.
4 Tatham Warter, D., *op. cit.*
5 *Ibid.*
6 *Ibid.*
7 *Ibid.*

Chapter 12

1 Tatham Warter DSO, Maj. D., *Dutch Courage & 'Pegasus'*, privately published *c.* 1991.
2 *Ibid.*
3 Tatham Warter Audio File, Leo Heaps Production Company, courtesy of Adrian Heaps (note: recording held by Imperial War Museum).
4 When describing these incidents in his book, *Dutch Courage and Pegasus*, Digby was particularly taken by one particular risky endeavour, as follows:

> A year or two before I met her, Bill had reason to believe that he had been betrayed to the Gestapo and, to escape their attentions, had gone underground for the best part of a year. This meant that Mrs. W. had to leave her home with her two children, Hilly and Dicky, and go into hiding with trusted friends in the countryside. Hilly, a bright and pretty little girl when I first knew her, was, at the time of their escape, possibly five years old. Dicky was a baby. To complicate matters Bill possessed a forbidden radio which was used to receive communications from British Intelligence and it was most desirable that this should go along too. The curfew was strict, and to move this at night was thought too dangerous. So they hit the idea of hiding the radio under Dicky in her pram. And so Mrs. W., the children and the radio moved freely through the German check-points around Ede with Hilly pushing her baby sister in the pram. The consequences of discovery are too awful to contemplate.

This incident did indeed take place, but Digby, when writing his memoir many years later, got things slightly muddled since this incident happened after Operation Pegasus, not before Digby's arrival (as confirmed by Dicky Wildeboer [the girl in the pram]). The Wildeboers must have told Digby the story at a later date, perhaps during his visit after their liberation, and he got mixed up when reminiscing.
However, Dicky told me that her father had indeed been on the run previously. In April 1943, he was recovering in bed after falling from his roof when removing an antenna that he had used to broadcast an illegal transmission. The Germans then put out a call for all men who had previously served in the Dutch armed forces to hand themselves in to be taken into military captivity. Bill was summoned to present himself on 7 May 1943. His wife had been due to give birth later that month and Bill, instead of answering the call, had gone into hiding. He returned several weeks later as a new father, sleeping in the secret underground shelter behind the house. Digby would come to know this shelter very well, for it was here where he himself slept during his stay.
5 Tatham Warter DSO, Maj. D., *Dutch Courage & 'Pegasus'*, privately published *c.* 1991.
6 *Ibid.*
7 *Ibid.*
8 *Ibid.*
9 Hackett, Sir J., *I Was a Stranger* (London: Chatto & Windus, 1977).
10 *Ibid.*
11 *Ibid.*
12 *Ibid.*
13 *Ibid.*
14 *Ibid.*

Chapter 13

1 Tatham Warter DSO, Maj. D., *Dutch Courage & 'Pegasus'*, privately published *c.* 1991.
2 Tatham Warter Audio File, Leo Heaps Production Company, courtesy of Adrian Heaps (note: recording held by Imperial War Museum).

3 Tatham Warter DSO, Maj. D., *Dutch Courage & 'Pegasus'*, *op. cit.*
4 Tatham Warter DSO, Maj. D., Evasion Report: 21 September to 23 October 1944.
5 *Ibid.*
6 Neave, A., *They have their Exits* (London: Hodder & Stoughton Ltd, 1953).
7 *Ibid.*
8 Neave, A., *Saturday at MI9* (London: Coronet Book, 1980).
9 *Ibid.*
10 Neave, A., *They have their Exits*, *op. cit.*
11 *Ibid.*
12 Tatham Warter Audio File, *op. cit.*
13 Tatham Warter DSO, Maj. D., *Dutch Courage & 'Pegasus'*, *op. cit.*
14 Dobie, Maj. D. Personal Account of Arnhem dated 9 September 1948. Note: Typed version copied from his original pencil notes together with his personal diary.
15 *Ibid.*
16 *Ibid.*
17 *Ibid.*
18 *Ibid.*
19 *Ibid.*
20 Tatham Warter DSO, Maj. D., *Dutch Courage & 'Pegasus'*, *op. cit.*
21 Heaps, L. *The Grey Goose of Arnhem* (London: Weidenfeld & Nicholson, 1976).
22 *Ibid.*
23 Tatham Warter DSO, Maj. D., *Dutch Courage & 'Pegasus'*, *op. cit.*
24 *Ibid.*
25 Tatham Warter DSO, Maj. D., Evasion Report, *op. cit.*
26 *Ibid.*
27 *Ibid.*
28 Van Eck, H., to author.
29 Unnamed newspaper article on Operation Pegasus quoting Brig. Lathbury.
30 Heaps, L., *op. cit.*
31 Tatham Warter DSO, Maj. D., *Dutch Courage & 'Pegasus'*, *op. cit.*

Chapter 14

1 Deane-Drummond, A., *Return Ticket* (London: Collins, 1953).
2 Tatham Warter DSO, Maj. D., *Dutch Courage & 'Pegasus'*, privately published *c.* 1991.
3 Dobie, Maj. D. Personal Account of Arnhem dated 9 September 1948. Note: Typed version copied from his original pencil notes together with his personal diary.
4 Tatham Warter DSO, Maj. D., *op .cit.*
5 *Ibid.*
6 *Ibid.*
7 Unnamed newspaper article on Operation Pegasus quoting Brig. Lathbury.
8 *Ibid.*
9 Tatham Warter DSO, Maj. D., *op. cit.*
10 *Ibid.*
11 Hibbert, T., audio file.
12 Tatham Warter DSO, Maj. D., *op. cit.*
13 Tatham Warter DSO, Maj. D., *op. cit.*
14 *Ibid.*
15 *Ibid.*
16 Heaps, L., *The Grey Goose of Arnhem* (London: Weidenfeld & Nicholson, 1976).
17 Dobie, Maj. D. Personal Account of Arnhem dated 9 September 1948. Note: Typed version copied from his original pencil notes together with his personal diary.
18 Heaps, L., *op. cit.*
19 *Ibid.*

20 *Ibid.*
21 Tatham Warter DSO, Maj. D., *op. cit.*
22 *Ibid.*
23 Hibbert, T., audio file.
24 Burgett, D., *A Screaming Eagle in Holland* (New York: Presidio Press, 1999).
25 Neave, A., *Saturday at MI9* (London: Coronet Book, 1980).
26 Heaps, L., *op. cit.*

Chapter 15

1 *Ibid.* Kooijman said: 'A week later Tatham Warter did join us again in London, where he told us of his plan to jump again over Ede or surrounding to evacuate the rest of the British soldiers (some 200 were believed to be still hiding somewhere)'.
2 Steer, F., *Arnhem: The Bridge* (Barnsley: Leo Cooper, 2003).
3 Peatling, R., *Without Tradition: 2 Para 1941–1945* (Barnsley: Pen & Sword, 2004).
4 As written by Digby on the letters he sent.
5 Tatham Warter, D., letter to the father of David Wallis.
6 Peatling, R., *op. cit.*
7 Original citation document (Digby's copy), courtesy of Jane Tatham Warter.
8 Frost CB, DSO, MC, Maj.-Gen., J., *A Drop Too Many* (London: Cassell & Co., 1980).
9 *Ibid.*
10 *Ibid.*

Chapter 16

1 Rooken-Smith, D., *Kenya Polo: Notes & Recollections.*
2 Tatham Warter, J., interview with author, January 2020, Nanyuki.
3 *Ibid.*
4 *Ibid.*
5 Charles Dobie as related to author, July 2020.
6 *Ibid.*
7 EuropeansinEastAfrica.co.uk (recollections from those who knew him).
8 Rooken-Smith, D., to author, *c.* 2020.
9 *Ibid.*
10 Fernandes, E., interview with author, January 2020.
11 *Ibid.*
12 *Ibid.*
13 Fitzgerald, D., *Many Parts* (London: The Radcliffe Press, 2007).
14 Parker I., *Last Colonial Regiment* (Moray: Librario Publishing Ltd, 2009).
15 *Ibid.*
16 Charters, D., memoir sent to author in private correspondence.
17 *Ibid.*
18 *Ibid.*
19 *Ibid.*
20 *Ibid.*
21 *Ibid.*
22 *Ibid.*
23 Charters, D., as related to the author *c.* 2020.
24 *Ibid.*
25 *Ibid.*
26 Charters, D., memoir, *op. cit.*
27 Rooken-Smith, D., *op. cit.*
28 Extract from a publication by Thady Ryan (title unknown), under the header 'The Years of Strife–Mau Mau and the Emergency' supplied by Tom Lawrence.

29 *Ibid.*
30 *Ibid.*
31 As related to author by Tim Holdcroft, Digby's son-in-law, *c.* January 2020.

Chapter 17

1 Barkas, A., written account to author *c.* 2019.
2 EuropeansinEastAfrica.co.uk (recollections from those who knew him).
3 Lathbury to CIGS, The National Archives, WO 216/892, 5 December 1955, quoted by Chappell, S., 'Air Power in the Mau Mau: The Government's Chief Weapon', *RUSI Journal*, February 2011).
4 Arbuthnot (*née* Lathbury), G., written account to author *c.* 2021.
5 Wildeboer, D., to author, *c.* 2020.
6 Tatham Warter DSO, Maj. D., *Dutch Courage & 'Pegasus'*, privately published *c.* 1991.
7 Tatham Warter, J., to author, Jan 2020.
8 Randle, J., to author, *c.* 2019.
9 *Ibid.*
10 Barkas, A., *op. cit.*
11 *Ibid.*
12 *Ibid.*
13 Rooken-Smith D., *Kenya Polo: Notes & Recollections.*
14 Holdcroft, C., (*née* Tatham Warter) to author, January 2020.
15 Barkas, A., *op. cit.*
16 Arbuthnot (*née* Lathbury), G., *op. cit.*
17 Gilly Littlewood (known as Gill Barnett and Gill Denison-Pender 'in those days') to author, January 2020.
18 *Ibid.*
19 Littlewood, G., *op. cit.*
20 *The Times*, 13 April 1993.
21 *The Daily Telegraph*, 30 March 1993.
22 Barkas, A., *op. cit.*
23 *The Times*, 13 April 1993.
24 Barkas, A., *op. cit.*
25 Arbuthnot (*née* Lathbury), G., *op. cit.*
26 *Ibid.*
27 Barkas, A., *op. cit.*
28 Holdcroft, C., *op. cit.*
29 *Ibid.*
30 *Ibid.*
31 Aschan, U., to author, January 2020.
32 *Ibid.*
33 *Ibid.*
34 *Ibid.*
35 Oldenburg, B., to author, January 2020.
36 *Ibid.*
37 Holdcroft, J., to author, January 2020.

Chapter 18

1 *The Times*, 13 April 1993.
2 Frost CB, DSO, MC, Maj.-Gen., J., *A Drop Too Many* (London: Cassell & Co., 1980).
3 *Ibid.*
4 *Ibid.*
5 *Ibid.*

6 Recollections of Graham Toze to author, *c.* 2020.
7 *A Bridge Too Far* (movie), directed by Richard Attenborough, 1977.
8 *Ibid.*
9 Frost, *op. cit.*
10 Ryan, C., *A Bridge Too Far* (London, Hamish Hamilton, 1974).
11 *Ibid.*
12 Halliwell was later recaptured. Fortunately for him, he was not recognised.
13 Frost, *op. cit.*
14 Sliz, J., *Engineers at the Bridge* (Printed by Amazon, 2010).
15 *Ibid.*
16 *A Bridge Too Far* (movie), *op. cit.*
17 *Ibid.*
18 Heaps, L. *The Grey Goose of Arnhem* (London: Weidenfeld & Nicholson, 1976).
19 This oft-quoted remark has been published in various places, all without reference to the primary source which I have been unable to track down or verify.

Chapter 19

1 Barkas, A., written account to author, *c.* 2019.
2 Wisley, J., *H Jones VC: The Life & Death of an Unusual Hero* (London: Arrow Books, 2003).
3 *Ibid.*
4 *Ibid.*
5 Barkas, A., *op. cit.*
6 *The Times*, 13 April 1993.
7 *Ibid.*
8 Aschan, U., to author, January 2020.
9 *Ibid.*
10 Holdcroft, C., to author, January 2020.
11 Letter from solicitor to Digby Tatham Warter threatening legal proceedings.
12 *Ibid.*
13 *The Times*, 13 April 1993.
14 Caldwell, R., to author, *c.* January 2020.
15 Kingscote, M., to author, *c.* 2019.
16 McCallum, D., to author, *c.* January 2020.
17 *London Gazette*, 8 October 1982.
18 Barkas, A., *op. cit.*
19 Arbuthnot (*née* Lathbury), G., written account to author, *c.* 2021.
20 Letter from 'Flip', 17 July 1984.
21 Wildeboer, D., to author, *c.* 2021.
22 *Ibid.*
23 Tatham Warter DSO, Maj. D., *Dutch Courage & 'Pegasus'*, privately published, *c.* 1991.
24 McCallum, J, to author, *c.* January 2020.
25 Tatham Warter DSO, Maj. D., *op. cit.*
26 Lawrence, T., *The Life and Mysterious Death of Jim Elkington.*
27 *Ibid.*
28 *Ibid.*
29 *Ibid.*
30 Brown, S., to author, *c.* January 2020.
31 *The Times*, 13 April 1993.

Bibliography

Publications

Airborne Forces: The Second World War 1939–1945 Royal Air Force, Issued by the Air Ministry (A.H.B), [Restricted publication]

Airborne Museum 'Hartenstein', *Escape Across the Rhine* (Oosterbeek, Airborne Museum, 1999)

Arthur, M., *Men of the Red Beret* (London: Hutchinson, 1990)

Beddington CBE, Maj.-Gen. W. R., *A History of the Queen's Bays (The 2nd Dragoon Guards) 1929–1945* (Winchester: Warren & Son Ltd, 1954)

Borden, M., *Journey Down a Blind Alley* (London: Hutchinson & Co. Ltd, 1946)

By Ait to Battle: The Official Account of the British Airborne Divisions.

Carter, R. S., *Those Devils in Baggy Pants* (Battery PR, 1979)

Chappell, S., 'Air Power in the Mau Mau: The Government's Chief Weapon', *RUSI Journal*, February 2011

Burgett, D., *A Screaming Eagle in Holland* (New York: Presidio Press, 1999)

Burgstrom, C., *Arnhem 1944: An Epic Battle Revisited*, Volumes 1 & 2 (Vaktel Books, 2017 & 2018)

Deane-Drummond, A., *Return Ticket* (London: Collins, 1953)

De Wiart, Sir A. C., *Happy Odyssey* (London: Jonathan Cape, 1950)

Dover MC, Maj. V., *The Silken Canopy* (London: Cassell Ltd, 1979)

Fairley, J., *Remember Arnhem* (Glasgow: Peaton Press, 1978)

Frost CB, DSO, MC, Maj.-Gen., J., *A Drop Too Many* (London: Cassell & Co., 1980)

Fitzgerald, D., *Many Parts* (London: The Radcliffe Press, 2007)

Fullick, R., *Shan Hackett: The Pursuit of Exactitude* (Barnsley: Pen & Sword, 2009)

Hackett, Sir J., *I Was a Stranger* (London: Chatto & Windus, 1977)

Heaps, L., *The Grey Goose of Arnhem* (London: Weidenfeld & Nicholson, 1976)

Hook, H., *Home From the Hill* (London: Penguin Books, 1987)

Howard, J., & Bates, P., *The Pegasus Diaries* (Barnsley: Pen & Sword, 2008)

Middlebrook, M., *Arnhem 1944: The Airborne Battle* (London: Viking, 1994)

Mordecai, T., *Private Memoir: Airborne Ordanance at Arnhem*, Airborne Assault, Duxford

Morgan, S., unpublished memoir via Debbie Betts later published as: (see below)

Morgan, S., *With a Machine Gun to Arnhem* (Lancashire: Brendon Publishing, 2020)

Neave, A., *They have their Exits* (London: Hodder & Stoughton Ltd, 1953)

Neave, A., *Saturday at MI9* (London: Coronet Book, 1980)

Nichol J., & Rennell T., *Arnhem: The Battle for Survival* (London: Penguin Books, 2012)
Oldfield, P, *Bruneval* (Barnsley: Pen & Sword, 2013)
O'Reilly, J., *156 Parachute Battalion: From Delhi to Arnhem* (Nottinghamshire: Thoroton Publishing Limited, 2009)
Ox & Bucks Chronicles 1937–1945 editions
Oxford Dictionary of National Biography
Parker I., *Last Colonial Regiment* (Moray: Librario Publishing Ltd, 2009)
Peatling, R., *Without Tradition: 2 Para 1941–1945* (Barnsley: Pen & Sword, 2004)
Ryan, C., *A Bridge Too Far* (London, Hamish Hamilton, 1974)
Sigmond, R., & van den Bosch, C., *Escape Across the Rhine* (Ooseterbeek: Airborne Museum 'Hartenstein', 1999)
Sims, J., *Arnhem Spearhead: A Private Soldier's Story* (London: Imperial War Museum, 1978)
Sliz, J., *Engineers at the Bridge* (Printed by Amazon, 2010)
Steer, F., *Arnhem: The Bridge* (Barnsley: Leo Cooper, 2003)
St George Saunders, H., *The Red Beret* (London: Michael Joseph Limited, 1950)
Tatham Warter DSO, Maj. D., *Dutch Courage & 'Pegasus'*, privately published, *c.* 1991.
Urquhart CB, DSO, Maj.-Gen. R. E., *Arnhem* (London: Cassell, 1958)
Wellintgon College Roll of Honour
Willett, P., *Armoured Horseman* (Barnsley: Pen & Sword, 2015)

Documents, Archives, Private Letters, Audio, Video, Unpublished Works, Correspondence

Barkas, R., Written Recollections
Battalion/unit war diaries—various (chiefly 2nd Parachute Battalion)
Charters, D., memoir
Dobie, D., evasion report
Dutch Operation Pegasus I documentary
Extract from a publication by Thady Ryan (title unknown), under the header 'The Years of Strife–Mau Mau and the Emergency' supplied by Tom Lawrence
Gelders Archive
Hibbert, T., audio clips (various)
Lawrence, T., 'The Life and Mysterious Death of Jim Elkington' article
Morgan, S., personal recollection recorded at Arnhem Bridge, Everist, R., & Everist, W, 2014
National Archives, WO 216/892, Lathbury to CIGS
Pegasus Journal, Volume xxvii, No. 1, January 1972
Tatham Warter, Maj. A. D., after-action report written in Holland, addressed to *The GOC 1 Airborne Division*
Rooken-Smith, D., Kenya Polo: Notes & Recollections
Ryan, C., Ohio University Archive (Back, F., account; Gough, F., account; Vlasto, R., account)
Tatham Warter, Maj. A. D., Arnhem Report Tatham Warter Audio File, Leo Heaps Production Company, courtesy of Adrian Heaps (note: recording held by Imperial War Museum)
Tebbutt, J., diary
Tin Hats & Silk Stockings, Hadfield Spears documentary, 1989

Newspapers

Daily Telegraph
The London Gazette
The Tatler
The Times
Western Times
The Western Gazette

Websites

Ancestry
British Newspaper Archive
EuropeansinEastAfrica.co.uk
Europeremembers.com
docplayer.net/amp/51915716-A-tribute-to-the-life-of-jack-grayburn.html
Pegasusarchive.org
Paradata
SaxonLodge
Shropshirehistory.org.uk
Walesonline

Interviews conducted in person by author

Ulf Aschan
Anthony Barkas
Sue Brown
Rose Caldwell
David Charters
Hiltje Van Eck
Eddie Fernandes
Caroline Holdcroft
Tim Holdcroft
Michael Kingscote
Gilly Littlewood
Michael Littlewood
Danny McCallum
Jo McCalllum
Steve Morgan
Irralie Murray
Binny Oldenburg
Jane Randle
Jane Tatham Warter
Michael Tremlett
Dicky Wildeboer